MW01073787

The ghost story, 1840–1920
A cultural history

Andrew Smith

Manchester University Press
Manchester and New York

distributed in the United States exclusively by Palgrave Macmillan

Published by Manchester University Press
Oxford Road, Manchester M13 9NR, UK
and Room 400, 175 Fifth Avenue, New York, NY 10010, USA
www.manchesteruniversitypress.co.uk

Distributed in the United States exclusively by
Palgrave Macmillan, 175 Fifth Avenue,
New York, NY 10010, USA

Distributed in Canada exclusively by
UBC Press, University of British Columbia, 2029 West Mall,
Vancouver, BC, Canada V6T 1Z2

British Library Cataloguing-in-Publication Data is available

Library of Congress Cataloging-in-Publication Data is available

ISBN 978 0 7190 8786 8 paperback

First published by Manchester University Press in hardback 2010

This paperback edition first published 2012

Printed by Lightning Source

For James Graham

Contents

Acknowledgements   ix

Introduction   1

1 Seeing the spectre: an economic theory of the ghost story   10

2 Dickens's spectres: sight, money, and reading the ghost story   32

3 Money and machines: Wilkie Collins's ghosts   49

4 Love, money, and history: the female ghost story   69

5 Reading ghosts and reading texts: spiritualism   97

6 Haunted houses and history: Henry James's Anglo-American ghosts   120

7 Colonial ghosts: mimicry, history, and laughter   143

8 M.R. James's Gothic revival   168

   Conclusion   186

   Bibliography   190

   Index   199

Acknowledgements

I would like to thank a number of friends and colleagues who read various draft versions of parts of this book and whose advice has been invaluable. In particular I would like to thank Diana Wallace, Martin Willis, Roger Luckhurst, Ian Scoones, Ben Fisher, and Tessa Hadley for their comments. I owe a debt of gratitude to Avril Horner, Sue Zlosnik, William Hughes, and Jerry Hogle, who have all contributed to my general thinking about the Gothic contexts of the ghost story. I would also like to thank Matthew Frost at Manchester University Press for his enthusiasm for the project, and Alison Kelly for her skilful copy-editing.

Various parts of this book have been delivered as conference papers at the 'Gothic Voyages' conference in Paris (2004), the International Gothic Association conference in Montreal (2005), the 'Nostalgia or Perversion' conference at Radboud University (2005), the 'Uncanny Media' conference at Utrecht University (2008), and the American Literature Association conference in Boston (2009). I am indebted to the delegates for their helpful questions and supportive comments. Aspects of the research were also delivered at staff research seminars at Cardiff University and Nottingham Trent University in 2007, and I would like to thank colleagues for their helpful questions and comments and Helen Phillips and Claire Jowitt for inviting me to speak at those seminars. Some minor parts of the book that have been previously published are acknowledged in the relevant endnotes.

Finally, as always, I would like to thank my wife, Joanne Benson, for her love, tolerance, and support throughout the writing of this book.

Introduction

In February 1848 Dickens reviewed Catherine Crowe's *The Night Side of Nature; or, Ghosts and Ghost Seers* (1848) for *The Examiner*. Crowe's collection of supposedly verifiable ghost stories was dismissed by Dickens on two grounds: the metaphysical and the literary. Dickens argued that spectres were not metaphysical entities but the product of organic disease by claiming that ghosts:

> always elude us. Doubtful and scant of proof at first, doubtful and scant of proof still, all mankind's experience of *them* is, that their alleged appearances have been, in all ages, marvellous, exceptional, and resting on imperfect grounds of proof; that in vast numbers of cases they are known to be delusions superintended by a well-understood, and by no means uncommon disease.[1]

Later he argues that 'it is the peculiarity of almost all ghost stories, as contra-distinguished from all other kinds of narratives purporting to be true, to depend, *as* ghost stories, on some one link in the chain of evidence, and that supposing that link to be destructible, the whole supernatural character is gone' (p. 89, italics in original). The unreality of the spectre is clear to Dickens: ghosts are the product of disease and their literary counterparts can only persuade on the basis of flimsy evidence. In a self-consciously sceptical book review, Dickens promised to resume the subject 'next week, to sum up what may be said in their [ghosts'] favour' (p. 82) – in an article that did not materialise.

It is not immediately clear what Dickens has specifically in mind as the 'by no means uncommon disease' that raises ghosts although he refers to their provenance within an 'imperfect state of perception, between sleeping and waking' (p. 83). The ghost is thus manifested somewhere between the unconscious and the conscious, which explains why its 'reality' is difficult to grasp. Dickens returned to this issue in 'Lying Awake', his account of insomnia, published in *Household Words* in October 1852:

> I wish the Morgue in Paris would not come here as I lie awake, with its ghastly beds, and the swollen saturated clothes hanging up, and the water dripping, dripping all day long, upon that other swollen saturated something in the corner, like a heap of crushed over-ripe figs that I had seen in Italy! And this detestable Morgue comes

back again at the head of a procession of forgotten ghost stories. This will never do. I must think of something else as I lie awake; or, like that sagacious animal in the United States who recognised the colonel who was such a dead shot, I am a gone 'Coon. What shall I think of? The late brutal assaults. Very good subject.[2]

Michael Slater has noted that the closing reference probably concerns a number of violent attacks on the police which had received recent coverage in *The Times*. Slater has also noted that Dickens's article recalls his travels in America in 1842 and that the reference to the ''Coon' relates to an anecdote about a racoon from Captain Marryat's *Diary in America* (1839).[3]

Dickens's liminal, ghostly semi-nightmare in 'Lying Awake' runs together a number of references which obliquely indicate that ghosts articulated some of the discrete political dramas of the period. Dickens's horror of the foreign, his feelings of being cornered in America, and anxieties about domestic dangers are here played out as a nightmare vision generated somewhere between waking and sleeping – the very site of the ghostly in his review of Crowe's book. That this vision is also a political one that articulates feelings of estrangement and alienation is confirmed by how the ghost story between 1840 and 1920 engages with a series of grand political debates about economics, national and colonial identities, gender, and the workings of the literary imagination. Dickens's odd waking nightmare can thus be read as a conceit for how the ghost story at the time incorporated a range of pressing social issues, an examination of which enables a reconsideration of the function of the ghost story and its political subtexts. This book explores not just the ghost story but also how images of spectrality (such as that suggested in Dickens's insomnia) are related to the politics of the time.

At one level Dickens's waking nightmare also points towards the fragile notion of the self in the period. The presence of the ghostly indicates a liminality which compromises models of a coherent, self-conscious and self-present, conception of identity. The ghost story also explores the ideological tensions and contradictions that the spectre introjects. Dickens's ghosts might, as in *A Christmas Carol* (1843), make visible the moral limitations of economic individualism but the tale also argues that economic activity provides the solution to such limitations. The spectre thus makes visible the invisible contradictions that are represented as ghostly political possibilities which are silenced or made absent by the dominant culture.

That these issues are rooted in the culture can be briefly clarified by how the history of ghosts in England helpfully contextualises their subsequent representation in the literary culture of the nineteenth and early twentieth centuries.

England's ghosts

Sasha Handley in *Visions of an Unseen World: Ghost Beliefs and Ghost Stories in Eighteenth-Century England* (2007) maps the development of the belief in ghosts from the medieval period to the eighteenth century. Her study outlines the connections between religious notions of the ghostly in both Catholic and Protestant contexts, arguing that although the Protestant Reformation of the sixteenth century typified ghost belief as a Catholic superstition, belief in ghosts nevertheless underpinned Protestant notions of an other world of spirits that would, on occasion, commune with the living. Such ghost beliefs were not eradicated in the Enlightenment as ghostly manifestations were tested with some empirical rigour in an attempt to account for spirit activity as an occulted aspect of the natural world. However, it is important to distinguish, as Dickens does, between stories about ghosts and the literary ghost story. Handley notes that tales of 'real' ghosts in the seventeenth and eighteenth centuries encoded 'principles of social justice' as the ghost was typically associated with a form of guilty conscience that bestowed on it a moral integrity seemingly absent in the terrestrial world.[4] Ghostly warnings about the need to modify behaviour are also reflected in the literary ghost story (witness Scrooge), but the culture of the early eighteenth century sought to discriminate between the two.

Handley identifies Defoe's *An Essay on the History and Reality of Apparitions* (1727) as a key Enlightenment text in which Defoe's record of ghostly encounters constitutes 'a consummate act of empiricism' (p. 102). However, as Owen Davies in *The Haunted: A Social History of Ghosts* (2007) has noted, subsequent late nineteenth-century attempts to subject ghosts to scientific evaluation (through the Society for Psychical Research, founded in 1882) tended to account for ghosts as randomly produced, meaningless entities that contrasted with the earlier notion of the morally instructive spectre. Davies notes that Andrew Lang, who collected tales of encounters with ghosts, claimed in 1894 that the ghost had become a 'purposeless creature' and 'appears nobody knows why; he has no message to deliver, no secret crime to reveal, no appointment to keep, no treasure to disclose, no commissions to be executed, and, as an almost invariable rule, he does not speak, even if you speak to him'.[5] The new 'science' had thus reduced the ghost to a meaningless, if baffling, aspect of the natural world. However, as Davies notes, the ghost narratives explored by the Society for Psychical Research tended to be middle-class in origin, leading him to conclude that, 'It is certainly evident that the ghosts reported by the Victorian middle classes were largely purposeless, but an examination of other sources, particularly newspapers and folklore, confirms the continued significance of purposeful ghosts in popular culture'.[6] Indeed writers such as Henry James and Vernon Lee consciously sought to distance their ghost stories from such pseudo-scientific approaches in order to reinvest ghostly narratives with historical and metaphysical significance.

For Handley, 'Ghost stories, whether real or imagined, were good for thinking with' (p. 137) because 'Despite attempts to transform the reality of ghost stories by cutting them off from empirical substantiation and objective "proof", they survived as a kind of disembodied knowledge, being reinterpreted and recycled into new, more abstract contexts' (p. 139). This model of the ghost story as a medium of epistemological interrogation is one pursued in this book.

During the nineteenth century the ghost story became *the* form in which conventional cultural assumptions about identity politics were challenged by a process of radical disembodiment. By transforming the self into the liminal form of the ghost the fragility of the self (as a social and cultural construct) is made apparent. In this respect the ghost story addresses the 'abstract contexts' of social narratives relating to class, gender, and national identity, which, as Handley notes, underlines the fundamentally abject function of the ghost. At one level the ghost represents the 'displacement of the human corpse' (p. 122) but in a more sophisticated way it also displaces cultural narratives about identity and so enables a re-evaluation of those constructions between 1840 and 1920.

It is noteworthy that early folktales included a diverse range of forms that were associated with haunting, such as werewolves and vampires, which were not ghosts. However, this indicates the importance of exploring the notion of the spectral in broad terms. Julia Briggs in her seminal *Night Visitors: The Rise and Fall of the English Ghost Story* (1977) acknowledges that the term 'ghost story' has some 'latitude' to it, and this current study explores not only hauntings by ghosts but also how characters are often rendered spectral in their encounters with plots, people, and political concepts.[7] Through these engagements the self frequently becomes spectralised in its encounter with othered versions of itself (as, for example, Scrooge who is forced into self-reflection through proxy encounters with his other possible selves), and this indicates that alienation characterises these moments of spectral doubling. Briggs sees this as a key aspect in understanding the nineteenth-century ghost story, concluding that 'Out of an alienation, to which the decay of supernatural beliefs contributed, there emerged the figure of the double, neither the self nor another, a powerful symbol of unresolved inner conflict' (p. 19). This book provides a reconsideration of some of the writers explored by Briggs, including Henry James, Vernon Lee, and M.R. James, however it also seeks to develop and move beyond her analysis by emphasising the politics of the ghost story.[8]

Reading ghosts

How to read the spectre is the principal issue addressed in this book as it explores alternative ways of decoding the central political visions of the period. Whilst the approach here is avowedly historical it is important to acknowledge that ghosts have close associations with deconstruction. The roots of this are to be found in Derrida's *Specters of Marx* (1994), in which he elaborates an account of radical politics that invests the ghost, and notions of haunting, with a powerful critical presence.[9] These issues were addressed in *Ghosts: Deconstruction, Psychoanalysis, History* (1999), edited by Peter Buse and Andrew Stott, which included explorations of how images of haunting (or hauntology) underpin Freudian psychoanalysis, urbanisation, models of history, and the postcolonial.[10] The ghost, post-Derrida, thus seemed to be transformed into a critically mobile figure whose presence helped to illuminate the complex origins and discrete political visions of a variety of intellectual contexts. The ghost in that respect escaped from its Gothic origins and infiltrated what had hirtherto been regarded as the more conventional aspects of cultural history. Julian Wolfreys in *Victorian Hauntings: Spectrality, Gothic, the Uncanny and Literature* (2001) refocused these issues in a Derridean inspired analysis of Victorian literature that, whilst exploring selected Gothic writings of Dickens and George Eliot, also examined images of the spectral in Tennyson's *In Memoriam* (1850) and Hardy's *The Mayor of Casterbridge* (1886).[11]

The ghost as a critical tool can also be used in more obviously historical ways, whilst also acknowledging the importance of deconstructionist accounts of the spectral, and this study explores how images of ghosts and the ghostly engage with some of the more significant political issues and literary concerns between 1840 and 1920. Chapter 1 develops a theory of spectrality that relates it to the specific field of economics. This is particularly relevant for a reading of the Victorian ghost stories of Dickens, Wilkie Collins, and Charlotte Riddell. The nineteenth century was subject to moments of acute economic crisis and it is noteworthy that images of specrality take on a peculiarly economic dimension during such periods. The links between economics and the ghostly relate to the perception of paper money at a time when such promissory notes were redeemed for gold. Paper money was perceived as spectral money (not 'real' money), which like the ghost had a liminal presence. By juxtaposing Marx with non-Marxist economic journalism and theories of political economy the context for this broad economically driven discourse of spectrality can be established. Derrida's reading of both Marx and Freud in *Specters of Marx* also helps to build connections between models of economic man and notions of the self. Chapter 1 thus attempts a new theorisation of the spectral which enables a re-reading of the economic contexts of the nineteenth century. This perspective is especially relevant to the first two chapters, on Dickens and Collins, and is not intended as a grand, all-encompassing theory of spectrality, but as one which develops the principal issues involved in reading ghosts as economic entities.

Chapter 2 outlines Dickens's view of the ghost story and provides close readings of *A Christmas Carol*, 'A December Vision' (1850), and 'The Signalman' (1866). Scrooge's miserliness should be seen within the context of the economic depression of the 1840s and the tale uses ghosts, paradoxically, to critique the economic system and to exonerate capitalism. Scrooge is a miser who takes money out of circulation and the solution, so the tale suggests, is that Scrooge needs to put himself back into social circulation and money into economic circulation. By doing so his happiness is assured and the strictly localised poverty of the Cratchits is alleviated. This conundrum is re-examined in 'A December Vision', where Dickens attempts to represent the ghost of the industrial economy as it spreads poverty throughout the country. This pessimistic view of industrialisation undoes the apparent optimism of *A Christmas Carol*. Dickens's fascination with the fundamentally allegorical mode of the ghost story and how to read such allegories (as political narratives) is addressed in 'The Signalman'.

In Chapter 3 images of spectrality are explored in Wilkie Collins's *The Woman in White* (1860), *No Name* (1862), *Armadale* (1866), and *The Haunted Hotel* (1878). Collins repeatedly turns his plotters into spectral subjects when their proximity to wealth is seemingly assured. For Collins, as for Dickens, money immorally or criminally acquired renders the self ghostly and makes visible the amorality of the economic system as a whole. These issues are given a particular inflection in an anonymously published but clearly Collins influenced tale, 'The Ghost in the Bank of England' (1879), which addresses the relationship between paper money and the ghostly. Reading the economy and accounting for the spectral thus runs throughout these texts.

It would be reductive to suggest that ghost stories in the nineteenth century should or could be read as little more than ciphers for periodic economic crisis. Collins's writings, for example, also explicitly address how gender issues impacted on models of economic power. Chapter 4 engages with these issues by acknowledging the crucially innovative form of the female-authored ghost story. This is not intended to isolate a specific issue about such tales, as writing by George Eliot and Flora Hayter is addressed elsewhere in this book. However, it provides an opportunity to explore how three writers, Charlotte Riddell, Vernon Lee (aka Violet Paget), and May Sinclair, active between the 1870s and 1920s, addressed themes of love, money, and history. Charlotte Riddell's work in the 1870s is influenced by Collins and Dickens and she shares with them an interest in the relationship between money and spectrality. However, she also moves beyond them, as in *The Uninhabited House* (1875), through an explicit engagement with how such ideas might be resituated within romance plots where the restoration of money enables a heroine's financial independence. The notion of romantic love is given an historical inflection by Vernon Lee in 'Amour Dure' (1887), where the beguiled male narrator, an academic historian, resurrects the past of the Renaissance Medea, on whom the story centres. The tale examines the presence of suppressed, and so ghostly, female histories and many of Lee's other tales explore the place of women's writing within male historical narratives, and rework and redirect late nineteenth-century theories of aesthetics (particularly those of Walter Pater). This questioning of the relationship between history and writing is taken up by May Sinclair, whose modernist ghost stories, such as 'The Finding of the Absolute' (1923), examine the relationship between history, authorship, and love.

The diverse voices of Riddell, Lee, and Sinclair cannot be subsumed into one coherent narrative concerning identity politics. However, they do give a representative indication of how a range of voices share certain preoccupations and gave shape to a gender-aware discourse of spectrality in the period. One of the issues raised in Chapter 4 concerns the interpretation of history, and the issue of how to read, and so critically decode, spectral messages is addressed in Chapter 5 through an analysis of the literary qualities of spirit messages. Eliot in 'The Lifted Veil' (1859) explored the relationship between the literary imagination and clairvoyance. The seemingly mysterious transmission of literary ideas is also examined through analysis of selected poems by Browning and via the perceived disjunction between the poetically inspired Browning and his apparently commonplace (real world) bourgeois identity. The disjunction was observed by Henry James in 'The Private Life' (1893) and by the ghost story writer A.C. Benson in *Escape and other Essays* (1915). Both ponder the seemingly mysterious ways in which Browning became haunted, or possessed, by poetic ideas. This model of inspiration underpins the receipt of certain spirit messages which is demonstrated through a reading of a spiritualist 'novel', *The Book of the Golden Key* (1909), by Hugo Ames and Flora Hayter (allegedly channelled to them by a spirit). The book repeatedly dwells on its construction and emphasises its intellectual ambitions by decoding its metaphors for the reader. That literary messages sent by spirits require acts of literary interpretation is also apparent from Sir Oliver Lodge's *Raymond* (1916), his account of messages allegedly sent to him concerning, and then by, his son Raymond, who was killed during the First World War. These messages are highly literary and initially hinge on the interpretation of some lines from Horace, with later messages accorded a literary complexity. How to interpret spirits messages are (in *Raymond* explicitly) reliant on a notion of the literary transmission of texts, an idea which brings together one aspect of the literary culture (Eliot and Browning) with the spiritual (Ames, Hayter, and Lodge).

Chapter 6 explores how representations of spectrality reformulate a model of national identity in Henry James. The inclusion of the American-born James (who became a British citizen in 1915) helps to elaborate a notion of national identity in which the ghost functions as the intermediary between British and American cultures. Readings of haunted houses (and hotels) in 'The Ghostly Rental' (1876), *The Portrait of a Lady* (1881, revised 1907), *The Turn of the Screw* (1898), *The American Scene* (1907), 'The Jolly Corner' (1908), and *The Sense of the Past* (1917) reveal how the historicity of the spectral articulates a nationally liminal Anglo-American identity politics. In addition, there persists a theme of money and spectrality that is familiar from Dickens, Collins, and Riddell and which relates to conceptions of national and economic power and powerlessness.

Whilst ideas about national identity are given a particular context in the reading of Henry James, they are explored in more emphatically colonialist terms in Chapter 7, which develops a comparative reading of Dickens, Sheridan Le Fanu, and Kipling. The diverse range of contexts explored – Dickens's reading of America, Le Fanu's Ireland, Kipling's India – all, at different levels of explicitness, argue that representations of mimicry challenge notions of colonial authority. Dickens's *American Notes* (1842) employs a ghost in the account of solitary confinement at the state penitentiary in Philadelphia in order to explain the feelings of isolation endured by a prisoner. However, it also represents a pivotal point in the narrative after which Dickens turns an increasingly confident, judgmental, colonial gaze on American institutions. The ghost stories of Le Fanu and Kipling utilise images of laughter and mimicry which problematise any attempt to accord them a coherent colonial perspective. By using ideas drawn from Homi K. Bhabha, and Avril Horner and Sue Zlosnik's conception of the comic turn within the Gothic, Chapter 7 examines how ghosts function as either complex critiques of the colonial, or provide a gloss on feelings of isolation, as in Dickens's American ghost.[12]

Chapter 8 explores the ghost stories of M.R. James and examines how the seemingly conservative Victorian and Edwardian world of James's tales conceals a critique of an apparently amoral modernism. Tales such as 'The Mezzotint' (1904) and 'The Haunted Dolls' House' (1925) also place particular demands on readers by rendering them complicit with the donnish worlds which, in 'The Mezzotint', seem to be at odds with the Gothic narrative played out in the engraving. Ultimately, James suggests that it is this donnish world which is truly Gothic because its vacuous contemplation of the unfolding pictorial Gothic narrative indicates an amoral lack of empathy which characterises James's version of modernism. James's ghosts thus provide a context which enacts a conservative critique of the modernist text. This chapter thus addresses how the modernist literary culture of the 1920s can be re-read through a discourse of spectrality.

The tales of spectrality explored here give a representative feel of the British ghost story during the period and indicate that spectres, like Dickens's waking nightmare, encode political and literary debates that enable us to rethink some of the principal dramas of the time.[13] What is constituted here is a long nineteenth century, and although this study is thematic rather than chronological it begins with Dickens and closes with M.R. James's peculiarly Victorian approach to the modernist text.

Notes

1 Charles Dickens, 'Review: *The Night Side of Nature; or, Ghosts and Ghost Seers* by Catherine Crowe' *The Examiner*, 26 February 1848; in Michael Slater (ed.), *Dickens' Journalism: The Amusements of the People and Other Papers: Reports, Essays and Reviews 1834–1851*, Vol. II (London: J.M. Dent, 1996) pp. 80–91, p. 83. Italics in original. All subsequent references are to this edition and are given in the text.

2 Charles Dickens, 'Lying Awake', *Household Words*, 30 October 1852; Michael Slater (ed.), *Dickens' Journalism: 'Gone Astray' and Other Papers from Household Words 1851–1859*, Vol. III (London: J.M. Dent, 1998) pp. 88–95, pp. 93–4.

3 See Michael Slater's commentary on the article, pp. 88–9.

4 Sasha Handley, *Visions of an Unseen World: Ghost Beliefs and Ghost Stories in Eighteenth-Century England* (London: Pickering & Chatto, 2007) p. 66. All subsequent references are to this edition and are given in the text.

5 Andrew Lang, *Cock Lane and Common-Sense* (London, [1894] 1896), 2nd edn, p. 95. Cited in Owen Davies, *The Haunted: A Social History of Ghosts* (Basingstoke: Palgrave, 2007) p. 8.

6 Owen Davies, *The Haunted: A Social History of Ghosts* (Basingstoke: Palgrave, 2007) p. 9.

7 Julia Briggs, *Night Visitors: The Rise and Fall of the English Ghost Story* (London: Faber, 1977) p. 12. All subsequent references are to this edition and are given in the text.

8 Another important study is Jack Sullivan's *Elegant Nightmares: The English Ghost Story from Le Fanu to Blackwood* (Athens: Ohio University Press, 1978). However, Sullivan predominantly focuses on Sheridan Le Fanu, M.R. James, and Algernon Blackwood and although he makes some telling points about James's style he does not consider him within the type of modernist context addressed here. Sullivan also explores Le Fanu's tales within the context of Ireland but he does not subject those tales to the close historical and political readings applied in this study.

9 Jacques Derrida, *Specters of Marx: The State of the Debt, the Work of Mourning, & the New International* (New York and London: Routledge, 1994).

10 Peter Buse and Andrew Stott (eds), *Ghosts: Deconstruction, Psychoanalysis, History* (Basingstoke: Macmillan, 1999). See Roger Luckhurst, ' "Something Tremendous, Something Elemental": On the Ghostly Origins of Psychoanalysis', pp. 50–71; Christina Britzolakis, 'Phantasmagoria: Walter Benjamin and the Poetics of Urban Modernism', pp. 72–91; Nigel Mapp, 'Spectre and Impurity: History and the Transcendental in Derrida and Adorno', pp. 92–123; Ken Gelder and Jane M. Jacobs, 'The Postcolonial Ghost Story', pp. 179–99.

11 Julian Wolfreys, *Victorian Hauntings: Spectrality, Gothic, the Uncanny and Literature* (Basingstoke: Macmillan, 2001).

12 See Homi K. Bhabha, 'Of Mimicry and Man: The Ambivalence of Colonial Discourse' in *The Location of Culture* (London: Routledge, 1995) pp. 85–92, and Avril Horner and Sue Zlosnik, *Gothic and the Comic Turn* (Basingstoke: Palgrave, 2005).

13 Although a broad range of authors are discussed in this study, there are some notable omissions due to space, including Oliver Onions, Margaret Oliphant, Walter de la Mare, and Algernon Blackwood.

1

Seeing the spectre: an economic theory of the ghost story

This chapter attempts a theorisation of the ghost story which outlines its associations with economics in the nineteenth century. Marx, political economists, and journalists writing on economic issues all worked to make visible the seemingly ineffable and the ghost story participated in a field of spectrality which was informed by these factors. The very different theories of political economy articulated by Jeremy Bentham in the 1780s and William Jevons in the 1870s elaborate a theory of desire which historically underpins Freud's account of pleasure and pain in *Beyond the Pleasure Principle* (1920). The model of the subject developed in these contexts is Gothic to the degree that it is shaped by a theory of the emotions that has its roots in an explanation, and attempted monitoring, of the relationship between pleasure and pain. The literary Gothic and these ostensibly objectively analytical contexts are bridged by images of spectrality generated within theories of economics and political economy, images that are reworked both within Freud's model of the subject and the ghost story.

In order to illustrate how the ghost story is linked to these matters it is first important to account for how a Gothic language was recycled in economic contexts. However, before exploring that specific link it is useful to delineate some of the more materialist critical approaches to the Gothic as they help situate the form within the wider areas of history and theories of class.

David Punter has noted that the Gothic developed against the background of the emergence of a laissez-faire economy in the eighteenth century.[1] Consequently the Gothic questions not just the Enlightenment rationality that supported the coming into being of the middle classes, but the very class contexts in which knowledge was produced. For Punter, this becomes transposed into the Gothic as a fascination with seemingly dead, antique, worlds in which social order appears in implied feudal hierarchies. According to Punter, the key question is 'whether it is an accident that an age marked by the breakdown of accepted class structure, and also by increasing consciousness of this phenomenon, should produce a literature which harks back obsessively to a time of rigid social hierarchisation' (p. 196). The past is alluring but unattainable and this suggests a degree of alienation from the processes of the new laissez-faire economy because 'the laws of economic activity and even personal success and failure were utterly mysterious to most of the population' (p. 194). These new 'laws of economic activity' were articulated in a particular strand of Enlightenment thinking: theories of political economy.

Adam Smith's *The Wealth of Nations* (1768) was the first text to synthesise an earlier tradition of political and philosophical writings in order to develop (rather than simply explore) the new rules for economic behaviour. Smith's Enlightenment vision of political economy was subsequently given a powerful expression in David Ricardo's *On the Principles of Political Economy and Taxation* (1817). Whilst such texts might appear to have only an oblique relationship to the Gothic they nevertheless inform a particular model of the Gothic imagination which appears in Dickens, Wilkie Collins, Charlotte Riddell, and more subtly, Henry James.

Punter identifies ambivalence as central to Gothic representations of class, desire, and history and it is also key to understanding the relationship between theories of money and the Gothic. The danger is that one could be crudely reductive in asserting a quasi-Marxist context into which a diverse range of Gothic narratives could be subsumed. Indeed, the assertion of the importance of an economic context requires a careful reading of that context. Theories of political economy and how they become Gothicised can be illuminated by Marx's analysis of commodity production. However this is not to develop a strictly Marxist reading because although such ideas enable the possibility of a materialist account of the Gothic, Marx's critique of industrial capitalism also uses a Gothic language of monstrosity and deformation in self-conscious ways.

Gothic Marx

Marx develops his theory of 'The Fetishism of Commodities' in *Capital* (1867), where he argues that an object, in the example of a table, contains the labour (life) which produced it. The question is one of visibility, an issue that is central to notions of spectrality:

> A commodity appears, at first sight, a very trivial thing, and easily understood. Its analysis shows that it is, in reality, a very queer thing, abounding in metaphysical subtleties and theological niceties [. . .]. Yet, for all that, the table continues to be that common, everyday thing, wood. But, so soon as it steps forth as a commodity, it is changed into something transcendent. It not only stands with its feet on the ground, but, in relation to all other commodities, it stands on its head, and evolves out of its wooden brain grotesque ideas.[2]

Objects become alive with 'grotesque ideas' because within them exist traces of the exploited labour that produced them. For Marx seeing is important because how one sees the object requires us to radically view it as the culmination of subjective endeavour. Commodities therefore contain within them the possibility of overcoming the system which produced them.

The animation of the inanimate draws Marx to a Gothic idiom as the most suitable vehicle for expressing his critique of theories of political economy because for Marx, it is not just capitalism which creates certain ways of mis-seeing, it is also the theories of political economy upon which such mis-seeing rests. His exploration of the 'rationality' of the system of production depends upon exposure of the irrationality which is inherent to the system, so that instead of the pristine commodity we see the 'grotesque ideas' which lurk within it.

A range of commentators have explored Marx's use of a Gothic argot. Terry Eagleton, for example, notes that in Marx:

> Capital is a phantasmal body, a monstrous *Doppelgänger* which stalks abroad while its master sleeps, mechanically consuming the pleasures he austerely forgoes. The more the capitalist forswears his self-delight, devoting his labours instead to the fashioning of his zombie-like *alter ego*, the more second-hand fulfilments he is able to reap. Both capitalist and capital are images of the living dead, the one inanimate yet anaesthetised, the other inanimate yet active.[3]

For Punter and Fred Botting, such ideas are manifested in the Gothic through a class-bound ambivalence about the past. A feudal past might represent seemingly secure hierarchies, but the Gothic fascination with demonised or otherwise maligned aristocrats suggests that the past is also a source of considerable horror. Botting notes that this process is closely associated with locating the middle classes within history, so that, 'The anxieties about the past and its forms of power are projected on to malevolent and villainous aristocrats in order to consolidate the ascendancy of middle-class values'.[4]

In Marx, fantastical or 'grotesque' ideas are part of his analysis of models of economics. However, he is also, in less ambivalent terms, critiquing this 'ascendancy of middle-class values', at least as they appear in theories of economics. This is another way of saying that Marx focuses directly on the perceived sources of economic and social power, whereas the Gothic more typically addresses the effects of such power as it is manifested in images of the family and versions of individualism. Nevertheless, this does not mean that Marx is merely using a Gothic idiom in order to demonise capitalism, rather he suggests that capitalism is a source of the demonic because it is inherently irrational. The Gothic fascination with malign aristocrats is in reality a version of this as it involves the projection of present-day anxieties on to constructions of the past. This explains why it also becomes necessary to enact a demonisation of that past because, as Punter notes: 'It could [. . .] be said that the middle "class" is largely an illusion, a frozen moment in which are collected together people and families on the way up and on the way down. And aspiration and fall are the abstract topics of Gothic fiction' (p. 201).

It might be tempting to claim that the Gothic is in reality little more than a by-product of late eighteenth- and early nineteenth-century middle-class anxieties.

However, the Gothic is so much more than this and to reduce the Gothic to a solely class-bound analysis is to ignore the aesthetic, national, and geopolitical context in which it emerged. Nevertheless such ideas help us to critically read specific issues about power which are relevant to a discussion of ghosts and money.

Marx's use of the Gothic has received some attention by scholars working on the Gothic, most notably Chris Baldick, whose *In Frankenstein's Shadow: Myth, Monstrosity and Nineteenth-Century Writing* (1987) includes a ground-breaking chapter on 'Karl Marx's Vampires and Grave-diggers'.[5] Baldick addresses the issue of spectrality in Marx's writings and its suggested continuing presence within a threatened bourgeois imagination. Baldick notes that Marx's beginning of *The Communist Manifesto*, 'A spectre is haunting Europe . . .' (p. 121), implies that communism has become a kind of 'bogy' to the supposedly rationally minded bourgeoisie. Baldick notes, 'Yet what such a figment is doing in the most rational, enlightened, and calculating culture known to history, and why the bourgeoisie having swept away all superstitions, should still be "haunted" by it ought to be a puzzle' (p. 121). He also observes:

> Throughout Marx's writings [. . .] some of the most gruesomely archaic echoes of fairy-tale, legend, myth, and folklore crop up in the wholly unexpected environment of the modern factory system, stock exchange, and parliamentary chamber: ghosts, vampires, ghouls, werewolves, alchemists, and reanimated corpses continue to haunt the bourgeois world, for all its sober and sceptical virtues. (p. 121)

Baldick therefore acknowledges that Marx's critique of capitalism evidences a Gothic challenge to Enlightenment notions of certainty, at least as they are mani-fested in systems of production and theories of economics. The wider concern is that the inherently Gothic quality of such a process of production recrudesces in the imagination. The subject under capitalism becomes turned into alienated, dis-embodied labour, in which objects are granted a life that resurrects the transformed subjectivity of the labourer. People become things and things become people because 'There is a definite social relation between men, that assumes, in their eyes, the fantastic form of a relation between things' (Marx, *Capital*, p. 436). The system thus perpetuates itself through a new mode of subjectivity that renders the subject inhuman. Considered in these terms the Gothic imagination enables us to see the system, the spectral presence of labour, in a new way. However, horror, as an appalled insight into the system, can seemingly only take place when the subject steps out-side of ideology.

Baldick's account of Marx is an invaluable starting point for a wider examina-tion of how issues relating to seeing and spectrality came to bear on the ghost story. It is also important to acknowledge that this view of Marx as a latent Gothic writer has become increasingly influential in criticism on the Gothic.

Tricia Lootens has coined the term 'Commodity Gothicism' as a label for the new economic processes of the nineteenth century.[6] Her analysis addresses how the spectrality of labour becomes visible in a range of Victorian texts including *Bleak House* (1854), *Dracula* (1897), and selected articles from *Punch*. She argues that the image of the ghost is frequently used in order to draw attention to the occluded presence of labour within the production of commodities. She also raises questions about the role that consumption plays in this, as it too brings into being objects that are transformed subjectivities and desires, and thus have a key role in conjuring the ghost. It is also important to acknowledge the work of Regenia Gagnier and Gail Turley Houston in this area, although my argument moves beyond Gagnier's focus on aesthetics and Houston's close focus on banking systems and forms of accountancy, in order to explore in detail how money and its abstractions shaped certain models of subjectivity.[7]

The Marxist account of spectrality, as developed by both Baldick and Lootens, provides a sophisticated and non-reductive way of reconsidering the Gothic. The role that the imagination plays in perceiving the commodity in Gothic terms suggests the presence of a radical scepticism which transcends both bourgeois formations of subjectivity and Marx's reading of capitalism. As we shall see in the following chapter, how to generate and account for this way of seeing is a principal theme in Dickens's 'A December Vision' (1850). Making visible what is invisible is an issue shared by the ghost story and Marxist praxis. However, so far our analysis has largely been confined to an exploration of this influence in a particular strand of Gothic criticism (Baldick and, briefly, Lootens) or in scholarship concerning some of the form's more generalisable socio-economic contexts (Punter and Botting). It is also crucial to see how such ideas can be related to readings of spectrality.

Reading the spectre

The first major contemporary study of the ghost story was Julia Briggs's *The Rise and Fall of the English Ghost Story* (1977), in which she explored not just the ghost stories of Dickens, Henry James, M.R. James, Vernon Lee, and Walter de La Mare, but also examined the more subtle ways in which images of ghostliness were exploited by realist writers such as E.M. Forster and D.H. Lawrence.[8] Briggs returned to the ghost story in an essay in *A Companion to the Gothic* (2000), where she noted that the ghost story 'constitute(s) a special category of the Gothic', because the supernatural is never explained.[9] The factual presence of the ghost is a given of the form and it is the notion of the return of the dead which, for Briggs, implies the presence of the Freudian uncanny.

The terms of Freud's discussion on the uncanny are the homely (*heimlich*) and unhomely (*unheimlich*). He claims that the two terms slide into each other in uncanny moments as the home is no longer the place where security can be guaranteed because it is the site where sexual secrets are generated within families. This view informs his reading of Hoffmann's 'The Sand Man' (1816) as a thinly disguised Oedipal drama, a drama that would 'normally' be enacted within the family. Therefore what is seemingly strange and distanced (demonically 'othered') comes to haunt the subject in the ostensibly private place of the home.

This exposure of family secrets bears a relationship to the issue of seeing which, for Marx, is a precondition for the emergence of scepticism. Within this debate about sight it is relevant that Freud's analysis of 'The Sand Man' focuses on the role of the optician Coppola and the threat of blindness which, for Freud, evidences the presence of a castration anxiety.

Freud recounts how Hoffmann's tale makes repeated associations between blindness and castration as Nathaniel, the narrator, is placed in a variety of situations where his sight becomes threatened (the lawyer Coppelius, for example, threatens to burn Nathaniel's eyes with hot coals) or linked to mental disturbance (as when Nathaniel looks through Coppola's spectacles and sees the dangerous presence of Coppelius). For Freud, the tale can only be understood as a reworking of Oedipal anxieties because otherwise it seems to concern little more than a series of irrational impulses produced by the inexplicably deranged Nathaniel.

Freud reads the tale for its ghostly symbolism by addressing how the persistence of the past is manifested through unresolved Oedipal desires. The tale is not an orthodox ghost story as it possesses a necessary ambivalence (that Nathaniel could be just 'mad') which casts doubt on any supernatural presence. However, it also suggests that ghostly aspects of the past should not be read literally because they function as allegories about particular anxieties. The spectral therefore configures a 'real' past to the extent that it symbolises the presence of real social and psychological issues. Hoffmann's tale is not a ghost story as conventionally understood but Freud does associate it with a model of the uncanny which is linked to a notion of the spectral when he claims that 'Many people experience the feeling in the highest degree in relation to death and dead bodies, to the return of the dead, and to spirits and ghosts'.[10] Nathaniel is in thrall to a spectral Oedipal past and so is ghosted by a particular anxiety that is represented in symbolic form.

The relationship between spectrality and forms of seeing is crucial. In Marx, to see the subjectivity contained within the object requires a moment of scepticism. In Freud it requires abreaction. Nathaniel cannot 'see' in any realistic way because, Freud suggests, of his anxious attachment to his father, which is manifested as a fear of other father figures such as Coppola and Coppelius. As in the ghost story, the problem is both the connection to the past and the inability to resolve the tensions that keep the past alive. As Briggs puts it, 'the concept of uncanniness [. . .] is clearly connected to disturbing interpretations and the discovery of resisted meanings' (p. 125). In the ghost story this may appear as an unresolved family drama. However, the concept of uncanniness also has links to Marx through a shared emphasis on a ghostly presence which inheres within the apparently inanimate.

Marx's account of commodity fetishism and Freud's model of uncanniness represent different philosophical versions of a tradition of intellectual enquiry which extends from Burke, through Kant to Marx and Freud, who are all united in attempting to explain the presence of the seemingly ineffable.[11] Freud's 'Uncanny' also registers a disillusionment about representing the phenomenon in anything other than literary terms, which compromises the idea of its reality and closely aligns the problem of 'seeing' with interpretation.

Jacques Derrida in *Specters of Marx* (1994) helpfully explores the relationships between Marx, the uncanny, sight, and spectrality.

Derrida's uncanny

Derrida's account of spectrality is rooted in his reading of *Hamlet* (1623), where he argues that the ghost functions as the purveyor of secrets. The ghost's coming into being suggests that haunting contains within it not just a personal message (about Hamlet's family) but also a political message (through images of statecraft and threatened political betrayal), and crucially it is sight which plays a role in this. For Derrida the ghost manifests its power through its ability to see us unseen. Derrida examines how in *Hamlet* there is much debate about whether the ghost can be seen or not, although there is agreement that its voice can be heard. In this way social power, here represented as the law of the father, can be imposed through this superior, secret, means of observation (in which the ghost becomes godlike). For Derrida, the visor on the helmet of Hamlet's father's ghost refers to a model of a shielded superior gaze which represents 'the supreme insignia of power: the power to see without being seen'[12] and he claims that this model of spectrality influenced the Shakespeare-loving Marx. Derrida also argues that in Marx's writing we 'are never very far from the specter. As is well known, Marx always described money, and more precisely the monetary sign, in that figure of appearance or simulacrum, more exactly of the ghost' (p. 45). The Marxist project therefore concerns the exorcism of the ghost, which functions in much the same way as abreaction does in Freud.

Derrida's concluding comments explicitly make this link with Freud, in an account of how objects (the dead) are rendered uncanny because they spring to life with the labour that produced them. The wider issue that he also addresses concerns how it is possible to develop a radical scepticism which can be generated by Marxist praxis.

For Derrida it is by welcoming the ghost that it, like the commodity, comes into being in a radically visual way. Scepticism constitutes a higher mode of perception, one which is the consequence of epiphany. However Derrida, like Marx, cannot account for this moment in strictly materialist terms. In his discussion of commodity fetishism and Marx's account of the table from *Capital*, Derrida notes that the problem is one of perception: 'One must see, at first sight, what does not let itself be seen. And this is invisibility itself. For what first sight misses is the invisible. The flaw, the error of first sight is to see, and not to notice the invisible' (p. 149). Invisibility here is the labour which has gone into the construction of the table. Derrida emphasises that the problem is one of accounting for this moment of epiphany in which 'at first sight' the object is exposed as the culmination of discrete subjectivities. He returns to this issue in his concluding discussion of the uncanny, where he implies that Marx's failure to account for scepticism is paralleled by Freud's inability to explain, with any scientific rigour, the roots of the uncanny. The problem of 'first sight' is that '*It is a matter* [. . .] of the passive movement of an apprehension, of an apprehensive movement ready to welcome, but where? In the head? What is the head before this apprehension that it cannot even contain?' (emphasis in the original, p. 172). Derrida locates this materialist aporia through an account of subjectivity. The problem might seem to exist as a purely theoretical one, but as exemplified by Dickens's ghost stories, it also exists as a particular nineteenth-century concern. Without producing a rational explanation for this moment of epiphany it becomes problematic, for Marx and indeed for Dickens, to develop a coherent political position which can ground such a radical scepticism.

This line of argument seems to depart from considerations about money and the Gothic, however Derrida's use of the uncanny introduces a specifically Gothic drama into Marx's analysis. As has been noted, Marx frequently used a Gothic idiom in his critique of capitalism. The connection that Derrida makes to Freud's 'Uncanny' (for many critics the great ur-text of the modern Gothic) further elaborates this by attempting to account for the uncanniness of a commodity Gothic in which 'things' become 'alive'. How this relates to money requires some clarification, but the issue of visibility and invisibility is closely related to changes in the perception of money from the late eighteenth century.

Seeing money

In her book *The Financial System in Nineteenth-Century Britain* (2003) Mary Poovey notes that from the late eighteenth century onwards there was, due to the emergence of a predominantly industrial economy, a shift in the perception of wealth. Crucially, whilst wealth had once been associated with land-ownership, it had now become less tangible, less visible, in part due to new forms of economic activity (such as the Stock Exchange) and partly because of the prevalence of paper money. According to Poovey:

> much of the wealth that fuelled Britain's spectacular growth in the nineteenth century was never available for its possessors to touch or count, for the gold that composed the wealth was characteristically rendered unnecessary by the paper that represented it, while the capital that wealth signified was typically at work elsewhere, awaiting collection at some future date.[13]

The processes of the money market were invisible and money itself seemed to disappear. Gold and silver were replaced by paper facsimiles. Profit was deferred against future financial speculation, so that the terms under which wealth was previously calculated (such as land-ownership) required revision.

How to make money visible therefore became an imperative to those debating the importance of these changes, but such debates also confronted the moral significance of such change. As we shall see in Chapter 2, this issue of the visibility of the economic system and how it relates to morality is central to Dickens's *A Christmas Carol* (1843). For Poovey, 'Making this system seem trustworthy – making it imaginatively visible – was the work of journalists and novelists who write about financial matters' (p. 3). Visibility is the key issue as writers struggled with how to represent money in ways which could be morally and intellectually comprehensible.

One obstacle was due to the vested interests of certain groups, such as, for example, unregulated stockbrokers, who wished to conceal their practices.[14] However, how to make the system 'appear' was not just conditioned by economic subterfuge, it also raised questions about how to communicate the complexities of the economic system to a reading public because 'ordinary Britons could not visualise how the market worked' (p. 4). There was thus a need to find an idiom through which the market could be manifested. However, investigative writings about the financial system could not only be thwarted by those with vested interests to conceal, but also by the rapidly changing nature of the markets. Such writing 'was an attempt to understand and interpret something that was only partially visible and constantly in a state of change' (p. 4), so that even apparently neutral sources of information such as McCulloch's *Dictionary of Commercial Navigation* (1832) 'need to be read as *interpretative descriptions*' (p. 5, emphasis Poovey's) rather than objective fact.

The problem of perception which for Marx (and Derrida) was closely related to commodity fetishism is thus central to understanding the system. Reading the commodity in sceptical terms and accounting for financial processes require exacting interpretive strategies which have much in common. This investigation was also staged within the literary culture and the apparently 'objective' analysis of the financial system frequently used literary devices in order to dramatise the effects of financial processes. Poovey states that as a result 'the line between factual reporting and fiction sometimes proves difficult to establish' (p. 29). Indeed, ostensibly economic investigations tended to be 'generically ambiguous' as they deployed techniques drawn from the 'melodrama, romance, the detective story, and sensationalism' (p. 33), the very elements which characterise the writings of Dickens, Wilkie Collins, and Charlotte Riddell. This blurring of generic distinctions also explains why the ghost story becomes so closely associated with accounts of economics. The ghost story's way of making the invisible visible is linked to this culture in which commentators were attempting to make the apparently secret processes of the financial system visible to a wider public.

The Stock Exchange

The relationship between the economic culture and the Gothic can be illustrated by the example of the Stock Exchange. The process through which wealth could be made and lost in apparently invisible ways dogged journalistic accounts of the system. In a wider sense images of racial, national, and class otherness were also developed in reactionary accounts of those involved in the Stock Exchange and a very similar language of 'otherness' was also elaborated within Gothic literature at the time. The two cultures, the economic and the literary, cannot be simply merged, but what is outlined here are suggested subtle points of contact between them which indicate how accounts of the Stock Exchange are rooted within a language of moral revulsion which demonises those associated with it. This cultural use of an implicitly Gothically inflected evaluation of the economic system indicates the covert relationship between the economic and literary cultures. Not all such imagery relates specifically to ghosts and haunted presences, but it does entertain a set of Gothic issues and labellings which underpin the form.

An example of how the literary Gothic infiltrated accounts of economics can be seen in W.E. Aytoun's 'The National Debt and the Stock Exchange', which was published in *Blackwood's Edinburgh Magazine* (a magazine with a history of publishing Gothic tales) in December 1849. Aytoun's initial concern is about the role of usury in generating credit, and he employs some popular anti-Semitic imagery in his discussion 'of those unconscionable Shylocks'[15] that he sees supporting the system. His history of the changes in British financial practices is coloured by a language of demonisation. Aytoun claims that the present financial problems (the 1840s was a decade of recession which culminated in a major financial panic in 1847) were the consequence of Whig mismanagement of the economy in the eighteenth century. For Aytoun the Whigs attempted to conceal their role in this, so that it becomes necessary to make visible their 'occult designs' (p. 131). Aytoun claims that such mismanagement resulted in financial irregularities and a widespread corruption whose pernicious influence could still be felt in the 1840s.

Aytoun notes that such a system has involved the 'conjuring [of] visions of unbounded and unbased wealth'. This has turned greed into the defining characteristic of the 'funding system' which 'has been pregnant with social and moral evils which have extended to the whole community' (p. 133). All of this is epitomised by the Stock Exchange, which has encouraged, according to Aytoun, an unprincipled gambling that underpins widespread secret financial transactions: 'No stranger, indeed, may enter the secret place where the prime mysteries are enacted' (p. 134). For Aytoun and other commentators of the time, this mystical, magical, place was presided over by Nathan Rothschild, who was subject to considerable anti-Semitic caricature at the end of the eighteenth century. Aytoun quotes with approval a contemporary account of Rothschild which referred to 'His huge and somewhat slovenly appearance; the lounging attitude he assumed, as he leaned against his pillar in the Royal Exchange; his rough and rugged speech; his foreign accent and idiom, [which] made caricature mark him as its own' (p. 145). Rothschild is thus the deserving recipient of mockery, but the description articulates Aytoun's underlying concern that the only winners on the Stock Exchange are 'the Capitalist and the Foreigner' (p. 148).

Aytoun uses anti-Semitic images in order to characterise the Stock Exchange as a disreputable institution which is both mysterious and morally corrupting. The mysteries cannot be properly exposed but are made visible in the caricature of Rothschild. Aytoun employs a language of sensationalism to make the financial system figuratively present even whilst the Stock Exchange is associated with loss and absence: of money, morality, Englishness, identity, and 'decency' – all registers which play an important part in the Gothic of the period.

The Stock Exchange attracted a particularly exaggerated form of moral censorship because it became synonymous with unprincipled gambling. The concern was that economic speculation in stocks and shares encouraged immorality, and this brought together a range of racial and national prejudices. The critique of the system was therefore frequently developed through a reactionary assumption about the moral probity of certain actors (such as Nathan Rothschild) rather than as a radical critique of the economic process (like Marx's).

An anonymously published article, 'Stockbroking and the Stock Exchange', which appeared in *Fraser's Magazine* in July 1876, reaffirms the view that the Stock Exchange had been 'taken advantage of by the Jews', who were responsible for the moral degradations generated by such licensed gambling.[16] The problems with the Stock Exchange were, however, varied; at one level it was merely a higher form of gambling, but at another level it enabled the otherwise socially and economically marginalised to gain wealth. Accounts of the Stock Exchange tended to be politic-ally reactionary assessments of an economic system that seemed to be dangerously empowering traditionally economically disempowered groups. The article proceeds to list such individuals as 'Betting-men, who have failed on the turf [. . .] loafers [. . .] Nondescripts from the Low Countries, Jews and Greeks from all parts of Europe and the Levant' (p. 155). This model of Britain under siege by other nations and races, and compromised by internal power shifts, echoes a concern with a reverse colonialism that is most clearly exemplified in *Dracula*'s (1897) account of an Eastern European (largely Jewish) invasion of modern Britain.[17]

It is difficult to isolate social, racial, and national prejudices from debates about the ownership of the economic system. Franco Moretti claims that Stoker's Count (a demonstrably anti-Semitic figure) 'is a rational entrepreneur who invests his gold to expand his dominion: to conquer the City of London'.[18] Ownership of a coun-try is therefore defined (by Stoker and financial commentators in the nineteenth century) by ownership of its economic system. The author of 'Stockbroking and the Stock Exchange' does not just address these issues in prejudicial terms that would later become reconstructed in *Dracula*; they also employ a language of moral censorship that demonises national and racial threats. The Stock Exchange is described as 'a prosperous gambling hell' (p. 155) and later as 'an elaborately organised gambling hell' (p. 160). It is a place where economic judgements compromise moral clarity, so that 'those who frequent it are unable to see clearly what is right and honourable from what is wrong and despicable'. As a consequence, decisions are taken which 'anyone with [a] sound moral vision would shrink from and shudder at' (p. 161). The implication is that it is only those 'others', the Jews, Greeks, Turks, or homegrown reprobates, who can thrive in such a system.

The alleged moral vacuity generated by the Stock Exchange was further explored by Alexander Innes Shand in 'Speculative Investments', published in *Blackwood's Edinburgh Magazine* in September 1876. In ironic mode, Shand noted that, 'If you are to hold your own, you must make a certain show, and do to others in the way of hospitality as you would that others would do unto you'.[19] He attributes this required backstabbing attitude to the seemingly occulted processes of the Exchange: 'With Stockbrokers it is a point of honour as of self-interest to keep the secrets of their chambers as punctiliously as consulting physicians' (p. 195). Such a view might not seem to be notably Gothic, but Shand also claims that 'Without taking a specially gloomy view of the world in general, we see that at least in its financial department and on the Stock Exchange, the powers of evil for the time are decidedly in the ascendant' (p. 193).

These accounts of the Stock Exchange illustrate how anxieties about new economic processes became developed by conservatively minded commentators at the time. Such commentators conistently employed a language of demonisation to mark out the apparent immorality generated by the presence of social and racial otherness within the British financial system. They also evidence despair that the Stock Exchange could ever be anything other than a place where immoral transactions take place. Ultimately, the Stock Exchange becomes 'othered' in its associations with an alien economic powerbase. In non-Marxist ways these commentaries evidence a different, although related, aspect of the Gothic imagination and its relationship to the economic system: one in which this Gothic language of demonisation conceals grander anxieties concerning disempowerment and displacement. The ghost stories of Dickens and Riddell in particular address this idea of displacement through an ambivalent response towards money.

In these accounts of the Stock Exchange there is a pervasive sense of alienation from power. There was a feeling that economic power had replaced any national or moral authority by empowering racial, national, and class 'others'. The demonisation of the 'other' is based on this feeling of alienation, and although Shand's is a politically reactionary evaluation of the system it nevertheless sketches the emergence of a new kind of economic subjectivity. The self is potentially disempowered by the new economic systems so that money *creates* social instability: 'As fortunes are made faster and faster, as incomes are dissipated more and more furiously, an impulse is given to extravagance which reacts on the remotest parishes, and makes

the quietest people conscious of the pressure, when it does not send them
staggering to the wall' (p. 174).

For Marx it is necessary to generate a radical scepticism which enables the
subject to see the commodity as the culmination of the labour which produced it.
For conservative commentators the instabilities of the system are all too apparent.
The acquisition of money becomes like a disease, one which spreads from
London to the 'remotest parishes' where people are sent 'staggering' by its touch.
It is therefore important to acknowledge that in the culture there was greater ambivalence about money than a strictly Marxist account admits. As we shall see in Dickens,
the problem he addresses is in part the Marxist problem of accounting for
scepticism. However, there is the additional concern, often implied, that money
generates immorality. Scrooge, for example, might be a wealthy wine merchant
but he lives in apparent poverty and is seemingly incapable of moral empathy.
How to envisage a new life, one in which Scrooge can remain a capitalist, is
the conundrum that Dickens addresses and it is one which has its roots in these
conservative readings of economics, and in a quasi-Marxist attitude towards the
commodity.

It is important to explore the level of explicitness at which this link between
money and ghosting is made. For Marx, the links between spectrality and the object
are clear. Seeing the ghostly presence of the labour required to make the object is
a necessary precondition for scepticism. Seeing the ghost therefore becomes a demonstrably political act. Freud recasts this issue of subjectivity so that in the 'uncanny'
the dead come back to life. For Freud the ghost is both familiar, a 'real' identifiable
and knowable person, and completely unfamiliar, because in abstract terms the ghost
is both dead and alive and so a kind of non-person. For both Marx and Freud objects
(tables, dolls) refuse to remain as objects as they invade the supposedly coherent
world of the unified self in order to destabilise it with alternative political and
psychological realities.

Contemporary accounts of the Stock Exchange provide a good, specific, example
of this anxiety about destabilisation. The triumph of the economic system becomes
not just the triumph of the industrial capitalist, but of the 'other', the foreigner,
the Jew, the British 'loafer', all of whom are granted access to power which had
traditionally been denied them. These accounts represent the insider's anxiety that
economic power could become democratically redistributed as the money market's
generation of a 'meritocracy' challenged social and economic hierarchies. This is
all, of course, a matter of political view and far removed from a Marxist critique.

The key register that requires exploration in these very different accounts of
economics and spectrality is emotion. Marx has to some degree a dispassionate
voice as he 'scientifically' deploys a Gothic idiom to illustrate the irrationalities of
the system. In Freud the scientific gaze breaks down as he confronts his inability
to objectively account for the conditions under which uncanniness occurs. Unlike
Marx, he is attempting to explain fear, anxiety, and feelings of loss: emotions rather

than economics define the self but they are ones which, for Freud, frustratingly elude final analysis. Accounts of the Stock Exchange might seem to be far removed from these considerations, but they too capture anxieties about disempowerment which illustrate how subjectivity was conceived in a money-based society. Freud and such commentators therefore address (Freud directly, the others obliquely) apparently newly configured experiences of pleasure and pain. Marx also addresses this idea of pleasure and pain in his account of alienation and how psychological self-realisation can be achieved. These accounts, at very different levels, therefore all address the possibility of happiness.

It would be crude to reduce all ghost stories to the level of economic parable. The ghost stories of Henry James and M.R. James do not directly address the economic system, and it is necessary to explore how and why, for example, Henry James explores models of subjectivity in predominantly psychological terms. However, as we shall see in Chapter 6, he is working within a tradition of the ghost story which has its roots in a particular economic sensibility from earlier in the nineteenth century, and consequently his work exhibits some of these concerns about economic, national, and cultural disempowerment. Pleasure and pain become one of the main, if implicit, themes of the ghost story and this has its point of origin in accounts of subjectivity that are related (or can be related) to economic factors.

Significantly, accounts of pleasure and pain are not just found in Marx, Freud, and journalistic assessments of the financial system. They are also essential factors in the underlying economic theories of the time, most famously in Jeremy Bentham's and William Jevons's theories of political economy.

Pleasure and pain: Bentham

Bentham's writings on utilitarianism emphasise the role of pleasure in guiding social actions. One of the texts that ghosts his account of pleasure is Edmund Burke's *A Philosophical Enquiry* (1757), which related pain to feelings of terror in a new theory of sublimity that influenced the eighteenth-century Gothic. Burke not only explored painful (and pleasurable) sensations but also, in his concluding comments, expressed a concern that words or modes of representation (including paintings) could synthetically articulate sublimity in a way which, necessarily, questioned the whole notion of a 'natural' sublime.[20] The issue of interpretation and representation also dogs accounts of political economy such as Bentham's and Jevons's.

Bentham in *An Introduction to the Principles of Morals and Legislation* (1789) expresses the idea of a virtuous act through a metaphor of economic balance:

> Sum up all the values of all the *pleasures* on the one side, and those of all the *pains* on the other. The balance, if it be on the side of pleasure, will give the *good* tendency of the act upon the whole, with respect to the interests of that *individual* person; if on the side of pain, the bad tendency of it upon the whole.[21]

Such a view suggests that moral actions can be gauged by how much pleasure they generate, so that how to calibrate happiness becomes a prime consideration for understanding motivation. Bentham's model of subjectivity is built around notions of pleasure and pain which are central to the Gothic's construction of pleasurable terror and notions of instability which are linked to the uncanny. The problem with Bentham's account of pleasure and pain is that, rather like Freud's account of *heimlich* and *unheimlich*, he cannot keep the two terms apart. Bentham lists a series of fourteen 'simple pleasures' which is followed by a list that reworks these 'pleasures' as 'pains', so that, to give one example, 'The pleasures of piety' are counterbalanced by 'The pains of piety' (p. 219). What is pleasurable can become painful, a view which ultimately compromises his schematic model of balance and loss.

The difficulty faced by Bentham is that the attempt to 'objectively' evaluate subjective emotions cannot fit an abstract notion of good and bad conceived of on putatively economic lines. Bentham acknowledges that 'in many instances the desire of pleasure and the sense of pain, run into one another indistinguishably' (p. 197), so that ultimately the problem becomes constituted as one of definition.

Bentham also inherits from Burke an issue about language which threatens to compromise the possibility of measuring the relationship between pleasure and pain. Burke in the *Philosophical Enquiry* notes of such feelings that 'People are not liable to be mistaken in their feelings, but they are very frequently wrong in the *names* they give them' (p. 30, my italics). Bentham addresses this problem of accurately naming an emotion in a footnote, where he comments, 'The great difficulty lies in the nature of the words; which are not, like pain and pleasure, names of homogenous real entities, but names of various fictitious entities, for which no common genus is to be found' (p. 131). The problem is thus one of transposition as not only are pleasure and pain potentially indistinguishable, but language itself is in danger of making them obsolete as words become devoid of meaning. Bentham returned to this issue in a discussion of how words can create 'a bad sense' of otherwise positive or at best indifferent emotions. In these circumstances an overly passionate use of language creates 'fictitious entities, which are framed only by considering pleasures or pains in some particular point of view' (p. 196). Earlier he commented on 'this imperfection of language' (p. 186) as it compromises his ability to coherently assert the idea that either pleasure or pain can be objectively represented. As with Freud's uncanny, the terms slide into each other but the additional problem is that the terms are themselves inherently unstable.

Bentham's account of pleasure and pain is thus conditioned by a subtext concerning how to locate them. The failure to define and locate such feelings implies that utilitarianism cannot be developed in pragmatic terms. Issues about representing the seemingly unrepresentable are not just confined to theories of political economy or notions of moral justice. The ghost story also intervenes in these moments of destabilisation as they address issues of representation, interpretation, and the inner life which refocus the cultural context that is articulated within utilitarian ideas.

Whilst Marx and Freud emphasise the notion of visibility, Bentham focuses on the idea of presence. As Marx attempts to make the ghosted labour appear within the product so Bentham searches for a language that can represent the ineffable. Freud attempts a psychological explanation for the ghost to try to make visible the reality that lurks within the symbol. All are thus concerned with the issue of visibility and presence, an issue also central to the ghost story as it explores how models of the unstable self can be represented and understood.

These cultural issues transcend their specific economic, political, and psychological contexts. The Gothic, in the form of the ghost story, is one such place where these issues are brought together in a series of debates about money, subjectivity, and pleasure. It is this latter issue which William Jevons was to readdress in his response to Benthamite utilitarianism in *The Theory of Political Economy* (1871).

Jevons's pleasure

Jevons's book provides an important reassessment of Bentham and a critique of David Ricardo. Ricardo in *On the Principles of Political Economy and Taxation* had argued that value was determined by the costs incurred in the labour process.[22] Jevons suggested a more psychological explanation of value by arguing that it was determined by the needs of the consumer. For Jevons, the consumer was the ultimate arbiter of a commodity's use-value and therefore the consumer determined the value of the product. This emphasises the role that psychology plays in determining value.[23] However, this poses a problem for Jevons (one which he inherits from Bentham), concerning how to scientifically measure a psychology of pleasure and pain which determines whether an individual will, or will not, purchase particular commodities. How to objectively calibrate subjective emotion becomes, for Jevons, the fundamental task for the economist. He states in the book's preface that he has 'attempted to treat [the] economy as a calculus of pleasure and pain'[24] and he notes of his methodology that, 'The nature of wealth and value is explained by consideration of indefinitely small amounts of pleasure and pain, just as the theory of statics is made to rest upon the equality of indefinitely small amounts of energy' (p. 44).

Jevons also proposes a refinement of Bentham's conclusions, which had tended to treat pleasure and pain as abstractions. For Jevons pleasure is a fluctuating emotion that depends upon demand because too much exposure to a commodity decreases the pleasure one derives from it, or as Jevons puts it, 'The natural law of pleasure is then clearly stated, somewhat as follows: *Increase of the same kind of consumption yields pleasure continuously diminishing up to the point of satiety*' (p. 60, italics in Jevons).

Too much of a good thing depletes the appetite, and Jevons develops a mathematical equation which plots the moment at which pleasure disappears. He elaborates on this in an account of symbols and how they represent the subjective state of pleasure. In Bentham the issue of presence was problematised by the function of language. However, for Jevons mathematics and linguistics are not incompatible as they come together to help make pleasure objectively visible. Jevons claims that 'the most complicated mathematical problems might be traced out by words', so that 'The symbols of mathematical books are not different in nature from language; they form a perfected system of language, adapted to the notions and relations which we need to express' (p. 79). Crucially, Jevons emphasises that this measures effects (actions) rather than causes (explanations of pleasure), acknowledging that, 'We can no more know nor measure gravity in its own nature than we can measure a feeling' (p. 83), even if we are aware of the effects of both. Jevons therefore attempts to keep the analysis within the realms of the strictly economic, rather than elaborate a sustained psychological explanation for desire.

However, Jevons does not fully dismiss the significance of the inner life. The problem is that the subject's pleasures, conceived of in mathematical terms, do not tell us very much about subjectivity. He emphasises that this type of analysis is beyond his exploration because 'there is never, in any single instance, an attempt made to compare the amount of feeling in one mind with that in another. I see no means by which such comparison can be accomplished' (p. 85). An additional problem is that 'Every mind is [. . .] inscrutable to every other mind, and no common denominator of feeling seems to be possible' (p. 85). The issue of visibility which was central to Marxist scepticism, Freud's uncanny, and writings on financial institutions is restated in this acknowledgement of the apparent inscrutability of subjectivity. Human actions can be calculated, according to Jevons, but they cannot be explained.

Jevons's theory of pleasure is couched in strangely dehumanising terms. The subject's inner life disappears because all that is manifested is an expression of desire that merely appears as an externalised action (such as purchasing a commodity). This echoes how mathematical symbols capture a view of the subject's actions but overlook the role that emotion may play in determining such acts. Subjects therefore become ghostlike as they are configured as versions of the living dead, in which abstract quantities of pleasure and pain appear to abstrusely influence their decision making in the marketplace.

Jevons's theory of the subject, one in which pleasure is too subjective, also makes it difficult for the economist to understand how subjective decisions influence particular buying practices. In his chapter on the 'Theory of Utility' he states:

> Pleasure and pain are undoubtedly the ultimate objects of the calculus of pleasure. To satisfy our wants to the utmost with the least effort – to procure the greatest amount of what is desirable at the expense of the least that is undesirable – in other words, *to maximize pleasure*, is the problem of economics. (p. 101, italics in the original)

Jevons conceives pleasure and pain only by how they relate to the economic system. In this regard he moves beyond Bentham by discounting the presence of other
forms of desire (such as sex, for example, which Bentham considers). This leads
Jevons to distil pleasure and pain into an algebraic theorem which concludes that,
'In a happy life the negative balance involved in production is more than cleared
off by the positive balance of pleasure arising from consumption' (p. 189). How
to define this new 'happiness' was an important, if implicit, issue of the time. The
self-realisation of the subject, in economic and psychological terms, conditions this
discourse of subjectivity and it becomes refracted through a certain type of ghost
story during the period.

The idea that the self can be conceived of in economic terms, and that economics
can be explained psychologically, provides the point of contact between these
seemingly opposed theories of pleasure and pain. It is a point of contact which
plays a prominent role in the ghost story as it addresses issues relating to presence, happiness, the past and the extent to which pleasure can be understood either
in abstractly economic terms (a theme which Dickens, and Wilkie Collins, repeatedly return to) or in psychological terms that incorporate a language of economic
loss and gain in their configurations of desire (a characteristic of Henry James's
ghost stories). A text that helps to illuminate some of these points of contact between
a rhetoric of economics and the world of the self is Freud's *Beyond the Pleasure
Principle* (1920), the final draft of which Freud completed in May 1919, the same
month that he finished writing 'The Uncanny'.

Freud's pleasure principle

Freud begins *Beyond the Pleasure Principle* with an account of psychoanalysis which
is Benthamite in both tone and content:

> In the theory of psychoanalysis we have no hesitation in assuming that the course
> taken by the mental events is automatically regulated by the pleasure principle. We
> believe, that is to say, that the course of these events is invariably set in motion
> by an unpleasurable tension, and that it takes a direction such that its final outcome
> coincides with a lowering of that tension – that is, with an avoidance of unpleasure
> or a production of pleasure.[25]

The language of finance is embedded in this. Pleasure is regarded as 'a
production' and that Freud has a rhetoric of finance in mind is illustrated in his
following comments on how to gauge pleasure in relation to pain. He claims that
in considering them relationally, 'we are introducing an "economic" point of view
into our work; and if, in describing those processes, we try to estimate this
"economic" factor in addition to the "topographical" and "dynamic" ones, we shall,
I think, be giving the most complete description of them' (p. 275).

Freud's approach to pleasure and pain is indebted to his concurrent thinking on the relationship between *heimlich* and *unheimlich*. For Bentham, the problem was that pain could also be pleasurable (as in the uncanny, *unheimlich* merges with *heimlich*), and this means that the language of economics starts to collapse when confronted by particular psychological processes. For Bentham the problem of how to separate pleasure from pain was largely a linguistic one. In Jevons, the subjectivity of the individual was ignored unless it could be quantified by action rather than intent. The self remains inscrutable (Bentham) or is simply lost (Jevons) in these deliberations and Freud's attempt to explain why pleasure can become painful is similarly occluded. He notes that 'The details of the process by which repression turns a possibility of pleasure into a source of unpleasure are not clearly understood or cannot be clearly represented' (p. 279). For Freud it is all the consequence of instinctive processes; the subject appears to be drawn to certain types of self-destructive behaviour in which pain replaces pleasure.

However, Freud also acknowledges that there are two problems with his analysis of pleasure and pain. The first is related to visibility because the instinctive drives that motivate the subject are inherently inscrutable and consequently cannot be observed by a properly located 'scientific' gaze. The second problem relates to the theory itself. As in 'The Uncanny', ultimately Freud cannot quite coherently explain the psychological experience. His theory of pleasure and pain incorporates an evolutionary explanation as to why the self might seek pain rather than pleasure (as a solipsistic protection from an alienating world), but he confesses some dissatisfaction with his findings: 'It may be asked whether and how far I am myself convinced of the truth of the hypotheses that have been set out in these pages. My answer would be that I am not convinced myself and that I do not seek to persuade other people to believe in them' (p. 332). The problem is one of economics. The model of balance and loss just does not seem to apply to psychological processes. The question one is tempted to raise is why apply such a model in the first place? The answer can be explained historically; it is a consequence of attempting to gauge happiness through the filters of the new conceptual system of the nineteenth century: the economically understood self.

This chapter has outlined how a series of seemingly disparate commentators, including Marx, Freud, Bentham, Jevons, and financial journalists, share certain preoccupations. How to account for pleasure and how to define the self through economics, politics, and psychology is what unites these figures. The ghost story is the form which reworks many of these ideas about pleasure, money, and subjectivity as it too addresses how such factors can be made visible by the seemingly invisible ghost. A certain strand in the ghost story is also defined by a focus on debates about money which underpins these new models of subjectivity. Readings of Dickens, Wilkie Collins, Charlotte Riddell, and Henry James will explore such issues.

It would, as mentioned earlier, be crudely reductive to argue that all ghost stories in the nineteenth century are little more than encrypted economic narratives. However, as we have seen, debates about economics are not just debates about money. In their own way political economists such as Bentham and Jevons are writing about desire and subjectivity. Writing about money therefore contributes to a wider attempt at explaining desire in the period.

The ghost story lies at the centre of this discourse. The ghost story addresses issues about subjectivity in ways which are familiar from materialist and psychological writings. Such tales provide us with a unique insight into the limits of that discourse by evidencing a typically Gothic scepticism about the dominant economic context. How to read the ghost story economically and psychologically, and how to Gothically read economics and psychology, are therefore the points of contact which enable an understanding of this wider discourse about desire.

First, it is necessary to discuss visibility, money, and scepticism. Dickens is the key figure here as it is his version of the ghost story which later writers had to contend with. How they either develop or move beyond his writings also indicates the extent to which debates about subjectivity shift in the latter part of the nineteenth century.

Notes

1 David Punter, *The Literature of Terror: The Modern Gothic* (London and New York: Longman, [1980] 1996) p. 194. All subsequent references are to this edition and are given in the text.

2 Karl Marx, *Capital* in David McLellan (ed.), *Karl Marx: Selected Writings* (Oxford: Oxford University Press, 1977) p. 435. All subsequent references are to this edition and are given in the text.

3 Terry Eagleton, *The Ideology of the Aesthetic* (Oxford: Blackwell, [1990] 2000) p. 200.

4 Fred Botting, *Gothic* (London: Routledge, 1996) p. 6.

5 Chris Baldick, *In Frankenstein's Shadow: Myth, Monstrosity and Nineteenth-Century Writing* (Oxford: Clarendon, 1987), see pp. 121–40. All subsequent references are to this edition and are given in the text.

6 Tricia Lootens, 'Fear of Furniture: Commodity Gothicism and the Teaching of Victorian Literature', in Diane Long Hoeveler and Tamar Heller (eds), *Gothic Fiction: The British and American Traditions* (New York: MLA, 2003) pp. 148–58.

7 Gail Turley Houston, *From Dickens to Dracula: Gothic, Economics, and Victorian Fiction* (Cambridge: Cambridge University Press, 2005); Regenia Gagnier, *The Insatiability of Human Wants: Economics and Aesthetics in Market Society* (Chicago: University of Chicago Press, 2000). The latter includes a very useful account of the move from classical to neoclassical economics; however, the particular inflection that I want to pursue here relates to the emotions in the Gothic rather than aesthetics.

8 Julia Briggs, *Night Visitors: The Rise and Fall of the English Ghost Story* (London: Faber, 1977).

9 Julia Briggs, 'The Ghost Story' in David Punter (ed.), *A Companion to the Gothic* (Oxford: Blackwell, 2000) pp. 122–31, p. 123. All subsequent references are to this edition and are given in the text.

10 Sigmund Freud, 'The Uncanny' in *Art and Literature: Jensen's* Gradiva, *Leonardo Da Vinci and Other Works*, trans. James Strachey, ed. Albert Dickson, vol. 14 Penguin Freud Library (Harmondsworth: Penguin, 1985) pp. 339–76, p. 364.

11 See my *Gothic Radicalism: Literature, Philosophy and Psychoanalysis in the Nineteenth Century* (Basingstoke: Macmillan, 2000), where I explore how the Gothic rewrites an Idealist tradition of thought from Burke to Freud. Marx does not feature in that analysis, and although his critique of materialism is grounded in a specific political view of the world, it nevertheless does encode a new form of idealism, one which can transcend the condition of false consciousness.

12 Jacques Derrida, *Specters of Marx: The State of the Debt, the Work of Mourning, & the New International* (New York and London: Routledge, 1994) p. 8. All subsequent references are to this edition and are given in the text.

13 Mary Poovey (ed.), *The Financial System in Nineteenth-Century Britain* (Oxford: Oxford University Press, 2003) p. 2. All subsequent references are to this edition and are given in the text.

14 There was much concern during the period with the Stock Exchange, which was often perceived as encouraging a form of gambling and therefore immorality. See Poovey, *The Financial System*, pp. 149–200.

15 W.E. Aytoun, 'The National Debt and the Stock Exchange', *Blackwood's Edinburgh Magazine*, 66 (December 1849), 655–78; in Poovey, *The Financial System in Nineteenth-Century Britain*, pp. 127–48, p. 128. All subsequent references are to this edition and are given in the text.

16 Anon., 'Stockbroking and the Stock Exchange', *Fraser's Magazine*, n.s. 14 (July 1876), 84–103; in Poovey, *The Financial System in Nineteenth-Century Britain*, pp. 149–73, p. 149. All subsequent references are to this edition and are given in the text.

17 See, for example, Stephen D. Arata's 'The Occidental Tourist: *Dracula* and the Anxiety of Reverse Colonialism', *Victorian Studies*, 33.4 (1990), 621–45, and Franco Moretti's 'Dialectic of Fear' in *Signs Taken for Wonders: Essays in the Sociology of Literary Form* (London: Verso, 1983) pp. 83–108.

18 Moretti, *Signs Taken for Wonders*, p. 84.

19 Alexander Innes Shand, 'Speculative Investments', *Blackwood's Edinburgh Magazine*, 120 (September 1876), 293–316; in Poovey, *The Financial System in Nineteenth-Century Britain*, pp. 173–200, p. 174. All subsequent references are to this edition and are given in the text.

20 Edmund Burke, *A Philosophical Enquiry into the Origin of our Ideas of the Sublime and the Beautiful*, ed. and introd. Adam Phillips (Oxford: Oxford University Press, [1757] 1998), see pp. 158–61. All subsequent references are to this edition and are given in the text.

21 Jeremy Bentham, *An Introduction to the Principles of Morals and Legislation* in *Bentham's Selected Writings on Utilitarianism*, introd. Ross Harrison (Ware, Herts: Wordsworth, 2001) pp. 73–309, p. 117. All subsequent references are to this edition and are given in the text.

22 David Ricardo, *On the Principles of Political Economy and Taxation* (London and Toronto: Dent, [1817] 1926). Regenia Gagnier, in *The Insatiability of Human Wants*, emphasises the importance of John Stuart Mill's *Principles of Political Economy* (1848) during the period. However, the emphasis here is on the implicit dialogue that takes place between Bentham and Jevons as two representative figures of particular versions of political economy.

23 Gagnier, *The Insatiability of Human Wants*, p. 4.

24 William Jevons, *The Theory of Political Economy*, ed. R.D. Collison Black (Harmondsworth: Penguin, [1871] 1970) p. 44. All subsequent references are to this edition and are given in the text.

25 Sigmund Freud, *Beyond the Pleasure Principle* in *On Metapsychology*, ed. James Strachey and Angela Richards, vol. 11 Penguin Freud Library (Harmondsworth: Penguin, 1984) pp. 275–338, p. 275. All subsequent references are to this edition and are given in the text.

2

Dickens's spectres: sight, money, and reading the ghost story

In *Bleak House* (1853) Lord and Lady Dedlock's housekeeper, Mrs Rouncewell, informs the socially ambitious Guppy that Chesney Wold's terrace is haunted: ' "The terrace below is much admired. It is called, from an old story in the family, The Ghost's Walk." "No?" says Mr Guppy, greedily curious; "what's the story, miss? Is it anything about a picture?" '[1]

Guppy's eager response suggests a familiarity with ghost stories – that they are stylised and conventional but nevertheless generate narrative expectations. However, there is also ambivalence here because Guppy has just realised that Esther Summerson resembles the portrait of Lady Dedlock, and his question thus infers a relationship between them. For Mrs Rouncewell the 'story has nothing to do with a picture' (p. 139) but is about class, as 'She regards a ghost as one of the privileges of the upper classes; a genteel distinction to which the common people have no claim' (pp. 139–40). Her view is in part tempered by the Dedlocks' ghost story, which concerns the marital discord between an earlier Lord and Lady Dedlock, who took different sides during the rebellion against Charles I. This earlier, republican, Lady Dedlock died in an accident when she went to lame the horses so that her husband and his followers would not be able to fight for the king. Mrs Rouncewell notes of this tale ' "that it *must be heard*" ' (p. 141, italics in original), and the ghost of Lady Dedlock is often heard walking on the terrace.

The subsequently insistent presence of this narrative develops Mrs Rouncewell's tale of marital disloyalty and confirms Guppy's implicit sense that 'the picture', or the relationship between Lady Dedlock and Esther, is connected to the narrative of the ghost. Later, when Esther discovers that she is Lady Dedlock's illegitimate child, she walks on the terrace and realises 'that there was a dreadful truth in the legend of the Ghost's Walk; that it was I, who was to bring calamity upon the stately house; and that my warning feet were haunting it even then' (p. 571). The past comes back to haunt, and so destabilises, the present, revealing a history which also represents a republican overthrow of the aristocratic Dedlocks. Alison Milbank has noted that this later scene forces Esther to 'flee in terror at the realisation that it is she who is its [Chesney Wold's] ghost, its alienated past, just as she is the embodiment of the absent Bleak House'.[2]

The point is that the ghost story is an allegory, an idea which will be pursued in this chapter. Whilst the principal focus here is on money, and more specifically allegories about money, it is also important to acknowledge that Dickens's major contribution to the development of the ghost story lies in how he employs allegory in order to encode wider issues relating to history, money, and identity. That Dickens is often self-conscious about this is apparent in his use of ghosting in *Bleak House*, where Guppy's reference to 'the picture' is both naive (a reader's expectations about narrative convention) and sophisticated (the suggested link between Esther and Lady Dedlock). Milbank notes of *Bleak House* that 'Allegory reveals the existence of meaning itself' (p. 93), and Dickens's ghosts are always about something other than just being ghosts in any conventionally, Gothically, understood way.

Dickens's contribution to the ghost story has not always received due acknowledgement. None of Dickens's tales is anthologised in *The Oxford Book of English Ghost Stories* (2002) and only one, the atypically non-allegorical 'To be Taken with a Grain of Salt' (1865), is included in *The Oxford Book of Victorian Ghost Stories* (2003). It is Dickens's more frequently unconventional use of ghosts which seems, at least apparently to anthologists, to distance him from his peers, a view which overlooks the considerable innovations that Dickens introduced into the ghost story.[3]

In 'A Christmas Tree' (1850), largely a celebration of family togetherness, Dickens provides a series of likely plot synopses of ghost stories which might be told by the fireside over the Christmas holiday. These synoptic plotlines include tales of aristocratic secrets, of people coming back from the dead to warn the living, of encounters with ghosts that anticipate a character's immediate demise, of meeting the ghost of someone recently deceased, and of being haunted by a child who had been maliciously treated by their guardian. Dickens notes of such tales that in them:

> There is no end to the old houses, resounding galleries, and dismal state bed-chambers, and haunted wings shut up for many years, through which we may ramble, with an agreeable creeping up our back, and encounter any number of ghosts, but (it is worthy of remark perhaps) reducible to a very few general types and classes; for, ghosts have little originality, and 'walk' in a beaten track.[4]

Dickens's apparent dismissal of the ghost story should not be taken too seriously as one of his principal ambitions is to translate the form into an allegorical mode, which whilst ostensibly telling one story (about the history of the Dedlocks, for example), is really telling another (about the problems confronted by the present Dedlocks).

That Dickens was particularly interested in ghost stories is also underlined by the frequency with which they appear as interpolated narratives in his novels. 'The Bagman's Story' in *The Pickwick Papers* (1837), for example, relates how a chair haunted by the spiritual guardian of a widow persuades Tom Smart, who is staying the night in the inn owned by the widow, to frighten away an undesirable suitor.

Tom does this and later marries the widow. The jocular, unconventional mode of the narrative enables Dickens to represent some form of spirit intervention, whilst simultaneously mocking the *faux* gravity of the ghost story. (Tom is initially not sure if the chair is really talking to him, or if it is a consequence of him having drunk too much punch.)

The Pickwick Papers includes other narratives such as 'A Madman's Manuscript', 'Containing the Story of the Bagman's Uncle', and perhaps the better-known 'The Story of the Goblins who stole a Sexton'. These loquacious tales whilst addressing issues about insanity and moral conduct do not, in keeping with the novel as a whole, take themselves too seriously. At the end of 'Containing the Story of the Bagman's Uncle', which centres on mail coaches, there is a punchline about the 'ghosts of mail-coaches' carrying 'dead letters'.[5] The implication is that the early Dickens cannot quite take the ghost story too seriously.

The point at which Dickens's writing develops a more sombre turn is usually seen as being marked by *Hard Times* (1854). However, a case can be made that it is in the Christmas books, especially *A Christmas Carol* (1843), that this darkening mood begins to appear because by this point Dickens is no longer exploiting the comedic possibilities of the ghost story. In *A Christmas Carol* the ghosts become, at some formal level, a device which enables Scrooge to envision different, potential, versions of himself. The apparently celebratory ending is not as unambiguous as it initially appears. Whilst the ghosts function as a formal device, at an allegorical level a rather different story is told.

As outlined in the previous chapter, how money comes to bear on the genesis of the Victorian ghost story is fundamental in appreciating why so many ghost stories of the period address, at different levels of explicitness, the role of money. It is when Dickens explores such issues that he develops a particular mode of allegory that identifies how consciousness is formed in a money-based society. This is not to say that the ghost story and models of the economy can be simply conflated, but rather it is to acknowledge that Dickens's ghost tales frequently function as allegories about how individuals negotiate their way around the financial system even whilst that system appears to psychologically 'possess' them (and ghost stories are *the* narrative form which concerns the possession of the self). It is when Dickens develops this allegorical mode that he introduces a new seriousness into his writings.

As we shall see, not only *A Christmas Carol* but also the lesser-known narrative 'A December Vision' (1850), which can be read as either journalised fiction or fictionalised journalism, develops an explicitly allegorical moral concerning money and industrialisation through its use of spectralisation.[6] This chapter discusses *A Christmas Carol* and 'A December Vision' and how they relocate the economic issues of the time, before concluding with a reading of 'The Signalman' (1866). 'The Signalman' is a tale in which allegory seemingly breaks down, and its deliberations and prevarications about meaning and where it is to be found both reflect a view of the industrial economy (through oblique references to investments in the railway system at the time) and raise issues about identity and interpretation which have significance for the account of Wilkie Collins in Chapter 3. 'The Signalman' can also be read as a deliberation on how to read the ghost story for its hidden political meanings. It has an important place in Dickens's writings because its self-reflexive character indicates Dickens's self-consciousness about how his spectral allegories needed to be read.

A Christmas Carol: seeing money

The putative morality of *A Christmas Carol*, one in which a social conscience and the rediscovery of an inner life become mutually supporting elements of a revitalised consciousness, indicates that change, whether political or personal, is dependent upon a matter of perception. The tale suggests that Scrooge needs to develop a form of social conscience that is generated through a rediscovered compassion for others. However, society is not transformed in this moment but merely reinterpreted as a set of unresolved problems which compassion identifies but can only partially alleviate. To some degree this is to assert a commonplace criticism of Dickens; namely that he is better at identifying social problems than he is at formulating solutions to them. However, the problem lies much deeper than this because the tale fails to explicitly confront the role of money, which is represented as both the source of the problem and its apparent solution. Scrooge's benign, seasonally redistributive capitalism implies a change at the social periphery (granted to employees, or staged within the family) which does not touch the central mechanisms of economic power.

However, at an unconscious level the text acknowledges the presence of unresolved issues about money which are displaced in the narrative as the language of money takes on a force of its own, influencing certain modes of representation which elude any formally rational explanation of them within the text. The key question which Dickens poses is what does the ghost make visible? It is a question which is intimately related to the process of perception, a process that indicates just how far the tale associates money with the ostensible requirements of moral change even as, at a more complex level, it implies the presence of a political unconscious through which these debates about money are expressed.

Dickens's explicit reference to ghosts glosses the Marxian model of the subject who becomes disembodied by an attachment to wealth. For Marx the self under capitalism ceases to have an ontological reality of its own, instead it substitutes within itself a series of object-attachments which replace any real (or otherwise economically non-motivated) sense of autonomy. This model of subjectivity is expressed in the representation of the chain which Marley's ghost drags along with him. We are informed that 'It was long, and wound about him like a tail; and it was made (for Scrooge observed it closely) of cash-boxes, keys, padlocks, ledgers, deeds, and

heavy purses wrought in steel'.[7] This litany of economically orientated objects contrasts with the insubstantiality of Marley, whose 'body was transparent: so that Scrooge,
observing him, and looking through his waistcoat, could see the two buttons on his
coat behind' (p. 57). The bringing together of Marley's chain and his liminal self
is effected through Scrooge's gaze as the narrative emphasises that what is important
is his observation of both; an observation which suggests a relationship between
the chain of objects and the spectre of Marley. In Marxist terms the encounter with
Marley makes visible what capitalism tries to render invisible, namely the labour
which is inherent to, and so sublimated within, the process of commodity production.
This is a key moment of identification for Scrooge because, as Marx acknowledged,
the notion that objects possessed an aura, or some inherent magical vitality of their
own, was a fundamental element of ideology in a money-based economy. As Lynn
M. Voskuil has asserted, in an argument specifically relating to the perception of
commodities, 'this vision of reality – in which products spring spontaneously to
life as commodities – is an ideological illusion. But that illusion is the lynchpin
[sic] of bourgeois production, willful blindness the key to the system'.[8] Scrooge is
thus confronted by objects whose 'vitality' contains the 'life' of Marley, who informs
Scrooge that 'I wear the chain I forged in life . . . I made it link by link, and yard
by yard' (p. 61) in what is a symbolic representation of his attachment to commodities and their production. The narrative emphasis on Scrooge's sight indicates
the desire to move beyond the 'wilful blindness' engendered by 'the system'.

The emphasis on seeing is used as a conceit in the tale for Scrooge's need
to develop a form of compassion which transforms his vision of the streets and
the social problems with which, ultimately, they are associated. Significantly the
description of the streets at the beginning of the tale suggests their spectrality: 'The
fog came pouring in at every chink and keyhole, and was so dense without, that
although the court was of the narrowest, the houses opposite were mere phantoms'
(p. 47). The phantom draws attention to the presence of a problem (here a social
one related to poverty) which at present is concealed from Scrooge. This idea of
a spectral atmosphere is later recycled in the opening description of the final of
the three spirits: 'When it came near him, Scrooge bent down upon his knee; for
in the very air through which this Spirit moved it seemed to scatter gloom and
mystery' (p. 110). However, after the final visitation Scrooge perceives the street
in a different way: 'No fog, no mist; clear, bright, jovial, stirring, cold; cold,
piping for the blood to dance to; Golden sunlight; Heavenly sky; sweet fresh air;
merry bells' (p. 128). The tale suggests that Scrooge's newfound compassion
creates a bridge between the world of money and the scenes of poverty which Scrooge
had, hitherto, consciously ignored or overlooked. However, the emphasis on
perception also suggests that there exist right and wrong ways of perceiving
the streets, and the latter becomes associated with alienation. Indeed, the tale
underlines this notion of estrangement when it grants Scrooge a vision of how this
alienation manifests itself through a form of ghostliness:

The air was filled with phantoms, wandering hither and thither in restless haste, and moaning as they went. Every one of them wore chains like Marley's Ghost; some few [. . .] were linked together; none were free [. . .]. The misery with them all was, clearly, that they sought to interfere, for good, in human matters, and had lost the power for ever. (p. 65)

What this represents is the disempowering of the economically powerful. On a more sophisticated level it also implies that the economically powerful have become disempowered *because* of their wealth. It also suggests that the economically powerful have failed because of their inappropriate use of wealth. The irony is that it is only when they have become ghosts that they recognise the insubstantiality of wealth. Dickens thus implies that once spectrality occurs (i.e. death), the power to change is lost. This explains why wealth in its spectral form has no power to change society for the better. Ultimately, the arrival of the ghosts is intended to offer Scrooge the chance to alter the spectral presence of wealth before he too becomes a spectre.[9] The question therefore concerns how money is to be used, or redistributed, for charitable ends. To this extent the ghosts, including the three Christmas spirits and Marley's, exist to engender compassion as well as fear. As Marley informs the terrified Scrooge, 'you have yet a chance and hope of escaping my fate. A chance and hope of my procuring' (p. 63). The point is to change the way that Scrooge perceives the streets; this change is dependent upon him seeing money, or how it can be used, in a different way.

The issue of perception is also related to seeing a link between wealth and poverty. It is important to acknowledge that during the period there emerged an often implicit debate which argued the case that poverty was the consequence of wealth, a debate which will be addressed shortly. The tale suggests that Scrooge cannot provide the solution to the problem which he has helped to create. Charity is not the real answer. However, the issue of perception cuts much deeper than this because the failure to acknowledge a link between product and labour required the act of wilful blindness that Voskuil, following Marx, suggests. Therefore what was seen was just as important as what was overlooked. *A Christmas Carol* uses sight as one of its controlling conceits for how the streets need to be reinterpreted. However, in this process a misperception of them is developed because of this refusal to see a link between wealth and poverty. At an unconscious level, the text acknowledges the presence of this misperception through a series of images which defy Scrooge's attempt to understand them, and which are related to the instabilities of money as a criterion of absolute value.

The issue of perception and misperception is linked to the idea of commodities. What is visible (the commodity) and what is invisible (the labour which forged the object, and the ghost) need to be forced into an alliance, as indeed they ostensibly are in the representation of Marley's spectre. The relationship between money and poverty is concealed within this image as it is expressed in predominantly theoretical terms (despite the insistent presence of the street). This other, more overtly political view of money is, nevertheless, also associated with a duality concerning the relationship between wealth and poverty that parallels, and potentially displaces, the relationship between the ghost and the object.

According to Christopher Herbert, the refusal to relate wealth to poverty can be witnessed in canonical anthropological and psychoanalytical texts from the period which unconsciously reveal the link between money and poverty even whilst they attempt to suppress it. Herbert claims, for example, that James Frazer's argument in *The Golden Bough* (1890–1915), concerning the blurring between the sacred and the profane in supposedly 'primitive' societies, relocates an association between money and dirt. For Herbert two essential, but quite different, ideas about money emerge at the time. The first acknowledges that money simultaneously creates wealth and poverty; and the second wilfully suppresses this relationship, or only admits it in transposed ways (such as in Frazer's projection of this tension back into the past). Herbert also explores Freud's analyses of the relationship between money and excrement, and how Freud's projection of this on to archaic societies aligns his work with Frazer. For Herbert, Freud fails to 'speculate upon the significance of his theory for the analysis of social phenomena under modern capitalism'.[10] By contrast, Ruskin in *Unto This Last* (1862) and Mayhew in *London Labour and the London Poor* (1861–2) make this suppressed link between wealth and poverty clear, leading Herbert to conclude that money in the period has 'two contradictory valences: it will function both as the index of all value and as the index of the nullification of value; it will be the sign of wealth and poverty alike' (p. 194). The issue is not properly resolved in *A Christmas Carol* because the final emphasis is on how Scrooge uses money for charitable purposes. Discussion of poverty is clearly marginalised because the emphasis is on how Scrooge needs to effect a compassionate change by becoming a *better* capitalist, as it is only through putting his money into circulation that, paradoxically, the inequalities generated by capitalism are alleviated. At the end, for example, when Scrooge awakens on Christmas day he instructs a passing boy to purchase a turkey from the butcher's: 'Go and buy it, and tell 'em to bring it here, that I may give them the direction where to take it. Come back with the man, and I'll give you a shilling. Come back with him in less than five minutes, and I'll give you half-a-crown!' (p. 129). Scrooge may have gone from miserable miser to jovial capitalist but this hardly transforms the system.

One additional irony is that Scrooge's wealth creates an illusion of poverty. Scrooge is a miser who hoards his money and lives in impoverished style, and this develops an alternative relationship between wealth and poverty. However, the vision of bounty which is associated with the spirit of Christmas present relocates the idea of object relationships which had conditioned earlier representations of Marley. When Scrooge awakens he finds that his drab residence has been transformed:

> Heaped up on the floor, to form a kind of throne, were turkeys, geese, game poultry, brawn, great joints of meat, suckling-pigs, long wreaths of sausages, mince-pies,

> plum-puddings, barrels of oysters, red-hot chestnuts, cherry-cheeked apples, juicy
> oranges, luscious pears, immense twelfth-cakes, and seething bowls of punch, that
> made the chamber dim with their delicious steam. (p. 86)

Such an accumulation of objects is meant, paradoxically, to replace the presence
of objects. However, this mountain of comestibles is later replaced by images of
starvation when the spirit introduces Scrooge to the children who represent
Ignorance and Want, and who seemingly exist within the folds of his gown. The
narrative therefore unconsciously forges a link between bounty and the 'degradation' that it produces. An argument which is ostensibly about the misuse of money
thus incorporates within it an implicit account about how money generates such
'monsters' (p. 108), and so makes visible the issues about money addressed by
Herbert.

In *A Christmas Carol* Scrooge's blurred, fog-laden view of the streets is
replaced by a sharper focus at the end, but the new, invigorated moral clarity which
is associated with this does not suggest that Dickens's wine merchant develops
a new perception of the system which has created his wealth. Nevertheless, the
narrative will elsewhere express – even if unconsciously – an anxiety about perception which implies that Dickens does not quite lose a grasp on this problem.
This can be seen when Scrooge encounters the ghost of Christmas past:

> its belt sparkled and glittered now in one part and now in another, and what was
> light one instant, at another time was dark, so the figure itself fluctuated in its dis-
> tinctness: being now a thing with one arm, now with one leg, now a head without a
> body: of which dissolving parts, no outline would be visible in the dense gloom wherein
> they melted away. And in the very wonder of this, it would be itself again; distinct
> and clear as ever. (p. 68)

Within the context of the tale and its economic obsessions the protean, shifting
form represents a desire to make the system visible. In this instance the occult
fluctuations of the ghost unconsciously represent the unpredictable nature of the
economy during a time of economic depression (the so-called 'hungry forties', which
has turned Scrooge into a miser). To some degree this image is also used to suggest the problem of memory, as Scrooge is subsequently confronted by the moment
in his life when he chose wealth over love. However, it also indicates a problem
with reclaiming that past, as this is one part of Scrooge's life that he cannot alter.
Herbert in his account of Frazer and Freud argued that they transfer to the past
a duality about money which has its place in the present. Money becomes something dirty, but in a more abstract sense money is prone to fluctuation. The very
protean quality of money, its non-objective status, becomes mapped on to the past
at this point in the tale. Crucially Scrooge cannot see this; instead he perceives a
confrontation with a changing, partially familiar form. As with Herbert's argument,
the abstract protean quality of money and the potentially undecipherable commodity
(identified by both Marx and Derrida) are projected out of the present and on to

an unreclaimable, although not unredeemable, past. Time and how it is related to the instabilities of money is thus a central issue in the narrative.

Time is money

A Christmas Carol overtly explores the disjunction between work and leisure. Bob Cratchit's request for time off to enjoy the 'holiday' period and Scrooge's claim that this will lose him money are clearly meant to indicate this. At another level the tale explores how Scrooge needs to reorientate himself in time in order to effect his transformation. Time to some significant degree therefore redeems Scrooge as he comes to inhabit a rather different kind of present than hitherto. However, this idea of present time is linked to the notion that Scrooge needs to put money into circulation rather than hoard his wealth.

Early images of Scrooge suggest that he is caught within the present because he is unable to look either back or forward. It is not just money which needs to be put into circulation but also Scrooge, and in this way Scrooge becomes like money, incorporating both wealth and poverty, miserliness and generosity, and degradation and compassion. Money only becomes of use once it is exchanged for the kinds of goods that help to keep the economy moving. Scrooge is only able to develop a conscience once he overcomes his life of splendid isolation and is put into social circulation. However, before this mobility takes place Scrooge becomes a time-traveller, and this suggests that an alternative, non-capitalist, model of time has an important bearing on how the system is re-evaluated.

In the tale it is the past which covertly articulates the images of projection which Herbert argued conditioned the work of Frazer and Freud. As we saw with the protean figure of the spirit of the past, at one level it represents the instability which Mary Poovey has noted as inherent to money at the time.[11] At the end the spirit faces Scrooge, and Scrooge 'turned upon the Ghost, and seeing that it looked upon him with a face, in which in some strange way there were fragments of all the faces it had shown him' (p. 83). Scrooge is haunted by the past but this encounter is also linked to money through the earlier image of the ghosts and their inability to offer charity to the poor, as both images share the sense of familiarity and strangeness as well as the unease that they represent an inner anxiety that Scrooge does not quite understand.

The point appears to be to reclaim the past so that Scrooge can begin the process of redemption. However, what is required is an ability to interpret the signs which these protean shapes possess as it will enable Scrooge to secure a different future. Scrooge, however, misreads them as the jumbled images of memory, even though the tale implies that Scrooge's consciousness reflects the protean aspects of money itself. Thus Scrooge's inner life becomes inherently associated with money, and this is the unconscious level at which the tale consistently expresses its unease about money. The problem is, as his earlier suitor had told him, that he looks upon the past as 'an unprofitable dream' (pp. 80–1) because 'the master-passion, Gain, engrosses you' (p. 79). Scrooge's inner life thus represents a personified and metaphoric attempt on Dickens's part to make money visible by showing how consciousness in a money-based society takes on the acquisitive aspects of money.

In *A Christmas Carol* there are unresolved tensions between the stress placed on the creation of a social conscience that will lead to charitable acts, and an unconscious acknowledgment that money cannot alleviate the problems it has created. However, there is also a more subtle way in which this is addressed: it is manifested through images of conceptual disorder, suggested by the fluctuating 'strange . . . fragments', which relocate the protean, Gothic, potentially destabilising qualities of money. The problem is how to read these moments because it requires a sophisticated reading of the semantics of money. How to read is also related to perception and whilst Dickens leaves the issue of money as an apparently unreadable element within the text, its significance is suggested by the anxiety which it generates.

Christmas revisited

Dickens returned to issues concerning identity and money in subsequent Christmas books, but his most explicit reworking of the incomplete ideas relating to money in *A Christmas Carol* are developed in 'A December Vision', published as a lead article on 14 December 1850 in *Household Words*. The opening of the article is strangely, and strongly, evocative of the opening of Marx and Engels's *Communist Manifesto* published two years earlier. Dickens writes, 'I saw a mighty Spirit, traversing the world without any rest or pause'. However, this is not the spectre of communism (a being coming into existence) but a spectre which represents the spirit of the industrial society. Dickens notes: 'It was omnipresent, it was all-powerful, it had no compunction, no pity, no relenting sense that any appeal from any race of men could reach'.[12] This pitiless spectre possesses an invisibility which glosses the difficulty in seeing money that characterised *A Christmas Carol*. Here industry introduces death into the world and at the very point at which one confronts it, its basilisk gaze is turned upon its victims: 'It was invisible to every creature born upon the earth, save one to each. It turned its shaded face on whatsoever living thing, one time; and straight the end of that thing was come' (p. 306).

Dickens emphasises that this is a spirit of the machine which carries out its mission without compassion: 'It had its work appointed; it inexorably did what was appointed to it to do; and neither sped nor slackened' (p. 306), it 'never rested from its labour' (p. 307). The fact that it is invisibly at work means, so Dickens suggests, that people are prone to ignoring its effects, consoling themselves with the slogan that 'IT WILL LAST MY TIME!' (p. 308) so that it becomes a problem for later generations to resolve. Dickens is trying to make visible that which a culture ignores. In *A Christmas Carol* visibility is unconsciously associated with money and with how to make its presence felt within a psychologically understood scopic field in which the effects of money upon consciousness could be made clear. In 'A December Vision' the privileged sight is, as the title suggests, granted to the narrator, who accounts for the actions of the spectre through quasi-biblical language which associates the mechanical spectre with an impending apocalypse that touches all classes: 'And, ever among them, as among all ranks and grades of the mortals, in all parts of the globe, the Spirit went; and ever by thousands, in their brutish state, with all the gifts of God perverted in their breasts or trampled out, they died' (p. 307).

At such moments the narrator sounds like a Marxian Saint John the Evangelist, in what is an attempt to forge a coherent political vision that combines insight into the dangers of industrialisation with a moral apprehension of how such dangers can be resolved. Dickens stresses the need to awaken some moral insight which can halt the spread of industrialisation. The role that money plays in this is, as it is in *A Christmas Carol*, marginalised even as it is given concrete form in these displaced visions of the machine. The issue of ownership of the machine is never questioned; instead the emphasis is on the industrial pollution which is generated and which transcends class boundaries. However, this is not as conservative as it seems; rather it implies the kind of relationship between wealth and poverty (here represented as the relationship between industrialisation and ownership) that, for Herbert, characterised the period. What is at issue is therefore the death of a money-based society which touches all:

> I saw the rich struck down in their strength, their darling children weakened and withered, their marriageable sons and daughters perish in their prime. I saw that not one miserable wretch breathed out his poisoned life in the deepest cellar of the most neglected town, but, from the surrounding atmosphere, some particles of his infection were borne away, charged with heavy retribution on the general guilt. (p. 308)

Dickens later developed such a view in his representation of the pestilential derelict housing of Tom All-Alone's in *Bleak House*. Wealth creates poverty which creates disease which kills the wealthy; society therefore self-destructs because of its inability to regulate the excesses of an industrial society. To this extent it might appear that 'A December Vision' is simply about self-destructive class relations rather than an implicit exploration of the formulation of unconscious experience in a money-based society. However, Dickens is concerned that the very invisibility of infection operates as a conceit for the spread of political complacency. Consciousness in this instance might not be related to the tacit fluctuations of the economy (an economic model of subjectivity personified by Scrooge), but it is formed out of the inability to develop scepticism about the notion of progress. In this sense a model of passivity and acceptance is politically produced by a society which seeks economic and intellectual conformity – a point which Dickens was to expand on at length in the debate about education in *Hard Times*.

In 'A December Vision' there are no individuals, merely types, but Dickens uses this in order to develop ideas concerning how the system generates a particular model of consciousness, rather than arguing that the system is an extension of consciousness. For this reason the spectre is machine-like, is manifested as a representative of a system which imposes itself because its great trick is that it also creates an inability to generate any alternative vision. Consciousness in this drama is fundamentally suicidal because it is trapped within its own tautologies, unable to see itself as it is. The moment of self-realisation, when the spectre looks upon you, coincides with the death of the subject because at this point the spectre has been exposed. The knowing subject is destroyed at the moment it gains consciousness.

Dickens suggests an aporia. In *A Christmas Carol* consciousness can never free itself from the dictates of the economy. This is unconsciously acknowledged in the text as an issue which it cannot properly address. The tale cannot generate the kind of scepticism that is required to see how money operates because the point at which this vision can appear is politically stifled by an alternative emphasis on charitable works which merely (in the implication that Scrooge needs to become a better capitalist) seems to extend the system by other means. How one can develop this scepticism is the subject of 'A December Vision', where Dickens explicitly links the problems of generating an alternative vision to the idea of visibility. It is a position which bears some similarity to Marx's view of the table in his account of commodity fetishism, discussed in Chapter 1. The problem is how can the necessary scepticism be generated? How can one look at the table in a new light and how can one 'see' the spirit of industrialisation? If Scrooge cannot quite see money, so society cannot look at the world in a different way as alternative perceptions are crushed by the machine; which in part explains Dickens's self-conscious apocalyptic tone in 'A December Vision'. As in *A Christmas Carol*, making money visible is not an option as the structure of the economic system (which turns people into types) is internalised to the point where seeing creates such devastation that the subject is erased in the process. And yet at the same time Dickens, like Marx, *is* outlining the emergence of a sceptical vision, one which is struggling to emerge against an apparently instrumentalist view of the world which closes down alternative perceptions of the system. In this way Scrooge becomes a better capitalist because that is the only option available to him. In 'A December Vision' Dickens revises this by exploring how a mode of scepticism needs to be evolved as an essential starting point for a social and economic alternative to capitalism.

The relationship between psychology and spectrality takes us back to Marx because the underlying problem is how to develop scepticism and so how to politicise money. Ultimately Dickens can only explore this state of mind rather than move beyond it. The fluctuations of money become superseded in Marx's reading of economics (an economic narrative addressed in *A Christmas Carol*) by a system based on labour but which merely, in its reconfigurations of the living and the dead, forms another

Gothic tautology. The system endlessly recycles itself and so keeps alienation and anxiety at the centre of modern consciousness, a point also made by Dickens: when you see the system for what it is, it destroys you because this newfound scepticism cannot be accommodated.

However, what is also at issue is how to read the ghost.

'The Signalman'

The nameless signalman's tale addresses feelings of alienation and estrangement which were implicit to *A Christmas Carol*. The signalman, like Scrooge, cannot fully comprehend his circumstances. Although Scrooge will gain some form of insight it is only a partial one as it fails to fully engage with how economic power could be distributed in an equal way. The signalman's incomprehension is more explicitly developed; indeed it is largely the subject of the tale. The narrator tells us of the signalman that 'He had been, when young (if I could believe it, sitting in that hut, – he scarcely could), a student of natural philosophy, and had attended lectures; but he had run wild, misused his opportunities, gone down, and never risen again'.[13] Instead of social advancement he finds himself in an intellectually limited world which is a consequence of his estrangement from certain sign-systems. In his hut, 'He had taught himself a language [. . .] if only to know it by sight, and to have formed his own crude ideas of its pronunciation' (p. 3). Also, 'He had worked at fractions and decimals, and tried a little algebra; but he was, and had been as a boy, a poor hand at figures' (p. 4). This estrangement from methods of interpretation, whether linguistic or mathematical, becomes linked to his inability to decode the apparently mysterious signs of danger that he periodically encounters. It also implies an estrangement from modes of analysis (relating to language and mathematics) which, as outlined in Chapter 1, had associations with models of political economy.

On three occasions the signalman sees a spectral figure that seems to warn him about an impending rail crash, and the signalman has difficulty in understanding whether such warnings are genuine or merely the product of his imagination. He informs the narrator that ' "what troubles me so dreadfully is the question, What does the spectre mean?" ' (p. 10).

The ghosts that Scrooge encounters are used to underline particular past dramas or ones which may occur, in order to create a better life for him. However, in 'The Signalman' the issue of interpretation is much more problematic. The tale at one level suggests, at least early on, that the signalman's anxieties are imaginary and possibly organic in nature. The narrator tries to convince him that a 'figure' he has seen waving violently near a tunnel had its origins 'in [a] disease of the delicate nerves that minister to the functions of the eye' (p. 7), which emphasises issues about seeing which were central to *A Christmas Carol* and analyses of the economic system (discussed in Chapter 1). In this way everything appears to be uncertain, even at this point reflecting the position of the reader, who cannot be sure what such indirection is meant to purport. Ultimately the narrator, like the reader, is forced into an implicit agreement with the signalman's anxiety: 'What does the spectre mean?' This view points towards the pivotal question of what repeatedly characterises Dickens's ghosts. The ghost is never simply a ghost, it always has an alternative function as an expression of concerns about money (*A Christmas Carol*) or an anxiety about industrialisation ('A December Vision'), and in this sense the ghost stops being a conventional narrative figure. As we saw in 'A Christmas Tree', Dickens is scornful of using ghosts merely as formal elements within a predictable ghost story. Such tales articulate an anti-Gothic ambience because far from expressing transgression they represent overly familiar literary devices which contain transgression, or reduce it to little more than narrative decoration. In 'The Signalman' the ghost serves to raise questions about interpretation because the tale is an alternative manifesto for the ghost story, one which invites the narrator and the reader to dwell on the problems of interpreting the ghost which more formulaic tales do not. What the ghost might actually mean is therefore subservient to the ability to ask the question about what it is supposed to mean. It is an attempt to generate the kind of sceptical and questioning attitude that Dickens sees as essential to an alternative politics. A problem occurs if one attempts to read the tale as a conventional ghost story, but Dickens emphasises the importance of reading it in an unorthodox way, and it is only by reading the earlier tales in a non-conventional fashion that they surrender their latent meanings. This is not to suggest that Dickens is consciously addressing this issue of readership. Rather, the hesitations and problems with interpretation are a consequence of his refusal to follow narrative convention. In this instance the refusal tells us something about how to read his tales.

The signalman is not sure whether the ghost is trying to warn him about an impending railway accident or not, and how can the ghost (arguably an inherently retrospective figure) represent the future? The subsequent death of the signalman in a railway accident means that his inability to read the signs costs him his life, but even the narrator does not know what the ghost really represented and consequently narrative closure becomes impossible.

At one level the tale can be related to issues about industrialisation. Critics have noted how the signalman becomes machine-like in the pursuit of his duties; according to Ewald Mengel 'he fulfils his duties like a mindless robot'.[14] John D. Stahl has related the signalman to contemporary railway documentation concerning the conduct of signalmen. One such publication, *Our Iron Roads* (1852), claimed: 'In the modern interlocking of signals the principle aimed at is, so far as possible, to supersede the man by the machine, to make him merely the motive power of the machine, and to render the machine as nearly as possible automatic'.[15] This ideal of the robotic employee suggests alienation from industrialisation because it propagates the kind of unthinking assimilation to the system which troubles

Dickens in 'A December Vision'. The problem for the signalman is that he cannot stand outside of the bureaucratic roles and duties which have been apportioned to him, and consequently he is not in a position to interpret, with any confidence, what the spectral signs and portents mean. This links to Dickens's wider, if implicitly formulated, concern about how the ghost story can function as a vehicle through which to see the system more clearly. As in the earlier tales, the fundamental concern is how a sceptical vision can be generated. Assimilating conventional narrative expectations (about the ghost story) and assimilating a rationalistic ideology (becoming a robot) are aligned in such a way that aesthetic considerations and political processes become conjoined. The revitalisation of literary form can therefore play a role in political revitalisation as it provides an alternative, sceptical, insight into how ideology functions to fend off awkward questions, and the tale achieves this by placing the whole idea of asking difficult questions in the foreground.

In our analysis of *A Christmas Carol* we noted how the conceit of seeing was used in order to address a debate about how one can 'see' the system. David Seed has explored how the conceit of seeing in 'The Signalman' is associated with an inability to locate meaning:

> . . . the narrator shouts down into the cutting. Strangely the signalman's reaction is to look along the railway-line when the other hails him and not upwards to the top of the cutting. Looking would be a predictable enough theme in a story of apparitions but Dickens relates the different lines of vision to the nature of the place.[16]

Seed notes how the tale repeatedly refers to sight either as blocked or misapplied. The narrator on his first encounter with the signalman comments on his unusual 'watchfulness' (p. 2) but also senses that this does not mean that he possesses a keen insight. As already noted, the signalman spends his free time trying to gain knowledge by reading about algebra and languages, but ultimately this pursuit of knowledge is largely superficial: the narrator comments that the signalman has 'taught himself a language' but 'only to know it by sight' (p. 3). As in *A Christmas Carol*, sight is partial or incomplete, and this explains the signalman's confused perception of what the ghost represents. How to see clearly in 'A December Vision' was obliquely related to how one can 'see' or generate a scepticism which transcends any ideological attachments to industrialisation, attachments which overlook the political significance of the spectre.

How to see the world differently is the factor which unites these narratives. The signalman's inability to decode the ghost becomes literally a matter of life or death – an issue which was rendered in more symbolic terms in 'A December Vision'. The role of sight in the ghost story has been explored by Srdjan Smajic, who acknowledges that sight is historically and politically inflected, claiming that 'theories of vision and ways of seeing are invariably contingent upon historical and cultural determinants'.[17] He goes on to argue that an analysis of seeing is central to any attempt at understanding the belief systems of the Victorians. The detective story and realist fiction might, so Smajic argues, indicate a confidence in 'the epistemological value of sight' (p. 1109) but the ghost story problematises this because unlike the detective the 'ghost-seer is typically caught in a disconcerting double bind between instinctive faith in the evidence of one's sight and the troubling knowledge that vision is often deceptive and unreliable: a subject precariously positioned at the crossroads of ocularcentric faith and anti-ocularcentric scepticism' (p. 1109).

The self-taught signalman is estranged from all kinds of knowledge, whether institutional or political. He is a lost figure baffled by a world which he knows to be dangerous, but he is unable to generate the kind of alternative vision which is required to transcend it. Also, as noted earlier, Dickens attempts to politicise the ghost story precisely so that it can incorporate such debates. As Smajic argues, it is by exploring how sight is used in such tales that their political message becomes clear, notwithstanding the fact that for most critics 'ghost stories are probably the last place one would think to look for evidence of how industrialisation, Darwinism, or colonial expansion affected Victorian society and culture' (p. 1108). It is the exploration of sight, certainly in Dickens, which enables us to identify how he developed his view on money and industrialisation.

Ghosts represent economic figures for Dickens and he uses them to explore changes in the perception of the economic system. In the texts examined here he employs images of ghosting in order to focus on how visibility and invisibility conceptually relate to economic ideas. The ghost story in these instances represents the desire to imaginatively construct narratives concerning the subject's formulation within, and relationship to, the prevailing economic system. Ultimately such ghosts, such abstractions, are not so otherworldly after all but constitute new attempts at encoding an understanding of the changing relationships between the subject and the economy of the time.

How to read signs, and how images of ghostliness influenced and destabilised some of the epistemological certainties of detective fiction and a money-based economy, are discussed in the following chapter on Dickens's friend and literary collaborator, Wilkie Collins.

Notes

1 Charles Dickens, *Bleak House* (Harmondsworth: Penguin, 1985) p. 139. All subsequent references are to this edition and are given in the text.
2 Alison Milbank in *Daughters of the House: Modes of Gothic in Victorian Fiction* (Basingstoke: Macmillan, 1992) p. 94. All subsequent references are to this edition and are given in the text.
3 However, there are anthologies which usefully bring together some of Dickens's ghost stories, including *The Signalman & Other Ghost Stories* (Stroud: Sutton, 1990), with an introduction by Sheila Michell.

4 Charles Dickens, 'A Christmas Tree', published as 'Christmas Ghosts' in *The Signalman & Other Ghost Stories* (Stroud: Sutton, 1990) pp. 110–16, p. 122.

5 Charles Dickens, *The Pickwick Papers*, ed. and introd. Mark Wormald (Harmondsworth: Penguin, [1837] 2003) p. 659.

6 My readings of *A Christmas Carol* and 'A December Vision' were originally developed in 'Dickens' Ghosts: Invisible Economies and Christmas', *Victorian Review*, 31.2 (2005), 36–55, special issue on 'Literature and Money', ed. Andrew Smith.

7 Charles Dickens, *A Christmas Carol* in *The Christmas Books*, vol. 1, ed. and introd. Michael Slater (Harmondsworth: Penguin, 1985) pp. 45–134, p. 57. All subsequent references are to this edition and are given in the text.

8 Lynn M. Voskuil, 'Feeling Public: Sensation Theater, Commodity Culture, and the Victorian Public Sphere', *Victorian Studies*, 44.2 (Winter 2002), 245–74, 257.

9 I am indebted to Martin Willis for helping to shape this view.

10 Christopher Herbert, 'Filthy Lucre: Victorian Ideas of Money', *Victorian Studies*, 44.2 (Winter 2002), 185–213, 187. All subsequent references are given in the text.

11 Mary Poovey (ed.), *The Financial System in Nineteenth-Century Britain* (Oxford: Oxford University Press, 2003) p. 4.

12 Charles Dickens, 'A December Vision', in *Dickens' Journalism: The Amusements of The People and Other Papers: Reports, Essays and Reviews 1834–51* (vol. II), ed. Michael Slater (London: Dent, 1996) pp. 306–9, p. 306. All subsequent references are to this edition and are given in the text.

13 Charles Dickens, 'The Signalman' in *The Signalman & Other Ghost Stories* (Stroud: Sutton, 1990) pp. 1–13, p. 4. All subsequent references are to this edition and are given in the text.

14 Ewald Mengel, 'The Structure and Meaning of Dickens's "The Signalman"', *Studies in Short Fiction*, 20 (1983), 271–80, 275.

15 Frederick S. Williams, *Our Iron Roads: Their History, Construction and Administration* (London: Frank Cass & Co., 1968) pp. 180–1. Cited in John D. Stahl, 'The Source and Significance of the Revenant in Dickens's "The Signal-Man"', *Dickens Studies Newsletter*, 11 (1980), 98–101, 99.

16 David Seed, 'Mystery in Everyday Things: Charles Dickens' "Signalman"', *Criticism*, 23.1 (1981), 42–57, 47.

17 Srdjan Smajic, 'The Trouble with Ghost-Seeing: Vision, Ideology, and Genre in the Victorian Ghost Story', *English Literary History*, 70.4 (2003), 1107–35, 1108. All subsequent references are to this edition and are given in the text.

3

Money and machines:
Wilkie Collins's ghosts

Wilkie Collins's sensation fiction drew upon a Gothic tradition, although he did not share Dickens's fascination with the ghost story. However, Collins did leave behind a variety of ghost tales which in their own way indicate an interest in how the form could be innovated.[1] Collins's most sustained attempt at a ghost story is his late novella *The Haunted Hotel* (1878), which addresses the issue of money and its relationship to identity which characterised Dickens's ghost stories. However, before discussing *The Haunted Hotel* it is important to examine some of Collins's major writings of his heyday in the 1860s – *The Woman in White* (1860), *No Name* (1862), and *Armadale* (1866) – as they foreshadow his later representations of the ghostly.[2] Both *The Woman in White* and *No Name*, for example, employ an oblique form of ghosting to explore how identity becomes lost when characters find themselves embroiled in financial plots. The chapter concludes with a reading of the anonymously published, but Collins influenced, 'The Ghost in the Bank of England' (1879), which helps to highlight how issues about identity, money, and spectrality are elaborated in Collins.

It is important to acknowledge that Collins is less a Gothic writer than a sensationalist one. The relationship between sensation fiction and the Gothic is relevant because it helps to consolidate Collins's influence on, and so familiarity with, Gothic tropes. Sensation fiction, the melodrama, and the Gothic played mutually supporting roles in developing the flavour of popular fiction in the mid-nineteenth century.

Sensation fiction

Winifred Hughes provides a neatly synoptic account of the literary provenance of the sensation novel, arguably *the* mode of popular fiction from the 1860s until the 1880s. She acknowledges the form's 'general affinity with the eighteenth-century Gothicism of Ann Radcliffe and "Monk" Lewis, the historical romance of Sir Walter Scott, the oriental tales of Byron, as well as with the more recent and somewhat more suspect performances of the Newgate novelists'.[3] Hughes also makes a convincing claim that the two earliest precursors to the sensation novel are Edward Bulwer-Lytton's *Eugene Aram* (1832) and Charlotte Brontë's *Jane Eyre* (1847).

The contemporary debates about the morality of sensation fiction were, as Hughes notes, underpinned by prevailing views concerning the nature of literary realism. For such critics the sensation novel appeared to compromise conceptions of literature which rested on the demarcation of the romance from the realist text. At one level the sensation novel contained recognisable 'realist' elements through its emphasis on place, class, and accounts of social mobility. However, the form was also seen by conservatively minded critics as pandering to low feelings, because the highly melodramatic incidents upon which these dramas so often turned implied the presence of an unreal, highly theatrical, mode of representation. Murderers, bigamists, and the 'insane' had no place in the realist novel and consequently there was considerable debate both about the form of the sensation novel and its likely moral impact on its readership. Indeed, such criticism tended to align the apparently immoral aspects of sensation fiction with an implied Gothic presence which also relegated it to a fanciful or fantastical (i.e. false) literary mode. Hughes quotes from *The Christian Remembrancer* (1863), which noted of the form's representation of bigamy that it was 'sensational as fully, though in a lower field, as are ghosts and portents; it disturbs in the same way the reader's sense of the stability of things, and opens a new, untried vista of what may be'.[4] Fantasy thus provides unacceptable political possibilities because it generates unacceptable versions of a literally unthinkable 'reality'.

The difficulty in aesthetically positioning the sensation novel was due to the importance which was accorded to literary realism. This is made clear, as Hughes notes, in G.H. Lewes's attempt to assert the distinctiveness of realism from romance. For Lewes realism should not focus on the mundane aspects of life: 'We are by no means rigorous in expecting that the story is to move along the highway of everyday life'. Nevertheless, 'if we are to travel into fairy-land, it must be in a fairy carriage, not a Hanson cab'.[5] Whilst one might speculate about what Lewes would have made of Amelia B. Edwards's ghost story 'The Phantom Coach' (1864), it is noteworthy that the sensation novel compromised such notions of literary propriety. In that regard the sensation novel played a similar role as the Gothic novel had for an earlier generation of critics and moralists.[6]

Literary confusion and moral anxiety become closely related and in many respects it is the continuing presence of the Gothic which effects this destabilisation. Alison Milbank has explored in depth how Wilkie Collins's novels rework many of the principal dramas of an earlier Female Gothic tradition.[7] This is a Gothic tradition which was as much theatrical as it was written and evidences how the popular stage melodrama informed the sensation novel, or as Collins put it in the preface to *Basil* (1852), 'one is a drama narrated [. . .] the other is a drama acted'.[8] Tamar Heller has also examined this Gothic presence in Collins's sensation fiction and has argued that even his early, seemingly non-Gothic writings such as his account of his father, *Memoirs of the Life of William Collins* (1846) and his first novel *Antonia* (1850) (ostensibly an historical romance), indicate an anxiety about paternal authority which has its provenance in the Female Gothic.[9] Heller also notes how Collins's status as a writer is often played out through images of anxious writers and artists (as in *Basil* and *The Woman in White*) who are seeking, as was Collins, a place for themselves in the literary marketplace. The attempts to assert this identity take place in the context of particular gender debates relating to the presence of female-authored sensation novels. The emphasis on economic success in Collins's writings was also, so Heller argues, an attempt to secure the legitimacy of his work when confronted by the adverse critical responses to the form. How money is manifested in Collins's images of spectrality is related to making legitimate the visibility of the work itself. This visibility might not become a critically endorsed one, but it is one which becomes possible in the marketplace: the sensation novel as product.

The theme of money and its rightful ownership is given some prominence in the sensation novel. Nowhere is this more explicit than in Charles Reade's novel *Hard Cash* (1863) (serialised by Dickens in *All the Year Round* as *Very Hard Cash*). His earlier novel, *It Is Never Too Late To Mend* (1856), focuses on the Australian gold rush. In Mrs Henry Wood's *East Lynne* (1861) a corpse is arrested for debt, and in *Aurora Floyd* (1863) Mary Elizabeth Braddon's eponymous 'heroine' is a banker's daughter. Such novels are not simply reworking Gothic elements but also some aspects of non-sensationalist popular literature that focused on money, such as Miss Mulock's *John Halifax Gentleman* (1856) and Catherine Gore's *The Moneylender* (1843), *The Banker's Wife* (1843), and *Men of Capital* (1846). Later in the century the ghost story writer Charlotte Riddell, discussed in Chapter 4, would also write popular novels about London's financial sector, such as *Mitre Court* (1885) and *The Head of the Firm* (1895). Norman Russell has explored how the pursuit of wealth for its own sake was associated with immorality because it failed to acknowledge the potentially socially ameliorative possibilities of wealth distribution (especially in relation to the poor). However, in this pursuit of wealth there was a wider danger that the allegedly dehumanising effects of selfish economic gain were also articulated *within* the pursuit itself, so that 'men became mere agents of a single economic urge, that of competition; emotions and spiritual yearnings had no place in the constitution of "economic man"'.[10] This sense of dehumanisation and money, or more specifically, the forms of ghostliness which it comes to inhabit, will provide the main context for the reading of Collins in this chapter. Characters become ghostly machines as they play out Carlyle's anxiety, expressed in 1829, that 'Men are grown mechanical in head and in heart as well as in hand'.[11]

The Woman in White: the spectral self

Heller has noted that *The Woman in White* generated a small commercial industry in which 'both text and author' were transformed into 'a seemingly endless series of commodities' (p. 110). Collins's earlier writings were republished with reference to him as 'the author of *The Woman in White*' (p. 110) and a variety of artefacts, bonnets, and perfumes were marketed as items associated with the novel.[12] However, as Heller notes, the novel in many respects resists such an easy commodification: 'The novel that achieved such success in the marketplace is animated by ambivalence about the marketplace and its process of commodification' (p. 111). This is because Walter Hartright represents an image of the artist who is struggling to gain financial independence and yet, at least initially, is represented as a wage slave, and one who is in the employ of women.

Such images of the market and their association with models of spectrality are suggested in Hartright's first encounter with Anne Catherick, the woman in white of the title. During an evening walk home she suddenly appears, seemingly from nowhere. His startled view of her is oddly dehumanising. He refers to her as an 'it' which has come from some other, definitively non-human world as if 'it had sprung from the earth or dropped from heaven'.[13] This initial view is a gauge of her potential moral character, whether she is spiritual ('heaven') or all too terrestrially physical ('from the earth'). He notes that in the road 'stood the figure of a solitary Woman, dressed from head to foot in white garments' (p. 47). His claims for this 'extraordinary apparition' are ones that dwell on his inability to locate her in either metaphysical or social terms. She is both high and low, as the first claim implies, and her demeanour is 'not exactly the manner of a lady, and, at the same time, not the manner of a woman in the humblest rank of life' (p. 48). She is an in-between being because she incorporates different social elements within her. In that regard she becomes an abstract presence – one which, for Heller, is used to subtly imply Hartright's disempowerment in the London marketplace which has necessitated his future employment in Limmeridge, so that when he records how 'her face bent in grave inquiry on mine, her hand pointing to the dark cloud over London' (p. 47), it represents his economic exclusion from London.

The mystery of Anne Catherick's identity will lead directly back to her mother. Hartright's subsequent encounter with her, when many of the dramas in the narrative are near resolution, emphasises the difference between old and new money. Hartright takes a train to Welmingham, a fictitious new town in Hampshire.

> Is there any wilderness of sand in the deserts of Arabia, is there any prospect of desolation among the ruins of Palestine, which can rival the repelling effect on the eye, and the depressing influence on the mind, of an English county town in the first stage of its existence, and in the transition state of its prosperity? (p. 503)

Welmingham, for Hartright, is little more than a ghost town, largely consisting of 'dead house-carcasses that waited in vain for the vivifying human element to animate them' (p. 503) and populated by 'tradesmen who stared after me from their lonely shops'.

This link between trade and emptiness is also suggested in a letter which Collins had written on 2 August 1847 to his mother after a visit to Rouen: 'As to

Rouen – I am glad we have left it – A more ghostly set of people than *Rouenuese* it has never been my misfortune to meet with [. . .] The people are all sordid trades people who sit behind their counters all day'.[14] This distaste for money earned through trade runs through Collins's work, which, as indicated earlier, has a fascination with how 'old' money can be legitimately returned to its rightful owners. Collins's schemers are invariably in pursuit of old money although, paradoxically, it is a pursuit which often renders them spectral as they become lost within financial plots, an issue which is developed in both *No Name* and *Armadale*. Hartright's distaste for this new money is emphasised in his description of Mrs Catherick's house, where he enters 'a little room, with a flaring paper of the largest pattern on the walls. Chairs, tables, chiffonier, and sofa, all gleamed with the glutinous brightness of cheap upholstery' (p. 504). The room is too full of crude acquisitions, which gives it a mood of shinning, sensuous overabundance. This physicality becomes embodied by Mrs Catherick, who 'had full square cheeks, a long, firm chin, and thick sensual, colourless lips. Her figure was stout and sturdy, and her manner aggressively self-possessed' (p. 504).

Throughout, the novel develops identity in terms of its ownership. The spectral vision of Anne Catherick on the road to London begins a mystery which leads to the coarse physicality of Mrs Catherick and her hypocritical pretensions to respectability. Ghosting in *The Woman in White* becomes emblematic of who controls, and so owns, identity. The spectral Anne Catherick is alternatively lost, found, is insane, and redeemed, a knower of partial secrets which she does not understand. She retains a marginality that makes her the absent presence of the narrative as she ghosts it with ideas about how identity needs to be read. These issues of control are not just about wealth and how its rightful possession creates a social cohesion dependent upon the confirmation of stable social identities; they also relate to how Hartright perceives identity. Clues about identity are generated from the outside as we witness Hartright (and before that Marian Halcombe) attempt to read the mysteries of identity and decode financial plots. *No Name* and *Armadale* rework this by addressing the issue of identity from inside out, as we watch, rather than vicariously decode through an amateur detective, the plots of Magdalen Vanstone and Lydia Gwilt.

These issues about identity are not solely related to money; they are also closely tied to conceptualisations of gender which appear to be either mocked or affirmed.[15] Hartright's initial perception of Marian focuses on her 'firm masculine mouth and jaw' (p. 58) and the fact that she appears 'to be altogether wanting in those feminine attractions of gentleness and pliability' (p. 59). Later he recounts a sketch he made of Laura Fairlie which seems to capture her heightened femininity and his feelings for her. However, he acknowledges that the drawing is a disappointment because it 'suggested to me the idea of something wanting' which 'At one time seemed like something wanting in *her*: at another like something wanting in myself, which hindered me from knowing her as I ought' (p. 76). This sketch of Laura is incomplete because it is lifeless and Hartright cannot explain why that should be.[16] Ultimately the narrative will imply that Laura *is* somewhat lifeless as she forms a largely abstract notion of femininity that Hartright and Marian come to protect. All of this becomes staged through Hartright's perceptions and pre-judices. However, the idea that people become abstractions supports Marx's idea that individuals in a money-based economy become depersonalised. Marx writes about this in ways that suggest an approach to romance – a gender-related theme which in *The Woman in White*, *No Name*, and *Armadale* becomes difficult to disentangle from financial intrigue.

No Name

If *The Woman in White* looks at plotting from the outside, through the efforts of Hartright and Marian, *No Name* explores the internal anxieties of Magdalen Vanstone as she seeks to take revenge upon those who have left her and her sister Norah financially destitute. Because Magdalen and Norah are born out of wedlock they lack the legal right to claim family money on the death of their parents. Magdalen's schemes for the restitution of this money, such as attempting to marry and then kill off the sickly distant relative, Noel, who inherits the wealth, have the effect of turning Magdalen into an oddly spectral figure. First, it is important to note that we learn from the start that Magdalen is a proficient actress, which at a technical level enables her to operate in disguise. On a more abstract level it suggests that Magdalen's personality is composed from a series of dramatic narratives, and it is her increasingly close association with such roles that gradually erodes her sense of self. However, the hollowing out of Magdalen's identity begins the moment she hears of the death of her parents in an accident: 'She stood, the spectre of herself. With a dreadful vacancy in her eyes'.[17] From this point she is illegitimate or legally absent: a 'No Name' who is no longer entitled to inhabit the social and economic world from which she comes. This turning of Magdalen into a spectral, liminal, presence is suggested by an implied change in her appearance in which her once wilful and lively face is turned into 'a white changeless blank, fearful to look at'. This also represents the erasure of any emotional life – 'Nothing roused, nothing melted her' (p. 83) – which also makes her ghostly.

However, *No Name* develops this language of spectrality by also suggesting that it is Magdalen's very associations with financial scheming that dehumanise her. There are repeated assertions that Magdalen's behaviour becomes increasingly mechanical, even in the midst of her grief. For example, her friend Miss Garth visits her and finds that Magdalen's 'large light eyes looked mechanically into hers, as vacant and as tearless as ever' (p. 85). These early scenes effectively strip Magdalen of her identity, before she seeks to enact her revenge through a narrative which also turns her into a figure that she cannot quite develop. Magdalen, so the novel suggests, repeatedly wrestles with her 'real' and 'acquired' self.

The link between plotting, disguise, references to money, and the loss of self, are all suggested in a key encounter between Mrs Wragge and Magdalen, when after an extensive shopping spree 'with a pile of small parcels hugged up in her arms' (p. 245) Magdalen's companion, Mrs Wragge, believes that a ghost of an old lady has entered the house (which is actually Magdalen returning in disguise after a visit to Noel Vanstone). Magdalen appears and the old lady has disappeared, leaving Mrs Wragge to exclaim: ' "I've heard tell of ghosts in night-gowns; ghosts in sheets; and ghosts in chains [. . .] Here's a worse ghost than any of 'em – a ghost in a grey cloak and a poke bonnet" ' (p. 246). The scene subtly suggests a link between spectrality and shopping when it notes of Mrs Wragge's precarious attempts at overcoming her agitation, 'The master passion of shopping might claim his own again – but the ghost was not laid yet' (p. 250). Laurence Talairach-Vielmas reads the figure of Matilda Wragge as linked to both the marketplace and to the images of the actress which are associated with Magdalen. She claims that 'Defining her being and her sense of femininity as an interplay with commodities, Matilda reveals the construction of the female self as hinged upon the market economy'.[18] The self is thus performed by money and it is this which renders characters ghostly. Talairach-Vielmas accounts for this ghosting of Magdalen in two ways because 'While the motif of the ghost metaphorizes Magdalen's name-lessness and lack of identity, for Matilda, the "Ghost" makes her head buzz again, as another embodiment of the spectral authoritative texts that fashion Victorian gender ideology' (p. 71). Mrs Wragge's self is shaped by a depend-ence upon fashionable clothes and Magdalen loses a sense of self by dressing to effect a disguise. The novel thus suggests that it is Magdalen's association with financial scheming that makes her ghostly and this is why Mrs Wragge sees her as a ghost.

As the plot develops and Magdalen becomes subsumed within her financial mach-inations she becomes increasingly associated with a language of spectrality. When she meets Captain Wragge to take his advice on how to proceed with the plot against Noel Vanstone it is noted that she 'glided into the obscurity of the room, like a ghost' (p. 342). Later, when Captain Wragge tells her of the day when the marriage with Noel should take place, a marriage which would constitute the culmination of her plotting, 'Her large grey eyes stared at him vacantly [. . .] her face stiffened awfully, like the face of a corpse' (p. 387). The closer she gets to the money, the more ghostlike, or deathly, she becomes. However, Magdalen is not the only spectral figure in the narrative. Noel's protector, the resourceful Mrs Lecount, who has been tricked by Captain Wragge and has left Noel vulnerable to Magdalen's plotting, is also associated with spectrality because she regards Noel as represent-ing her future financial security due to the service she has rendered him. When she returns to Noel, at the point where his doom seems inevitable, she is much changed: 'Was it the spectre of the woman? or the woman herself? Her hair was white; her face had fallen away' (p. 442).

Images of illness and commercial enterprise are implicitly linked throughout the novel. These links become clear in the closing chapters, which concern the financial triumph of Captain Wragge, who has made his wealth by playing upon fears of illness. As he tells Magdalen, ' "I have shifted from Moral Agriculture to Medical Agriculture. Formerly, I preyed on the public sympathy; now, I prey on the public stomach" ' (p. 585). Such a view indicates that bodily ailments have replaced emotional anxieties and literalises how Magdalen's physical decline is bound up with a prevailing economic mood which, in Marxian terms, generates models of alienation and self-estrangement. Captain Wragge with his bogus medical remedies illustrates the moral vacuity of those who control consumer society and who generate the very ills that they promise to solve. As Wragge tells Magdalen, ' "Here I am, a Grand Financial Fact" ' (p. 585). Later he says to her, ' "Don't think me mercenary – I merely understand the age I live in" ' (p. 590). *No Name* thus develops the hostility towards money made in trade that was implicit to *The Woman in White*. It also indicates that it is men like Wragge who own the economic system and that women such as Magdalen cannot, seemingly, ultimately control financial plots because involvement within them requires surrendering the kind of 'Moral Agriculture' that Captain Wragge so readily gives up. Collins has no solution to this problem other than a sentimental one. It is ultimately Captain Kirke's love for Magdalen which provides the possibility of redemption, so the novel suggests, because love, or any positive emotion, is necessarily written out of the economic schemes in the novel. The final lines suggest that it is love which also enables Magdalen, after a severe bout of illness, to return to her body, when she says to Kirke, ' "Say what you think of me, with your own lips" ' and 'He stooped, and kissed her' (p. 610). Magdalen may at the end be in a love plot rather than a financial one, but the final act still suggests an element of male control.

No Name uses a language of spectrality in order to examine the dehumanising effects of money. Money supplants affection and Collins's gender scripts interrogate how the ownership of money empowers men but seems to destroy women. The ghost is thus a gendered figure in Collins. The ghost represents a projected reality for many aspiring women of a certain class; like them it is liminal, disempowered, and not really part of this (economic) world. It is an image of ghosting that Collins returned to in *Armadale*.

Armadale

In *Armadale* Lydia Gwilt is repeatedly associated with a criminal mentality, although explanations are given for her behaviour. Her propensity to criminal activity is grounded in a series of emotional disappointments which have seemingly left her bereft of any fellow feeling. She represents an instrumentality that rearticulates the amoral financial acquisitiveness of a money-based society. Whilst in *No Name* identities became lost within financial plots, in *Armadale* identity appears to be multiple and confused. Ultimately the novel suggests that Lydia has to choose between the two Allan Armadales, the one she wishes to murder for his money and the other that she loves and has married. The final scenes of the novel take place in Doctor le Doux's sanatorium. Lydia is introduced in disguise to visitors of the sanatorium as a victim of ' "Shattered nerves – domestic anxiety" ', which ironically is a correct diagnosis of Lydia's emotional turmoil.[19]

Lydia plots the murder of one Allan Armadale, whilst the thought of the other 'haunts me like a ghost' (p. 719), and the tension between the desire for money and the demands of love indicates how Collins regards the pursuit of money as inimical to genuine happiness. In order to achieve this he relies upon a notion of an essential humanity (one that is reawoken in Lydia) which becomes lost in such financial pursuits. This is a position illuminated by Marx's *Economic and Philosophic Manuscripts of 1844*, where he developed an early model of alienation which argued that individuals become estranged from a notion of human essence. For Marx, money:

> transforms the *real essential powers of man and nature* into what are merely abstract conceits and therefore *imperfections* – into tormenting chimeras – just as it transforms *real imperfections and chimeras* – essential powers which are really impotent, which exist only in the imagination of the individual – into *real powers* and *faculties*.[20]

Money represents for Marx an abstract sense of value, which because of its very abstraction helps generate a dehumanisation that encourages individuals to 'lose' themselves in its pursuit. Moreover, it means that genuine feeling is made to appear as if it were abstract or unreal, so that emotions seem to be devoid of meaning. Therefore money:

> appears as this *overturning* power both against the individual and against the bonds of society, etc., which claim to be *essences* in themselves. It transforms fidelity into infidelity, love into hate, hate into love, virtue into vice, vice into virtue, servant into master, master into servant, idiocy into intelligence and intelligence into idiocy. (p. 130, italics in original)

Money, in other words, effects a highly conservative revolution which 'makes contradictions embrace' (p. 131).

Lydia Gwilt embodies these tensions when it seems as though she will choose money over love and thus replace genuine feeling with an abstraction. However, she nearly kills her husband because he has changed rooms with her intended victim. She rescues him from the poison that she has been pumping into the room and takes her own life. It is a moment of self-sacrifice and a final gesture of love. Her pursuit of money had, in Marxian terms, nearly destroyed love because love and money are incompatible, and significantly Marx concludes his chapter on 'The Power of Money in Bourgeois Society' not with a synopsis of his theory of money, but with an account of love:

Every one of your relations to man and to nature must be a *specific expression*, corresponding to the object of your will, of your *real individual* life. If you love without evoking love in return – that is, if your loving as loving does not produce reciprocal love; if through a *living expression* of yourself as a loving person you do not make yourself a *loved person*, then your love is impotent – a misfortune. (p. 131, italics in original)

There is no obvious solution to the dilemma posed in the novel, other than that proposed, some what naively, by the wealthy Allan Armadale: ' "What I can't beat into my thick head [. . .] is the meaning of the fuss that's made about giving money away. Why can't people who have got money to spare give it to the people who haven't got money to spare, and make things pleasant and comfortable all the world over in that way?" ' (p. 71). Allan's notion of a socialistic charitable redistribution seems like a too simple solution to a complex problem because one of the complicating factors in this, as in the other texts discussed here, is that Collins also examines the relationship between gender and economic power. Lydia Gwilt is, at one level, a survivor who has managed, if precariously, to maintain an appearance of a gentlewoman by gaining proximity to economic power. In the end she, like Magdalen Vanstone, is unsuccessful. Also, whilst *Armadale* does not employ a language of spectrality that is as explicit as in *No Name*, it covertly develops this through repeated references to lost or hidden identities which are intimately associated with the type of financial plotting to be found in *No Name*. Issues concerning money, gender, and ghosts are all foregrounded in the later *The Haunted Hotel*, where the meaning of the ghost plays a central role in determining the limits of the financial plot.

The Haunted Hotel

The Haunted Hotel was first published in *Belgravia* magazine in November 1878. When published as a book it was released in a single volume with another novella, *My Lady's Money*. Both texts concern missing money and financial deception and have a character in common, a lawyer named Troy who helps to investigate some of the mysteries.

The Haunted Hotel reads like a sketch of a longer novel and its very brevity highlights Collins's reliance on the drama in the construction of his texts. The novella is in four parts with a postscript, and the chapters within the parts can be read as scenes. In addition within the novella there is a sketch of a play, titled *The Haunted Hotel*, which is written by one of the principal protagonists, the conniving Countess Narona, which reveals the secret concerning the murder of her husband, Lord Montbarry, and the disappearance of their courier, Ferrari. The play reveals that the countess had married Montbarry for his money. His life was insured for £10,000 and shortly after the wedding, during a stay in Venice, he was murdered by the Baron Rivar, the countess's brother. The baron is an alchemist and the insurance money is used to finance his experiments, or rather money is gained in order to experiment with making more of it. However, the baron is concerned that a doctor would be able to tell that poison had been administered to Montbarry. He and the countess persuade their courier, Ferrari, who is struck with a terminal bronchial attack, to pretend to be him in exchange for £1,000, which is sent to his widow on his death. By doing so they can gain a legal death certificate and have the insurance money released.

This basic plot becomes linked to financial speculation when a syndicate is formed to turn the building in which Montbarry is murdered into a hotel. Montbarry's brothers, Henry and Francis, and their sister, Mrs Norbury, individually visit the hotel and are disturbed by some noxious smells that emanate from a particular room (which is above the room where Montbarry was murdered). Agnes, who had been betrothed to Montbarry before he married the countess, stays in the room, the countess enters it and they are disturbed by a spectral severed head. The countess writes a play which explains what happened to Montbarry and Ferrari; a play which she has written for money because the £10,000 insurance money has been spent on the baron's experiments. The countess, who is physically and emotionally unwell, dies and so escapes justice.

Throughout this complicated plot the links between money and spectrality are consistently asserted. The countess, on the eve of her wedding, visits a Doctor Wybrow because she wants ' "to know, if you please, whether I am in danger of going mad" '.[21] In this encounter the countess seems like a liminal figure who is both vital and deathly. The doctor notes 'The startling contrast between the corpse-like pallor of her complexion and the overpowering life and light, the glittering metallic brightness in her large black eyes' (p. 4). This image of the living dead glosses the abstract quality of money which Marx had proposed in the *Economic and Philosophic Manuscripts of 1844*, where money takes on a vitality that it does not, because it is an abstraction, possess. The novella suggests that the countess makes visible an attitude about money and financial speculation which is otherwise legitimated in the discussions about investing in the hotel. In effect the countess makes money seem tainted. When she leaves his surgery Wybrow is both attracted and repulsed by her, leading him to wonder if 'the woman [had] left an infection of wickedness in the house, and had he caught it?' Crucially he refuses to keep her fee: 'He sealed it up in an envelope; addressed it to the "Poor-Box" ' (p. 10). She represents what happens when money goes 'bad'.

The novella repeatedly focuses on individuals' financial positions. From Lord Montbarry to servants, everyone is closely linked to money and forms of financial speculation. When Ferrari's disappearance is investigated the countess (now Lady Montbarry) claims ignorance of his whereabouts but expresses hope that he can be found so that his salary can be paid. Tensions appear between the baron and

Montbarry because Montbarry refuses to lend him money and Ferrari recounts in a letter to his wife Emily that the baron even attempted to borrow money from him. Finally Emily receives a banknote for £1,000 in the mail with a note that it was '*To console you for the loss of your husband*' (italics in original, p. 27). This creates an implicit link between money and absence which runs throughout the text. Troy, who is investigating Ferrari's disappearance, suggests that Ferrari has been paid to stay out of the way and literalises this absence (which nevertheless can be read in more metaphorical terms) when he states that the 'bank-note there on the table is the price of his absence' (p. 29). Money makes the self disappear, as it did in both *No Name* and *Armadale*. Wybrow intuits this when he unconsciously links the countess to money, death, and disease (i.e. to immanent absence). It is also the case that money, like the characters, seems to keep disappearing. The baron quickly gets through the insurance money, and there are concerns about financially investing in the hotel. Money is repeatedly represented as precarious because it seems to lack solidity and becomes ghostlike. The strange suggestion is that although everyone appears to be in pursuit of money, it lacks any obvious utility. The baron's alchemical experiments appear to lampoon this as he wastes money in attempting to make more of it.

Attitudes to money also colour Emily's reservation about touching her missing husband's £1,000. Emily's lack of money means that she is unable to help progress the investigation into Ferrari's disappearance, but 'Mrs Ferrari shrank from the bare idea of making use of the thousand-pound note. It had been deposited in the safe keeping of a bank. If it was even mentioned in her hearing, she shuddered and referred to it, with melodramatic fervour, as "my husband's blood-money!"' (p. 33). As Wybrow had noted, money is in danger of becoming tainted. Emily eventually encounters the countess after the death of her husband and notes that 'her face had fallen away to mere skin and bone' (p. 43). Tellingly, the countess says to her, ' "What do you want with me? [. . .] Do you want money?" ' (p. 43).

The overt debate about money is continued in the following discussion between Henry (Montbarry's brother) and his nurse, who has been left some money in Montbarry's will and intends to speculate with it by buying a small interest in the hotel. Again, there is a sense that the money is tainted. The nurse says to Henry, ' "I don't care about this bit of money – I never did like the man who has left it to me, though he *was* your brother" ' (italics in original, p. 54). The text notes an irony in this because now 'the nurse, following Henry's mercenary example, had her pecuniary interest, too, in the house in which Lord Montbarry had died' (p. 55). When Henry visits the hotel he is struck by its splendour and 'began to share the old nurse's view of the future, and to contemplate seriously the coming dividend of ten per cent' (p. 69). However, he stays in a room which is above the chamber in which Montbarry was murdered and he has a restless night. Henry leaves the hotel and the room is occupied by his sister, who has a series of vivid nightmares about Montbarry:

She saw him starving in a loathsome prison; she saw him pursued by assassins, and dying under their knives; she saw him drowning in immeasurable depths of dark water; she saw him in a bed on fire, burning to death in the flames; she saw him tempted by the shadowy creature to drink, and dying of the poisonous draught. (p. 72)

These multiple deaths – stabbed, drowned, burned alive, and poisoned – come to haunt Mrs Norbury, who learns from her maid that Henry had found it difficult to sleep in those rooms and that Lord Montbarry had lived in them when the hotel was a run-down palace. Rumours begin that room 14 might be haunted and this concerns the manager because 'He instantly saw that the credit of the hotel was in danger, unless something was done to retrieve the character of the room' (p. 73); a danger he averts by turning it into room 13A. However, all this indicates is how the financial speculation upon which the hotel depends is haunted by a murder which was carried out in order to help finance alchemical experiments designed to magically create more wealth. Supposedly respectable financial speculation is thus ghosted by other financial plots and the novella subtly links the two by suggesting that the amoral pursuit of wealth dehumanises individuals, such as the countess, but also to an extent Henry.

The murder plot therefore makes visible what is concealed within supposedly legitimate financial schemes. These links are made clear by Francis's desire to visit the hotel after discussing with Henry and Mrs Norbury their respective experiences. Francis has made his money by investing in the theatre. For Francis this sounds like the grounds for a possible commercial venture: 'The circumstances related to him contained invaluable hints for a ghost-drama. The title occurred to him in the railway. "The Haunted Hotel." Post that in red letters six feet high, on a black ground, all over London – and trust the excitable public to crowd into the theatre!' (p. 74). However, Francis is struck by a noxious smell which pervades the room but does not link this to Montbarry. Francis is an economic pragmatist, indeed 'a thorough materialist' who is concerned that the smell might be playing tricks with his imagination. However, much of this is expressed in terms which suggest that such an experience does not enhance the cause of any possible play: ' "A terrible smell from an invisible ghost is a perfectly new idea. But it has one drawback. If I realise it on the stage, I shall drive the audience out of the theatre" ' (p. 77). This type of amoral approach, as stated earlier, reflects the amorality which leads to Montbarry's murder. The countess makes these links clear when she refers to the hotel as ' "The old hell, transformed into the new purgatory" ' (p. 79). She also tries to see if Francis would be interested in buying a play from her because she needs money. He is surprised by this: ' "Surely you don't want money!" he exclaimed. "I always want money" ' (pp. 80–1), she replies. He requests that she perhaps try ' "a drama with a ghost in it?" ' (p. 82).

These issues about money are constantly foregrounded by the hotel. Francis, for example, discovers that it only seems to be his family who are affected by the mysterious room. However, the manager is content to let the room out to other guests because, he tells Francis, ' "I am the servant of the Company; and I dare not turn money out of the hotel" ' (p. 87). Later there is an encounter between the countess and Agnes (who had been engaged to Montbarry before he broke it off to marry the countess) in the room. They are suddenly confronted by an apparition of a severed head.

> The hair on the skull, discoloured like the hair on the face, had been burnt away in places. The bluish lips, parted in a fixed grin, showed the double row of teeth. By slow degrees, the hovering head (perfectly still when she first saw it) began to descend towards Agnes. (p. 97)

The countess is seemingly deranged by this visitation and begins working hard on producing the play in order to provide financial support to the baron. However, as she and the others know, the baron has died (although she psychologically refuses to acknowledge this). The countess thus explains through a play (partly inspired by the 'ghost' of Montbarry) the financial reasons for Montbarry's murder; all in a drama written to make money for a dead alchemist. This somewhat overdetermined language of spectrality functions to make visible the invisible workings of finance.

Henry and the hotel manager examine the room where the spectral head appeared and discover a hidden chamber which contains the much disfigured head of Montbarry, which means that Henry fails to recognise it as his brother. The ever pragmatic manager says, ' "If this frightful discovery becomes known [. . .] the closing of the hotel and the ruin of the Company will be the inevitable results. I feel sure that I can trust your discretion, sir, so far?" ' (p. 105). However, even Henry suspects that it would not be possible to conceal the discovery and shortly afterwards the manager is detected by some guests whilst trying to remove the head to another part of the hotel.

The countess's play functions as a confession and explains the presence of the head (if not its strange apparitional appearance). She dies, but even this, in keeping with her death-in-life state, is ambiguous. Henry visits her whilst she is under medical care and it is noted that 'From time to time, she drew a heavy stertorous breath, like a person oppressed in sleeping' (p. 119). Henry asks the doctor, ' "Is she likely to die?" ', to which he replies, ' "She is dead [. . .] Those sounds that you hear are purely mechanical – they may go on for hours" ' (p. 119). Death and money pervade the text, and until her last moments the countess was rewriting the play which she conceived of as a popular commercial venture.

When Henry reads the play he confesses to Francis (who is now Lord Montbarry), ' "I felt for him to-night, what I am ashamed to think I never felt for him before" ' (p. 123). Henry, at last, is able to move beyond the apparently all-pervasive amorality which governed all social relations until this point. The metaphysical mystery is never properly explained. Francis dismisses it as a delusion and the text concludes with the terse, 'Is there no explanation of the mystery of The

Haunted Hotel? Ask yourself if there is any explanation of the mystery of your own life and death – Farewell' (p. 127).

The novella, however, can also be read as incorporating references to popular commercial culture through images of writing. The countess's play foregrounds such issues, which obliquely refer to Collins's concern about the place of the artist in the marketplace. Tamar Heller saw this concern as underpinning many of the anxieties about money in *The Woman in White*. Collins was a commercial writer who frequently had his work published in serial form before publication in the novel format, and was thus involved in a particular type of financial speculation. Selling novels in a serial, or piecemeal, way glosses the idea of speculative financial investment. This idea is associated with the Haunted Hotel as a place within the text and as a play about the hotel which, like the novella, has certain commercial ambitions. Money and writing are thus tentatively linked in a drama about murder, ghosts, and financial plots. The publication of the novella with *My Lady's Money* emphasises that such issues were becoming increasingly important to Collins. These issues can be related to an anonymously published ghost story, 'The Ghost in the Bank of England', which if not by Collins, can certainly be read as heavily influenced by him.

'The Ghost in the Bank of England'

> I can see him still in fancy as I saw him once in visible fact, receiving what, by the ghostly error of a ghostly clerk, he mistook for a ghostly cheque drawn by a dead man from the hands of one who looked like a ghost, so worn out was I by the shadow of death through which I had so lately gone.[22]

Andrew Wilson, the narrator of the tale, acknowledges that at the end he is still haunted by the memory of a spectral cashier in the Bank of England. The tale concerns how Wilson, a recently qualified doctor with financial difficulties, is forced to pander to the wealthy Julius Mendez, an apparent hypochondriac. Mendez lives in the West Indies and is convinced that he will die before his fifty-seventh birthday, but that if he survives the day he will live for a further forty years. Wilson leaves his pregnant wife, Annie, in Britain and stays with Mendez (whom he had met whilst a ship's surgeon in the West Indies) for the two months leading up to his birthday. After seeing Mendez through the mental tortures of his birthday he leaves him but falls ill with yellow fever before he can return to England. When he has partially recovered and is able to undertake the journey home he finds that Annie has had the child and is living with her brother Tom. Wilson joins them, but is still conscious of their penury when some months later he discovers a letter from the West Indies sent by Mendez, which Annie had neglected to open. In it he finds a cheque for £1,000 and goes to the Bank of England, where he cashes the cheque with a strange-looking cashier and uses the money to help set up his country practice. All goes well until it is discovered that the banknote that he received is listed as having been destroyed by the bank. This means that the note appears to be a fake and Wilson, unable to identify the cashier, is charged with forgery. At this point a Mr Deacon, an octogenarian who lives in the same village as Wilson and who worked as a cashier in the bank (and whose son is Wilson's solicitor), is able to identify the mysterious cashier who cashed the cheque.

Mr Deacon recounts how some sixty years earlier he had been friends with a cashier named Fred Hawes. Fred's sister, Nancy, was the love interest for a number of cashiers until an older cashier, Isaac Ayscough, attempted to bring her under his influence by getting Fred involved in some trouble at the bank. Ayscough's intention was only to leave Nancy temporarily vulnerable to him whilst Fred was in prison, but the trouble involved fraud and Fred was sentenced to death. Nancy became deranged by Fred's death and the other cashiers shunned Ayscough, who despite some initial promise was never promoted and led a lonely existence until his death. It transpires that the cheque submitted by Wilson had been postdated by Mendez, who drowned in an accident the day after his birthday and was dead before the date on the cheque. The tale speculates that the ghost of Ayscough appears when dead people's cheques are cashed because they are usually forgeries and he gives them money which is likely to lead to their conviction (and damnation). A more prosaic explanation is that the number on the banknote had been incorrectly listed as destroyed by the bank, or that a cashier had kept a new £1,000 note drawn on Mendez's cheque whilst giving Wilson a banknote that should have been destroyed. Wilson is cleared but the tale still haunts him.[23]

Wilson begins by marking out the Gothic possibilities within an institution seemingly 'built upon the rock of strong fact' (pp. 242–3) rather than set 'in some ruined Rhenish castle' (p. 242). Wilson grants money a vitality that Marx had suggested in the *Economic and Philosophic Manuscripts of 1844*, when he suggests that 'mosses of memory gather about gold' (p. 242). However, it is around the banknote, or the notion of paper money, that ideas of spectrality are more clearly developed. The connections between paper money and absence are suggested by Mendez's cheque. The banknote is also not real, or perceived as a forgery. The banknote as a facsimile of money reworks the issues about money and absence found in *The Haunted Hotel*, where Ferrari's £1,000 banknote is closely related to his disappearance. In the tale it is developed in the relationship between Wilson and Mendez, which invites a Marxian reading. Wilson notes:

> It was almost as if he had decoyed me to his detestable sugar plantation, where all sorts of wild notions and strange practices lingered [. . .] in order that he might convey to himself the additional years of health and life which had been given to me – as if there were only a certain amount of human vitality in the world, so that when one man gains he must needs take from another. Of course I knew such a fancy to be the merest nonsensical nerve-trick; but I seemed at that time to see and hear everything more clearly than one can in a normal state of the brain, so that substances often became shadowy, and shadows substantial. (pp. 252–3)

Given that the relationship between them is, at least for Wilson, fundamentally an economic one, these images take on the peculiar properties which Marx had seen as accruing to money. If money ascribes value and quality to 'things' then this represents a misplacing of value which effects a conservative, or monetary, anarchy in human relations. Here Mendez appears to parasitically consume the life and energy of Wilson. This generates an emotional turmoil in Wilson that precisely replicates the overthrow of 'normal' relations that for Marx money effects, in which 'substances often became shadowy, and shadows substantial'. In a wider sense this also reads as a thematic synopsis of the tale in which the past, in the guise of Ayscough's guilt, is brought back to life. However, much of this imagery is constituted through association with money, rather than with a mishandled romance (Ayscough) or the irritations posed by pandering to a hypochondriac (Wilson). Money is thus an explicit theme of the tale and it also inhabits metaphors of possession and ownership which are familiar from *The Haunted Hotel* and images of money and lost identities that characterise *No Name* and *Armadale*.

These concerns about money and possession are also developed in Mr Deacon's recounting of his time as a cashier in the bank. He tells Wilson: ' "I wonder when I think of it if a bank desk doesn't feel itself to be the real body and soul of the whole thing, and the clerk behind it only a pair of hands that it gets new from time to time" ' (pp. 257–8). This functions as an unconscious gloss on Marx's famous account of the table, discussed in Chapter 1, which he used to illustrate how commodity fetishism operates, whereby the desk comes alive with the power of the system and the worker is merely an alienated adjunct to the process. This is also what happens to Ayscough when the other cashiers shun him after Fred's death: ' "He was punctual in all his duties; he turned into a sort of machine" ' (p. 262). When Wilson describes the cashier, the ghost of Ayscough, who serves him, the description is a mixture of the impersonal and the intimate. He initially notes of him that 'he was nothing to me save in his capacity of an automaton for paying me a thousand pounds on demand' (p. 264). Yet the corpse-like Ayscough, whose 'head seemed to be degenerating, before death, into a living skeleton', provokes an extreme emotional response in Wilson because of his appearance as a figure that seems to possess 'a corpse look which had murdered not only bodies, but brains, hearts and souls' (p. 266).

Given the earlier suggested links between the power of money and depersonalisation, Ayscough figuratively represents those who are lost to the system. He is both thing (an automaton, a corpse) and yet animated and possessing a spectral agency which is inherent to paper money. Wilson also comes to this conclusion when he deliberates on whether the banknote issued to him should, or could, have been destroyed because money, in abstract terms, seems all-powerful and indestructible: 'Burn a bank-note as thoroughly as you will, its particles are not destroyed, and may be restored by the process of ghostly cohesion, which, if such a thing be at all, is just as applicable to paper and to engraver's ink as to flesh and bone' (p. 286).

Finally Wilson sees that the ghost merely makes visible what is inherent to paper money because the ghost and money are intimately related: 'The body may die but the corpse may live; the paper may be burned, but the written words are not to be blotted out merely by man-kindled fire' (p. 286). Such a conclusion transfers Marx's view of the commodity to money itself. Marx had commented on how the product is 'a very queer thing, abounding in metaphysical subtleties and theological niceties', because it is ghosted by the labour which produced it.[24] 'The Ghost in the Bank of England' finesses this by suggesting that money itself is the abstract form which governs, and ghosts, social relations. Revealingly Wilson also suggests that he has mentally incorporated Ayscough: 'I know in my inner brain stands the corpse of Isaac Ayscough, in his habit, in his sin, and in his remorse as he lived, honouring with burned bank-notes the cheques of dead men' (p. 286). Money – its circulation and apparent mystique – is ultimately psychologically and emotionally assimilated by Wilson through the image of Ayscough, who, paradoxically, enables the abstract spectrality of money to be seen. As in Dickens, seeing how the system works and attempting to change it are not always compatible, but a tale such as this illustrates how consciousness in a money-based society internalises and so reproduces a metaphorics of money that underpins the system.

Spectrality works at a covert level in much of Collins's writings. It implicitly inhabits a language of money which is linked to representations of gender. Often, of course, his texts are also love stories. The relationship between romance, money, and gender is given a particular emphasis in the ghost stories of Charlotte Riddell, which are discussed alongside tales by Vernon Lee and May Sinclair in the following chapter.

Notes

1 See Wilkie Collins's *Mad Monkton and Other Stories* (Oxford: Oxford University Press, 1998), ed. and introd. Norman Page, which includes many of Collins's ghost stories.

2 The key omitted text here is *The Moonstone* (1868), a novel which explicitly addresses issues about orientalism. This places it somewhat beyond the discussion of literature and money which is the principal focus of this chapter.

3 Winifred Hughes, *The Maniac in the Cellar: Sensation Novels of the 1860s* (Princeton: Princeton University Press, 1980) p. 7.

4 Quoted in Hughes, *The Maniac in the Cellar*, pp. 55–6. Referenced by Hughes to 'Our Female Sensation Novelists' from the *Christian Remembrancer*, repr. in *Littell's Living Age*, 22 August 1863, p. 353.

5 G.H. Lewes, quoted in Hughes, *The Maniac in the Cellar*, p. 54. Referenced by Hughes to the *Edinburgh Review*, 1850.

6 See Robert Miles's discussion of the critical reception of the early Gothic in *Ann Radcliffe: The Great Enchantress* (Manchester: Manchester University Press, 1996) pp. 34–56.

7 Alison Milbank, *Daughters of the House: Modes of Gothic in Victorian Fiction* (Basingstoke: Macmillan, 1992).

8 Wilkie Collins, *Basil*, ed. and introd. Dorothy Goodman (Oxford: Oxford University Press, [1852] 2000) p. xli.

9 Tamar Heller, *Dead Secrets: Wilkie Collins and the Female Gothic* (New Haven: Yale University Press, 1992). All subsequent references are to this edition and are given in the text.

10 Norman Russell, *The Novelist and Mammon: Literary Responses to the World of Commerce in the Nineteenth Century* (Oxford: Clarendon, 1986) p. 11.

11 Thomas Caryle, quoted in Russell, p. 13. Referenced by Russell to the *Edinburgh Review*, 49 (June 1829), 440.

12 Heller, *Dead Secrets*, p. 110.

13 Wilkie Collins, *The Woman in White*, ed. and introd. Julian Symons (Harmondsworth: Penguin, [1860] 1985) p. 47. All subsequent references are to this edition and are given in the text.

14 Wilkie Collins, in William Baker and William M. Clarke (eds), *The Letters of Wilkie Collins*, vol. 1: 1838–65 (Basingstoke: Macmillan, 1999) p. 45.

15 There is a strong case to be made that Collins is deliberately lampooning traditional gender scripts. Note the representation of Mr Fairlie in *The Woman in White*.

16 I have also discussed the gender implications of this in *Victorian Demons: Medicine, Masculinity and the Gothic at the Fin de Siècle* (Manchester: Manchester University Press, 2004) pp. 126–7.

17 Wilkie Collins, *No Name*, ed. and introd. Mark Ford (Harmondsworth: Penguin, [1862] 1994) p. 82. All subsequent references are to this edition and are given in the text.

18 Laurence Talairach-Vielmas, 'Victorian Sensational Shoppers: Representing Transgressive Femininity in Wilkie Collins's *No Name*', *Victorian Review*, 31.2 (2005), 56–78, 67, special issue on 'Literature and Money', ed. Andrew Smith. All subsequent references are to this edition and are given in the text.

19 Wilkie Collins, *Armadale*, ed. and introd. Catherine Peters (Oxford: Oxford University Press, [1866] 1989) p. 769. All subsequent references are to this edition and are given in the text.

20 Karl Marx, *Economic and Philosophic Manuscripts of 1844* (Moscow: Progress Publishers, [1844] 1967) p. 130, italics in original. All subsequent references are to this edition and are given in the tex.

21 Wilkie Collins, *The Haunted Hotel: A Mystery of Modern Venice* (New York: Dover, [1878] 1982) p. 5. All subsequent references are to this edition and are given in the text.

22 Anon., 'The Ghost in the Bank of England' in *Victorian Ghost Stories* (London: Senate, [1936] 1996) pp. 242–87, pp. 285–6. All subsequent references are to this edition and are given in the text.

23 'The Ghost in the Bank of England' has a number of factors in common with Collins's writing: not only the theme of money and ghosting, which was clearly a topic of his

writing at the time, but also some formal elements such as references to sea travel and a characteristically sardonic view of marriage. Annie's maiden name is Burdon and when he is ill with yellow fever Annie's family suspect that his disappearance is because he 'had deserted her to relieve myself of a burden' (pp. 251–2). Many of the character portraits – especially of Tom Burdon, who 'was a young Englishman of the sort that makes a point of never being surprised at anything, or glad to see anybody' (p. 251), and the eccentric old Mr Deacon – seem to bear Collins's imprint.

24 Karl Marx, *Capital* in David McLellan (ed.), *Karl Marx: Selected Writings* (Oxford: Oxford University Press, [1977] 1984) pp. 415–507, p. 435.

4

Love, money, and history:
the female ghost story

It is crucial to acknowledge the major contribution that women writers made to the ghost story during the period. The selection of authors discussed here is necessarily limited but gives a representative flavour of how women writers engaged with the specific issues of love, money, and history. There is the danger that such a thematic approach simplifies the range of the female-authored ghost story and it is not claimed that these are the sole issues involved in reading such tales. However, this approach helps to identify the shared concerns that enable a comparative reading of three significant authors: Charlotte Riddell, Vernon Lee, and May Sinclair, whose writings span the 1870s–1920s.[1]

This period is noteworthy because, as Vanessa D. Dickerson has stated:

> The ghost stories written after the 1850s, but especially in the last decades of the century, would be written in a climate of change and reform marked by such developments as the agitation for women's rights to education, employment, and suffrage; the passage of the married women's property bills; and the rise of the New Woman.[2]

Dickerson argues that this context repositioned a popular narrative such as the ghost story, after the later sensation fiction of Mary Elizabeth Braddon and Ellen Wood had taken a moralistic and politically conservative turn in the 1860s. The female-authored ghost story filled this vacuum by reasserting the important use of the fantastic in exploring the issues confronted by women. Diana Wallace has also claimed that 'The ghost story as a form has allowed women writers special kinds of freedom, not merely to include the fantastic and the supernatural, but also to offer critiques of male power and sexuality which are often more radical than those in more realist genres'.[3] The symbolic mode of the ghost story allows for this freedom whilst, paradoxically, such symbolism helps to encode (or encrypt) these critiques.

This chapter examines how women writers reflect on gender matters by focusing on a selection of ghost stories that self-consciously explore how constructions of art and literature relate to ideological and historical factors such as love, money, and history.

Chalotte Riddell: ghosts and money

Charlotte Riddell (or 'Mrs J.H. Riddell', the name under which she often published) was the author of some fifty-two books beginning with *Zuriel's Grandchild* in 1856 and concluding in 1902 with *Poor Fellow!* During the 1870s she was also the editor of the *St. James's Magazine*. Her output consists of novels, novellas, and collections of short stories. Her Irish background was occasionally explicitly addressed in novels such as *Maxwell Drewitt* (1865) and *Berna Boyle* (1882), as well as in ghost stories such as 'Hertford O'Donnell's Warning' (1867), 'Diarmid Chittock's Story' (1894), and 'Conn Kilrea' (1899). Riddell also produced a series of what were well-known novels concerning the financial sector, including *City and Suburb* (1861), *George Geith of Fen Court* (1865), *The Senior Partner* (1881), *Mitre Court* (1885), and *The Head of the Firm* (1892). Her Gothic novellas consist of *Fairy Water* (1873), *The Uninhabited House* (1875), *The Haunted River* (1877), and *The Disappearance of Jeremiah Redworth* (1878). Her collection of Gothic tales, *Weird Stories*, was published in 1884 and includes many important ghost stories.

Benjamin F. Fisher has noted that Riddell was 'one of Great Britain's leading novelists during the 1860s–1870s' although her work has now largely been forgotten.[4] Her tales bear comparison with the work of Wilkie Collins as their repeated focus on money reworks a connection between money and spectrality that was, as we saw in the previous chapter, a characteristic of both Collins's ghost writings and the implicit images of the spectre that were employed in his sensation fiction. (Riddell's sensation novel, *Above Suspicion*, was published in 1876.)[5] That Riddell shares a context with Collins is suggested by S.M. Ellis's tellingly entitled *Wilkie Collins, Le Fanu, and Others* (1931), which includes a chapter on Riddell. More recently, Fisher has explored in some depth the debt that Riddell owes to Collins. In particular Fisher notes that her non-Gothic writings are characterised by a strange Gothic ambience which also shapes her use of language, and which suggest points of contact with Collins. Fisher, for example, argues that Collins's *The Woman in White* (1860) established themes which reappear in Riddell's more realistic writings, where 'We see no hapless victims walled up alive to suffer physical and emotional horrors accompanying a slow death, but figurative live burials [that] enrich many of the novels' (p. 176). Fisher also identifies this as a characteristic of Riddell's novels about the financial sector, in which 'commercial men' feel 'that their workplaces as well as their daily routines resemble graveyards in which they are buried' (p. 184) – an issue she explored in *The Uninhabited House*.

The Uninhabited House initially focuses on the legal practicalities of renting out River Hall, a haunted house. The legal firm involved is successfully sued for having attempted to conceal that River Hall is haunted and Patterson, a clerk from the firm who narrates the tale, agrees to reside there in an effort to identify the source of the ghostly activity. It is revealed that the house is haunted by a previous owner, a Mr Elmsdale, a wealthy and unscrupulous money-lender who had attempted to ruin a Mr Harringford, who in a moment of rage had shot Elmsdale. The sight of Elmsdale's ghost is recounted by Colonel Morris, the successful litigant in the court case. He records how one evening when walking outside the house he heard a noise within:

> I rushed to the nearest window and looked in. The gas was all ablaze, the door of the strong room open, the table strewed with papers, while in an office chair drawn close up to the largest drawer, a man was seated counting over bank-notes. He had a pile of them before him, and I distinctly saw that he wetted his fingers in order to separate them.[6]

This spectral attachment to money implies a form of disembodiment that is elaborated through Harringford, who tells Patterson: ' "From the hour I left him lying dead in the library every worldly plan prospered with me" '. However, ' "I had sold my soul to the devil" ' and as a consequence ' "One after another, wife and children died" ' whilst he became lame and prematurely aged (p. 163). In the end wealth is restored as the dying Harringford leaves his money to Elmsdale's daughter, who marries the narrator. These links between money and ghosts are familiar from Collins and there is an emphasis on how the mystery requires the kind of decoding that only a detective can make. However, the apparent 'clues' discovered by Patterson are conveyed to him via dreams which in symbolic form explain why Elmsdale's spirit is so restless (because he wants Harringford punished). In the first dream Patterson recounts being led to a graveyard and looking into an empty open grave whilst its occupant sits on a nearby tombstone 'looking at me with wistful, eager eyes' (p. 130). This figure commands him to look at 'something flitting away into darkness' to which Patterson could give 'no shape or substance' (p. 131), but which is meant to indicate Harringford. In a subsequent dream there 'was a vague feeling I was pursuing a person who eluded all my efforts to find him; playing a terrible game of hide-and-seek' (p. 146). Later, when Harringford has been discovered loitering in the vicinity of the house, the narrator notes 'This was the hiding figure in my dream, the link hitherto wanting in my reveries concerning River Hall' (p. 154). The psychic message sent to Patterson seems, so the tale suggests, to emanate from the spectral Elmsdale whose intervention ensures that wealth is passed on to his daughter by the guilty Harringford. How money is used defines moral character in the novella in ways which echo Collins's concern about money and its proper restoration. However, unlike Collins, Riddell's tales do not dwell on feelings of revenge but on the unravelling of the mystery.

At times Riddell's engagement with Collins seems to be more or less explicit. *The Haunted River*, for example, explores the relationship between two sisters who have been disinherited and who move from a house in Yorkshire to Surrey. There they rent a haunted house which has associations with abduction, murder, and female incarceration in an asylum, which makes the novella seem like an amalgam of *The Woman in White* and *No Name* (1862). There is even an echo of Walter Hartright's horror of Welmingham when Riddell's narrator refers to a new town and notes the presence of ' "carcases" – that is, I believe, the correct and technical expression – of various shops and houses in a more or less forward state of incompleteness'.[7] *Fairy Water*, like *The Uninhabited House* and *The Haunted River*, also addresses the difficulties in renting out a haunted house and this recurring theme, which is also a feature of many of Riddell's ghost stories such as 'The Open Door' (1882), indicates a reiterated concern about money, houses, and threatened or actual dispossession.

These issues are not gender neutral because although many of the texts have male narrators who are in need of money, such an ascription of powerlessness to those narrators cannot disguise that their participation in a romance plot (as in *The Uninhabited House*) is intended to cater for a female audience.[8] In a subtle way Riddell attempts a repositioning of Collins's spectres by frequently letting them go unpunished, and by focusing the narrative through a language of romantic love that often embraces marriage as a form of textual closure. By contrast, Collins's scepticism about marriage as a social and economic contract frequently unsettles such closures. Riddell might therefore seem to be more conservative on such matters than Collins, but it is noteworthy that the men in Riddell's tales, whether they are narrating or not, have to prove their moral worth in order to secure the woman. The issue of money as a means of ensuring power thus appears to be set aside as other forms of identity, which are not touched by such ghostly economic plots, are established.

Riddell's emphasis on the romance plot could be construed as a conservative correction of Collins's problematisation of gender scripts.[9] However, as we shall see, there is an engagement with ideas about money and art that forms a counterpoint to Collins by emphasising the role and status of the woman artist. As discussed in the previous chapter, Walter Hartright in *The Woman in White* represents an image of a threatened male artistic endeavour, and Riddell reworks this in her representation of the links between spectrality, money, and the female artist. Before discussing these links it is worth noting that the relationship between money and spectrality was also given prominence in Riddell's rewriting of Dickens's model of the male miser from *A Christmas Carol* (1843), which also suggests her critical engagement with such male-authored texts.

In *The Uninhabited House* Elmsdale and Harringford's wrangling over money indicates that ownership of wealth is not in itself a virtue. As in *A Christmas Carol* it is necessary that such wealth is redistributed for positive ends, which also means that Elmsdale (and Harringford) can make moral (and financial) restitution from beyond the grave. However, this transfer of money from one generation to the next is also intended to empower Elmsdale's previously impoverished daughter and secure her a husband who has to demonstrate his moral credibility. To that degree the movement of wealth into a female-orientated romance plot and away from a male revenge narrative is intended to exonerate the role of money as it supports female emotional development and grants a level of financial independence.[10]

That Riddell may have had Dickens's tale in mind is also indicated by one of her Christmas tales, 'The Old House in Vauxhall Walk' (1882).[11] The tale centres on Graham Coulton, who as a consequence of a quarrel with his father has been left financially destitute, the opening line referring to him as ' "Houseless-homeless-hopeless!" '.[12] Coulton has a gentleman's background but is now described as an urban tramp, as one of 'the waifs and strays of struggling humanity that are always coming and going, cold starving and miserable' (p. 85). He is discovered in this condition by William, a former family servant who has made money and who resides in a grand house that he has been forced to leave due to ghostly activity which, although it had unsettled his wife, he had not personally experienced. Coulton is permitted to stay in the now partially empty house and encounters the figure of a female ghost who functions as a female version of Scrooge. He wakes from a dream and describes seeing:

> . . . the outline of a female figure seated beside the fire, engaged in picking some-thing out of her lap and dropping it with a despairing gesture.
> He heard the mellow sound of gold, and knew she was lifting and dropping sovereigns. (p. 91)

Unlike Scrooge she seems to be beyond redemption because she is trapped by her despair: ' "Oh! My lost life – for one day, for one hour of it again!" ' (p. 92). This is occasioned by her inability to use her wealth to improve the lot of the poor, and to that extent she resembles Dickens's ghosts, who could only observe rather than alleviate poverty. Coulton records that: 'out from the dreary night, with their sodden feet and the wet dripping from their heads, came the old men and the young children, the worn women and the weary hearts, whose misery that gold might have relieved, but whose wretchedness it mocked' (p. 92).

As this spectral narrative unfolds Coulton sees that it revolves around the miserly woman and her more charitable brother, who had been happy together as children before 'the accursed greed for gold had [. . .] divided them' (p. 93). As with Scrooge her miserliness induces a form of self-inflicted poverty as Coulton describes her 'walking slowly across the floor munching a dry crust – she who could have purchased all the luxuries wealth can command' (pp. 92–3). The scene plays out the brother's request for money 'to avert some bitter misfortune' (p. 93), which he is denied. The woman is described as possessing a pitiful soul that is 'contaminated with the most despicable and insidious vice'. This places her beyond physical mortification because 'the greed of the miser eats into the very soul' (p. 93). Coulton notes her peculiar poverty including a four-poster bed without hangings in which she sleeps 'with her claw-like fingers clutching the clothes, as though even in sleep she was guarding her gold!' (p. 94). William informs Coulton that the woman was murdered and that the landlord is her brother. Struck by the ghostly encounters,

Coulton indicates a willingness to stay in the building and attempts to solve the mystery of her murder.

On the second night he sees the old woman again but observes a confrontation between her and a seemingly identical female spirit which steps out from behind a large mirror in the drawing-room, 'at the sight of which the first turned and fled, uttering piercing shrieks as the other followed her from story to story' (p. 98). The following day Coulton returns to the house in the evening, when 'the pavements were full of people going marketing, for it was Christmas Eve, and all who had money to spend seemed bent on shopping' (p. 99). On his return he discovers two robbers who have been searching for the old woman's gold (and who seemingly have been responsible for her murder). Coulton is assaulted by them but they are apprehended by the police. Subsequently there is a loud noise emanating from the drawing-room. Mr Tynan, the landlord, rushes to the room:

> When he unlocked the door, what a sight met his eyes! The mirror had fallen – it was lying all over the floor shivered into a thousand pieces; the console table had been borne down by its weight, and the marble slab was shattered as well. But this was not what claimed his attention. Hundreds, thousands of gold pieces were scattered about, and an aperture behind the glass contained boxes filled with securities and deeds and bonds, the possession of which had cost his sister her life. (pp. 100–1)

The key to this narrative relates to the scene where Tynan's sister is scared away by an image of herself that is both reflected in the mirror and associated with the money which is behind the mirror. The second figure represents what she has become, a soulless miser whose spectral status is a result of associating herself too closely with money which is both abstract (coined) and real (gold). By looking into the mirror she has symbolically become money and so has been depersonalised. The horrified self-reflection in the mirror thus emphasises her despair. However, the language of the scene implies that it enables Coulton to exercise a self-mastery in which 'he recovered his self-possession' (p. 98) even whilst the first ghost loses hers. The miser learns that gold unused is, like her, buried and beyond social (and economic) circulation. Scrooge may overcome this plight through a series of enforced epiphanies but it takes the arrest of the robbers to liberate the money.

The fact that Tynan shares some of this wealth with Coulton reinstates him in a position which he would have maintained if he had not argued with his father. The money is thus used to restore Coulton rather than to improve the lot of the poor. However, the tale closes with Coulton becoming reconciled with his father after William disabuses him of the view that his father disliked Coulton's mother. In reality, William tells Coulton, ' "he was over fond of your mother" ' (p. 90). In an elision which appears elsewhere with the mirror, Coulton regains his 'self-possession' by overcoming the feelings of the 'lost life' that are associated with the spectral Miss Tynan. He is confronted by his father, who asks if Coulton has lost his senses and he replies, ' "No, sir, I have found them" ' (p. 101).

The 'lost' world of Miss Tynan is thus compensated by the now wealthy Coulton's desire to ' "make a better thing of my life" ' as a consequence (p. 101). Miss Tynan thus lives through Coulton, but the clear gender implications of this move suggest that the woman is lost, or denied, at the expense of male entry into the public sphere. A reconciliation between Coulton and his father will only work if Coulton can convince his father of his bravery (his father had called him a coward before their estrangement (p. 90)). Even Tynan is exonerated because the apprehension of the killers removes a suspicion that had fallen upon him. The conclusion of the tale implies that it is Miss Tynan who is lost to a world of public money and social decorum because it is a world that is 'owned' by men. Riddell's rewriting of *A Christmas Carol* portrays the public sphere as a discriminatory arena that Scrooge can rejoin but from which the already dead Miss Tynan is estranged. The language of reconciliation which overcomes financial and personal estrangement is played out in a male public domain because that, seemingly, is the only place where it can be properly accommodated. This radical, if subtle, reappropriation of Dickens's tale indicates an issue which is also addressed in terms of artistic authority through images of art which appear elsewhere in Riddell's ghost stories.

Peg, the narrator of *The Haunted River*, makes a living as an artist. Her reflections on her art suggest abstract associations with the ghost story and a more general sense of an artist's place within a wider market. She decides to paint an abandoned mill on the edge of what turns out to be a haunted river and applies a Gothic aesthetic as she wanders 'about the ruined building, trying to decide from which point the grey, moss-covered walls, the broken wheel, the foaming water, the precipitate banks, the weird, solemn-looking pines, grouped themselves most effectively' (p. 41). She also senses that within such a Gothic scene exists a narrative that becomes, if only vaguely, communicated to her: 'I felt that under my fingers, not merely a landscape, but a story was growing – a story of wrong, of mystery, and disaster' (p. 41). Her imagination reworks the story of a tragic death which had taken place near the river and she attempts to arrange the scene so that it articulates an appropriate mood: 'What almost unconsciously I wanted – what I desired – was to give to my picture a meaning beyond that contained in the mere natural components which constituted the actual details' (p. 41). The ambition is to make it clear that 'everyone who looked hereafter at the scene depicted would understand each adjunct said, "As plain as whisper in the ear! The place is haunted!"' (p. 41). Peg thus registers the wider aesthetic intent of the Gothic writer who rearranges certain formal conventions and associated images of ruins as structural elements within a Gothic plot. Later, Peg self-consciously reflects on her place in the art world, regarding herself as a fundamentally commercial artist because her 'gift' is 'a somewhat adaptable gift' (p. 69). This arguably registers Riddell's appraisal of the different forms of popular writing (realist, financial, and supernatural) with which she was associated. Peg notes that her art is one that will 'give pleasure'

rather than innovate the art world. The interpolated narrative about art is revealing because it suggests a self-consciousness about writing which also conditions
Riddell's appropriations of Collins and Dickens. Peg also evinces an acute sense
of writing for a market where a badly executed idea means that one 'dies a
bankrupt' (p. 69).

That Riddell was conscious of her market position has been explored by Linda
H. Peterson, who has argued that Riddell's novel *A Struggle for Fame* (1883)
examines the link between female authorship and romantic artistic genius which
was central to Gaskell's *Life of Charlotte Brontë* (1857).[13] *A Struggle for Fame*
acknowledges the difference between an early, Brontësque, model of the writer
and the professionalisation of the writing culture which existed towards the end
of the nineteenth century. Such professionalisation generated a literary celebrity
culture which, so the novel argues, stifled innovative art in the name of identifying
marketable brands of writing. Peterson argues that the novel attempts a balance
between evoking the earlier myth of the writer as a Romantic genius whilst admit-
ting that the current literary culture is now unavoidably driven by economics.
Ultimately the novel acknowledges the new complexities confronted by the woman
writer who wishes to be financially successful (like Peg with her 'so little genius'
(p. 69)) and yet retain some form of artistic credibility. These issues about writing
and appropriation overlap with repeated themes of money in Riddell's ghost stories
which also indicate a self-consciousness about literary appropriation. How the woman
writer can find her place within such a culture forms one of the important strands
in the ghost stories of Vernon Lee.

Vernon Lee: aesthetics and history

If there is an engagement with art and the marketplace in Riddell's work, Lee's
writings emphasise an engagement with history in which art functions as the crucial intermediary between the past and the present. Whilst Riddell's tales follow
a fairly conventional line on ghosts to the degree that they concern laying the
past to rest, with Lee the ghost is often used to resurrect the past. Lee's work needs
to be seen within the context of late nineteenth-century debates on aesthetics
(she was a close friend of Walter Pater) and a Victorian fascination with the
Renaissance (she was, for a time, on friendly terms with the Italian Renaissance
scholar, Bernard Berenson). Vernon Lee (real name Violet Paget) was domiciled
for much of her life in Italy (although of partly British descent), and her writings
between the 1880s and 1930s consist of forty-three books on a number of topics
including the history of the Italian Renaissance, theories of aesthetics, travel
writing, philosophy, literary criticism, ghost stories, and novels. She was, for a while,
close friends with Henry James (whose ghost stories she influenced) and she
knew a number of artists in the Pre-Raphaelite circle.[14] She was largely rejected
by modernist writers because her association with a refashioned Paterian aesthetic

seemingly linked her to old-fashioned Victorian concerns about art. As we shall see, however, Lee's aesthetic principles are not quite so hostile to modernist experimentation and her aesthetic pursuits are echoed in the ghost stories of May Sinclair, which have a self-conscious modernist air to them.

In recent years Lee has also received considerable critical attention (unlike Riddell) which has considered how these issues about history and aesthetics might relate to Lee's sexuality. This topic was explored by Burdett Gardner in his PhD thesis in 1954 (published in 1987), and more recently by Martha Vicinus and Kathy Alexis Psomiades. Psomiades claims that Lee 'produced a theory of the aesthetic grounded in the congress between female bodies'.[15] It is also important to acknowledge just how innovative her ghost stories are. Her main collections of ghost stories are *Hauntings* (1890), *Pope Jacynth and other Fantastic Tales* (1904), and *For Maurice: Five Unlikely Stories* (1927). In her preface to *Hauntings* she outlines a manifesto for the ghost story by claiming that it needs to cultivate an historically evocative ambience through reference to the 'vague shroud of moonbeams that hangs about the haunting lady, the glint on the warrior's breastplate, the click of his unseen spurs'.[16] This view of the ghost story explicitly places it beyond the 'modern ghost-experts' associated with the Society for Psychical Research, where 'you can always tell a genuine ghost-story by the circumstances of its being about a nobody' (p. 38).[17] Rather Lee's tales 'are things of the imagination, born there, bred there, sprung from the strange confused heaps, half-rubbish, half-treasure, which lie in our fancy' (p. 39). Her ghosts transcend the specific circumstances that give rise to them when she claims that the 'remote Past [. . .] is the place to get our ghosts from' (p. 39). However, significantly this is not a dead past because such ghosts, 'very vague and changeful, are perpetually to and fro, fetching and carrying for us between it [the past] and the Present' (p. 39). The implication is that the ghost story aesthetically functions to bring the past back to life. Its associations with a particular mood also rework Lee's view, in her historical writing, that the past can be evoked by our empathy with it. There has been considerable critical discussion of Lee's views on gender because despite her essay 'The Economic Parasitism of Women' (1902), which marked her conversion to feminism as politics, she appeared to have little to say on the matter. Her tales demonstrate ample evidence, however, of a radical position on gender issues. Aesthetics, history, gender, and the function of art tend to become elided in her tales and 'Amour Dure' (1887) provides an interesting example of these points of convergence.

The tale is narrated in a diary format by a young Polish historian, Spiridion Trepka, who is visiting Italy to write a history of the city of Urbania. However, it is clear from the opening lines that his engagement with history is personal rather than professional. 'I had longed, these years and years, to be in Italy, to come face to face with the past', he states, only to find that his approach is conditioned by a dry historical scholarship that constitutes a 'modern scientific vandalism'.[18] His researches, however, lead him to explore the story of the sixteenth-century Medea, an apparent femme fatale who was forcibly married into a prominent Urbanian family and who left behind her a line of dead lovers before she was executed by the order of Duke Robert. Trepka likens her to Lucrezia Borgia and the more he discovers of her history the more beguiled he becomes. Later he has a brief encounter seemingly with Medea, who promises to come to him if he destroys a consecrated silver image that Duke Robert had hidden within a bronze statue of himself. This silver image protects the duke's soul until Judgement Day whilst guaranteeing Medea's eternal damnation. Trepka carries out the task but is discovered the next morning dead of a stab to the heart.

Early in the tale Trepka becomes aware that in his beguilement he has discovered a means of emotionally gaining access to the past through an empathetic bond which challenges his conventional idea of historical enquiry. One diary entry notes: 'I can't free myself from the thought of this Medea da Carpi. In my walks, my mornings in the Archives, my solitary evenings, I catch myself thinking over the woman. Am I turning novelist instead of historian? And still it seems to me that I understand her so well; so much better than my facts warrant' (pp. 55–6). This thinking implies that fiction animates the past rather than historical writing and this develops a theme about the role of art which is also suggested in a portrait of Medea that Trepka had seen earlier:

> The face is a perfect oval, the forehead somewhat over-round, with minute curls, like a fleece, of bright auburn hair; the nose a trifle over-aquiline, and the cheek-bones a trifle too low; the eyes grey, large, prominent, beneath exquisitely curved brows and lids just a little too tight at the corners; the mouth, also, brilliantly red and most delicately designed, is a little too tight, the lips strained over the teeth. Tight eyelids and tight lips give a strange refinement, and, at the same time, an air of mystery, a somewhat sinister seductiveness; they seem to take not to give. The mouth with a kind of childish pout, looks as if it could bite or suck like a leech. (pp. 51–2)

Critics such as Mary Patricia Kane, Angela Leighton, and Christa Zorn have noted that Pater's infamous description of the Mona Lisa played a role in Lee's reconstruction of his 'vampire'.[19] In Pater's famous description the Mona Lisa:

> is older than the rocks among which she sits; like the vampire, she has been dead many times, and learned the secrets of the grave; and has been a diver in deep seas, and keeps their fallen day about her; and trafficked for strange webs with Eastern merchants: and, as Leda, was the mother of Helen of Troy, and, as Saint Anne, the mother of Mary; and all this has been to her but as the sound of lyres and flutes, and lives only in the delicacy with which it has moulded the changing lineaments, and tinged the eyelids and the hands. The fancy of a perpetual life, sweeping together ten thousand experiences, is an old one; and modern thought has conceived the idea of humanity as wrought upon by, and summing up in itself, all modes of thought and life. Certainly Lady Lisa might stand as the embodiment of the old fancy, the symbol of the modern idea.[20]

Kane argues that Lee engages and reworks Pater's model of the Mona Lisa in order to put back the kind of historical approach that is lost in his emphasis on an impressionistic sense of beauty which simply turns 'Lady Lisa' into a 'modern idea'. For Kane:

> Lee recognised the portrait's potential for providing a point of contact in narrative discourse between the past and the present – a space in which the two could be made to coincide. But where Pater saw Leonardo's portrait as the quintessential Renaissance representation of human desires over the centuries, Lee approaches the authoritative representations of portraiture with an eye to uncovering the stories that had been left in the shadows or suppressed.[21]

Lee also incorporates in her aesthetics a series of points that were central to the notion of beauty which Pater had attempted to formulate synoptically in his preface to *The Renaissance* (1873): 'Beauty, like all other qualities presented to human experience, is relative; and the definition of it becomes unmeaning and useless in proportion to its abstractness' (p. xxix). How to find a model which represents this beauty 'in the most concrete terms' is for Pater 'the aim of the true student of aesthetics' (p. xxix). This objectivity can be developed, according to Pater, by asking ourselves a series of questions when attempting an aesthetic evaluation: 'What is this song or picture, this engaging personality presented in life or in a book, to *me*? What effect does it really produce on me? Does it give me pleasure? and if so, what sort or degree of pleasure? How is my nature modified by its presence, and under its influence?' (p. xxix).

To some degree Lee's notion that empathy enables an engagement with history reworks Pater's emphasis on impression as the key to evaluating artistic affect. Art for Lee, in the instance of Medea's portrait, represents a history which Trepka responds to in a spirit of Paterian impressionism that brings history back to life through his empathetic engagement with Medea. However, as Kane notes, in an observation that recalls Pater's emphasis on the subjective evaluation of beauty, 'The empathetic relations that her characters have with the subjects of portraits ultimately reveal more about the characters themselves than about the illusive objects of their gaze' (p. 23). The question begged by this view concerns what type of resurrection is effected through such an empathetic evocation of the past. Pater remains implicit to this resurrection because Pater's account of the Mona Lisa, as Leighton has noted, 'turn[s] history into a body', specifically a female body for a male gaze.[22] However, given the Mona Lisa's vampiric qualities this 'is a resurrection of the body without spiritual promise or moral reassurance' (p. 225).

As a counterpoint to this, Lee's famous rebuttal of Ruskin's dismissal of Renaissance art on the grounds of immorality comes to mind, because for her the Renaissance mixture of high art and low morality (Leonardo *and* the Borgias) is key to understanding the complexity of the period which is echoed in the complexity of human empathy. As Lois Agnew notes, Lee also dismissed the Ruskinian view of an objective inner beauty which inheres to objects by suggesting in *The Beautiful: An Introduction to Psychological Aesthetics* (1913) that beauty is understood through 'a particular group of mental activities and habits'.[23] The role of history in this is sketched, as Catherine Maxwell has claimed, in Lee's essay on 'The Lake of Charlemagne' (1887), where Lee states that 'in our perceptions of nature and of art there usually exists a kind of phantom of the past'.[24] This version of the past suggests that we become ghostly in our encounters with it and that this is a necessary precondition for conjuring the past. Such engagements therefore, as in Trepka's, might seem to be highly personal, or overly subjective, but the past that is conjured concerns a lost or obscured history of Medea in which Trepka's revitalised view of the past is objectively re-embodied in her resurrection.

Trepka's attempt to bring Medea conceptually back to life is suggested by his moving beyond formal public documents and the type of historical readings that they conventionally invite, in order to locate the 'real' Medea. He discovers a batch of her letters concerning some unimportant business. Trepka is disappointed by their content, 'But they are her letters, and I can imagine almost that there hangs about these mouldering pieces of paper a scent as of a woman's hair' (p. 58). These associations with death (mould) and life (scent) are elaborated within the tale as Medea's return compromises notions of public history. Ultimately, Trepka might be the catalyst for this resurrection but it is one which depends upon moving beyond the historical method and interests that as a professional historian no matter how embittered, he is constrained by. As Diana Wallace has noted, the problematics in the text are not finally resolved because although Medea becomes freed from the past she has no voice of her own: 'at no point [. . .] do we hear the female or feminine voice unmediated by the male narrator'.[25] However, all of this is mediated by (typically in Lee) an unreliable, hysterical male narrator so that the mediation of Medea as a disturbed male construction is emphasised, even if at one level Medea is also the figure behind the painting.

Patricia Pulham has identified a recurring movement in Lee's work where art and ghosts become conflated so that such 'physical counterparts lend Lee's "ghosts" a solidity: they become "art objects" in their own right'.[26] The animation of history thus depends on an animation of art in which it too comes to life. By gendering art (and by association history) in this way an argument about the politics of representation becomes staged, one which revolves around issues of sexuality and gendered identities. In order to appreciate this it is necessary to take a step back from the Renaissance into a more mythological world because, as Pulham claims, even Lee's Renaissance, Jacobean, or eighteenth-century ghosts 'have mythic qualities of their own, and find their counterparts in the pagan figures of Athena, Marsyas, Venus, and the Sphinx' (p. xix). Crucially for Pulham such figures are 'associated with forms of hybridity'. An examination of how Lee represents Lamia provides a reconsideration of Lee's aesthetics and how they relate to formations of gender.

Lamia

In 'Amour Dure', as he longingly awaits a visit from Medea, Trepka writes about it in negative terms: 'And I, for what am I waiting? I don't know; all seems a dream; everything vague and unsubstantial about me, as if time had ceased, nothing could happen, my own desires and hopes were all dead' (p. 74). Trepka thus takes a troubling step outside of history, where 'time had ceased', because the tale implies that he is about to encounter the pagan, and in Pulham's terms mythic, figure of Medea. The irony that history takes you out of history is only a superficial one because it relates to art as a form which is both real (tangible, an object) and unreal (made up) and which yet functions to resurrect the past. References to the myth of Lamia are made in 'Prince Alberic and the Snake Lady' (1896),[27] and critics such as Diana Wallace, Ruth Robbins, Martha Vicinus, and Kathy Psomiades have argued that the snake lady of the title should be seen within the context of nineteenth-century representations of Lamia. Robbins has claimed that the tale recalls not only ancient myth but Keats's *Lamia* (1820) and Dante Gabriel Rossetti's 'Eden Bower' (1869), which forged links with the myth of Lilith that George MacDonald was to elaborate in his novel *Lilith* (1895). Such associations imply that Lee's tale should be seen within the context of counter-myths such as that of Lilith, who according to Hebrew Apocrypha was the first wife of Adam and according to some ancient myths was linked with Lamia. Robbins, however, suggests similarities between the tale and Keats's *Lamia*, as 'Keats's poem has much the same outcome as Lee's story, with both lover and lady dead at the end'.[28] This is a point of contact with Keats which will be developed as it provides an example of how Lee's aesthetics should be seen within the context of existing (here Romantic) models of creativity and how she moves beyond them through a gender-aware aesthetic.[29]

The tale is not explicitly a ghost story, although it does engage with the idea of a spectrally present history that is familiar from 'Amour Dure'. There are other, more formal ghost stories of Lee's such as 'Oke of Okehurst' (1886) and 'A Wicked Voice' (1887) which also explore the relationship between art and the spectral. However, Lee's reworking of Keats is helpful to consider here as it enables an exploration of how she redirects a male-authored conception of art which also underpins her engagement with Pater in 'Amour Dure'.

The tale focuses on the orphaned Prince Alberic, who is raised by his grandfather, Duke Balthasar Maria, at the Red Palace. The boy develops an attachment to a tapestry in his room entitled *Alberic the Blond and the Snake Lady Oriana*, which is removed by his uncle and replaced with a more morally instructive (Christian) tapestry: *Susanna and the Elders*.[30] The young prince, who has become emotionally attached to the earlier tapestry, is distraught by this substitution and destroys the replacement. His punishment is to be banished to the Castle of the Sparkling Waters where he is befriended by a godmother who takes charge of his education and where he discovers a harmless grass snake. Family legend reveals that Alberic the Blond had rescued the Fairy Oriana by kissing a snake inside which she had been imprisoned. However, for the charm on Oriana to be fully removed it was necessary that he be loyal to her for ten years, a task in which he failed. A second Prince Alberic also failed. The prince in Lee's tale is moved by this narrative and kisses the snake, which is transformed into his godmother, who is Oriana. His attempts at staying faithful are, however, thwarted by his grandfather, who recalls him to the Red Palace so that he may marry an heiress. The prince refuses to do so and is imprisoned. It is discovered that there is a snake in his cell and this is killed by the duke's supporters. The snake turns into the dead and horribly mutilated body of his godmother and the prince starves himself to death.

Robbins's observation that Keats's *Lamia* and Lee's tale share a similar conclusion suggests that Lee had Keats's poem in mind. The structure of Lee's tale, in which the pagan world of the snake lady's tapestry is superseded by a more modern and morally enlightening *Susanna and the Elders*, is echoed in the structure of Keats's poem. The first part of *Lamia* dwells on the pagan world of Lamia and Hermes (the latter allowing Lamia to regain human form in exchange for information concerning the whereabouts of a nymph that he is sexually pursuing). The second part focuses on the modern and human world which Lamia, like the snake lady in Lee's tale, is seeking to infiltrate. Keats's description of Lamia dwells on her associations with colour, which becomes the medium through which the natural and the artificial are elided:

> She was a gordian shape of dazzling hue.
> Vermilion-spotted, golden, green, and blue:
> Striped like a zebra, speckled like a pard,
> Eyed like a peacock, and all crimson barr'd:
> And full of silver moons, that, as she breathed,
> Dissolv'd, or brighter shone, or interwreathed
> Their lustres with the gloomier tapestries –
> So rainbow-sided, touch'd with miseries,
> She seem'd, at once, some penanced lady elf,
> Some demon's mistress, or the demon's self. (Part I, ll. 47–56)[31]

Lamia's command over nature is elaborated in Part II in her transformation of the banquet room for her wedding feast with Lycius. Lamia:

> Mission'd her viewless servants to enrich
> The fretted splendour of each nook and niche.
> Between the tree-stems, marbled plain at first,
> Came jasper pannels: then anon, there burst
> Forth creeping imagery of slighter trees,
> And with the larger wove in small intricacies.
> Approving all, she faded at self-will. (Part II, ll. 136–42)

Lamia is thus a force of nature and a force which commands it. Significantly she represents a spirit of creativity as she physically constructs a version of pastoral

which is rooted in her imagination. To that degree the poem is about the trans-
formative energies of the Romantic imagination. Such a model of creativity is also
associated with a self-conscious aura of mystery which is contrasted with scientific
accounts of nature.

In Part I the description of Lamia's colouration suggests the rainbow. The
scientific evaluation of the rainbow (Keats clearly having in mind Newton's work
on optics) thus constitutes an implied assault on Lamia:

> Do not all charms fly
> At the mere touch of cold philosophy?
> There was an awful rainbow once in heaven:
> We know her woof, her texture: she is given
> In the dull catalogue of common things.
> Philosophy will clip an Angel's wings,
> Conquer all mysteries by rule and line,
> Empty the haunted air, and gnomed mine –
> Unweave a rainbow, as it erewhile made
> The tender-person'd Lamia melt into a shade. (Part II, ll. 229–38)

This position is elaborated at the end when she encounters Lycius's philosophy
tutor, Apollonius: 'the sophist's eye / Like a sharp spear, went through her utterly'
(Part II, ll. 299–300). The love story between Lamia and Lycius thus forms a
pretext through which Lamia can enter into and creatively transform the human
world as the poem works through its central theme concerning the respective claims
of art and science. Significantly, the imagination is represented as female (an issue
subsequently addressed in the cultural links between Lamia and Lilith) and it is a
gendered conceptualisation of the imagination that Lee also addresses in her tale.

A striking aspect of 'Prince Alberic and the Snake Lady' is the repeated references to forms of representation. Lamia's association with tapestries in Keats's poem
is elaborated from the start of the tale, which emphasises the narrative figurations
within the tapestry. The prince's account of the tapestry variously refers to the
snake lady as possessing 'the colour of [. . .] moonbeams' (p. 186) and having
'a beautiful gold chain, and patterns in gold [. . .] all over her bodice' (p. 187).
By removing a crucifix and a chest of drawers that stood in front of the tapestry
and which had concealed her lower half, her tail is revealed. It is described as
having 'scales of still most vivid [. . .] green and gold' (p. 187). Such colours recall
the gold, green, and silver moons of Keats's Lamia. When the prince is initially
banished to the Castle of the Sparkling Waters he finds himself in a place which
resembles the tapestry: 'Alberic rambled on, from discovery to discovery, with the
growing sense that he was in the tapestry [. . .] that the tapestry had become
the whole world' (p. 193). When he first encounters the snake he notes its green
colour and 'small golden eyes', colouration which aligns it with the snake lady from
the tapestry. The green dress worn by his godmother also aligns her with the tapestry
and what it records 'began to haunt his dreams; only it was now a vaguely painful

thought; and while dreading still to know more, he began to experience a restless, miserable craving to know all' (p. 204). The uncomfortable knowledge that he inherits relates to how previous princes had reneged on their promise to wait ten years for the snake lady and he also inherits a place within that narrative. As in *Lamia* art and the imagination are associated with a female provenance which in this instance indicates the snake lady's control over history.

In 'Amour Dure' Trepka is pulled into a history that he has in part conjured. In 'Prince Alberic and the Snake Lady' the prince is effectively seduced by a model of history in which the past is associated with male betrayal, even whilst it accords art a transcendent quality that keeps alive those uncompleted, betrayed, narratives. Art thus becomes a politicised form through which the past is reconsidered and 'owned' by figures such as Medea and the snake lady. The killing of the snake lady at the end represents the destruction of art, imagination, history, and love, which means that the historical and artistic narrative is incomplete. The final lines note that 'the house of Luna [to which the prince belonged] became extinct' and this is reflected in the family estate, where 'the mosaic chapel remained for ever unfinished' and the 'rockery also was never completed' (p. 227). This curtailment of history is also echoed in the destruction of the snake lady tapestry, which has been cut up and used to cover chairs and make curtains for 'the porter's lodge of the now long-deserted Red Palace' (p. 228). History is brought to a premature end and art is destroyed in a dispersal that suggests that female history only exists in fragments.[32]

The themes of art and history are clearly gendered in 'Prince Alberic and the Snake Lady'. The connection between the prince and the snake lady suggests a narrative about heterosexuality which might appear normative. However, Vicinus argues that Prince Alberic 'is another of Lee's effeminate heroes', and that his life with his godmother constitutes 'an isolated, self-contained idyll of sensual love that needs no sexual consummation'. For Lee, claims Vicinus, this was 'the ideal lesbian romance'.[33]

This link is also suggested through the figure of Lamia. In *Miss Brown* (1884) Lee had parodied the aesthetic movement and those associated with it (the novel includes thinly veiled portraits of Walter Pater and a number of Pre-Raphaelites). Anne Brown, the principal protagonist, evidences a hostility towards the apparently amoral and sexualised behaviour of such figures and the sexual overtures that certain men make to her. She is befriended by Sacha Elaguine and theirs is a particularly intimate friendship in which Anne is attracted and repelled by Sacha, who is associated with Lamia. At one point Sacha is described as 'putting her arm around Miss Brown's neck, in her childish way, and which yet always affected Anne as might the caress of a lamia's clammy scales'.[34] However, as Psomiades has noted, this clamminess 'is also Sacha's body and Sacha's sex' and this 'makes Anne hot, rather than cold' (p. 26). This is indicated in the lines 'her face [was] still burning from this strangling embrace' (3:202).[35] This ambivalent sexualising of the relationship between Anne and Sacha is also seen by Psomiades as closely linked to an ambivalent sense of the aesthetic because 'these embraces are profoundly aestheticist at the same time as they stand in opposition to aestheticism's hetero-sexual plots, profoundly textual as the same time as they are visceral' (p. 26). This idea helps to support the critical position developed here, that Lee's version of the spectral incorporates within it a debate about how to redirect aesthetics so that they construct a model of desire which infiltrates and challenges hetero-normative models of desire *and* history. Lee achieves this by creatively challenging the aesthetics of both Pater and Keats.

Discussions about art and literature play a central role in Lee's tales. They represent a different type of engagement with textuality from that found in Riddell. Whilst Riddell's tales introject otherwise external debates about literature and the marketplace, Lee addresses the way that art reconstructs and reanimates the past. Whilst a modernist such as Woolf sought to distance herself from Lee, Denis Denisoff has noted that Woolf's work owes a debt to her.[36] Indeed Kane has argued that the stylistic innovations of Lee's work and its engagement with myth and history indicate modernist preoccupations and that the modernist dismissal of her makes Lee 'one of modernism's most undeserving victims' (p. 17). The roots of this modernist sensibility are to be found in her tales because, for Kane, 'She was one of the few writers in her generation to truly understand the use to which the lingering traces of the high gothic genre could be put in the constitution of the modern fragmented subject' (p. 46). What an explicitly modernist female ghost story might look like can be illustrated by the tales of May Sinclair. Sinclair engages with notions of art and history which are similar to Lee's but which move us beyond their development in Lee.

May Sinclair: love, history, and the modernist spirit

May Sinclair was the author of twenty-four novels, poems, and over forty short stories in a writing career which extended from the late nineteenth century to the 1930s. She also wrote on Kant and Hegel and was committed to the suffragette cause. Her early work is characterised by social realism but she later developed a very active engagement with modernism, principally via her developing interests in Freudian psychology, and wrote on (and produced) Imagist poetry. During this later period she knew Ezra Pound and Virginia Woolf. Novels such as *Mary Olivier: A Life* (1919), *Life and Death of Harriett Frean* (1922), and the *History of Anthony Waring* (1929) carry a clear modernist imprint in terms of their aesthetic ambitions and the psychological states that they explore. Her two principal collections of supernatural tales are *Uncanny Stories* (1923) and *The Intercessor and Other Stories* (1931). *Uncanny Stories* consists of ghost stories written between 1912 and 1923. The later collection includes the important long tale, 'The Intercessor', which reworks images of ghostliness from *Wuthering Heights* (1847). The Wordsworth edition of *Uncanny Stories* published in 2006 includes 'The

Intercessor' as an implicit acknowledgement that it seems to sit logically with the earlier tales and seems slightly at odds with the more orientalist tales that characterise much of the 1931 collection. Sinclair also had an interest in the Brontës and wrote a critical account of their work, published as *The Three Brontës* in 1912.[37]

Laurel Forster has noted that Sinclair started work on her supernatural stories during a period which coincided with her journal reviews of Imagist poetry.[38] Additionally, in 1917 Sinclair wrote the introduction to *The Closed Door*, a collection of Imagist verse written by Jean de Bosschère. Also a novelist, painter, and illustrator, Bosschère produced the haunting line drawings which illustrate the tales in *Uncanny Stories*. Sinclair's explicit engagement with modernism is conditioned by how she uses aspects of the supernatural in general, and images of ghosts in particular. David Seed has also noted that Sinclair's interests in the activities of the Society for Psychical Research, which she joined in 1914, indicated an enthusiasm for how theories of psychology could be related to a sublimated spirit world.[39] Seed notes that 'The supernatural was not a marginal concern' for Sinclair because it 'was central' to her 'attempts to relocate the importance of the mind'.[40] In this way the 'other world' of the spirits represents an attempt to reach out to the human world and this is a key element in the tales which make up *Uncanny Stories*.

Richard Bleiler has argued that the tales in *Uncanny Stories* should be read as an integrated series because they individually develop or conclude issues which are progressed throughout the collection. Bleiler has also noted that the predominant theme of the collection relates to 'presentations of appropriate versus inappropriate love' (p. 127). The opening tale, 'Where Their Fire Is Not Quenched', focuses on a soon fatigued affair between a woman and a married man that is continued after death and which transforms their now eternal relationship into a type of hell. 'The Token', which will be discussed at length below, provides a more optimistic sense of love as it suggests the importance of a positive emotional intensity which transcends the everyday, mundane and material world. 'The Flaw in the Crystal', which bears a clear indebtedness to Henry James, explores how a supernatural ability to help the sick becomes compromised if the emotional attachment contains an impurity or flaw. 'The Nature of the Evidence' focuses on a widower haunted by the ghost of his first wife, who successfully intervenes in his attempts at consummating his marriage with his sensual and seemingly immoral second wife. 'If the Dead Knew' and 'The Victim' concern ghosts who grant forgiveness to those who have done them harm, and 'The Finding of the Absolute', which will also be discussed at length below, examines how a recently deceased metaphysician's conversations with Kant obliquely suggest their location in a hell which was constructed in the first tale.

Such tales use models of love as the means through which to explore the relations between the living and the dead. Many of them, such as 'The Nature of the Evidence', also explicitly explore conjunctions and disjunctions between sex and love. To that degree the tales exemplify Sinclair's interest in Freudian psychology whilst she displaces such issues on to the relations between the living and the dead, a move which implies a spiritualist influence. It should also be noted that many of her ghosts are not intended to be frightening; they are frequently conjured in response to some unanswered need or to console those in torment. To that degree her ghosts, whilst uncanny, do not always appear to be demonstrably Gothic, or evil, at least in *Uncanny Stories.*[41]

'The Token' recounts how Donald Dunbar becomes haunted by his wife Cicely, who is looking for confirmation, via a sign or a token, that he loved her. The tale is narrated by Donald's sister, who observes the relationship between Donald and Cicely's ghost. Whilst Sinclair's tales might, generally considered, appear to be far removed from the economic concerns of Dickens and Collins, or beyond Riddell's implied focus on writing and the marketplace, such issues do play a role in 'The Token'. We discover that Donald had suppressed his feelings of anxiety during Cicely's final illness by working devotedly on a book entitled *Development of Social Economics*. On his writing desk Donald has a paperweight, referred to throughout as the Token, 'a white alabaster Buddha painted and gilt' which had been given to him and inscribed by the author George Meredith.[42] Whilst alive, Donald's emotional reticence upset Cicely and led her to believe him to be indifferent to her. She had complained to the narrator, ' "He cares more for that damned paper-weight than he does for me" ' (p. 56). Donald replies, ' "Well – George Meredith gave it me" ', to which Cicely rejoins, ' "And nobody gave you me. I gave myself" '. This prompts the retort from Donald: ' "It can't have cost you much [. . .] And I may remind you that the paper-weight has *some* intrinsic value" ' (p. 56). The tale makes clear that Donald retreats from a world of emotions by replacing it with research and writing about economics. Such an attachment to a material world superficially, and so only temporarily, enables him to push genuine feeling aside. The transformation of the Buddha into a token of materialism stands as a knowing ironic comment for how Donald replaces the spiritual with the material.

A further irony in 'The Token' is that the ostensible materialism endorsed by Donald implicitly forms a paradigm for a factual, putatively objective, knowledge of the world which is transposed on to the spirit of Cicely, who is also looking for an objective verification of Donald's love. The narrator notes of Cicely's ghost that 'With a longing unquenched by death, she had come back for certainty' (p. 72). This also emphasises the theme of knowledge which runs throughout the tales. Evidence of fidelity, love, and empathy is constantly required, and tested, before spirits can gain peace. Knowledge of the other world thus requires some form of objective validation which confirms the presence of either a spiritual or an emotional reality. It is as if Sinclair has taken the pseudo-scientific aspects of psychical research and in 'The Token' inverts them by having a watchful spirit require evidence from the physical world rather than vice versa.

This implicit, and non-economic, language of exchange becomes linked to the Token, which Donald has kept hidden in a locked drawer of his writing table since

Cicely's death. Donald does not know that Cicely's spirit can be seen by the narrator, who ultimately feels compelled to tell Donald about her presence. Cicely's ghost searches through a number of drawers in the desk only to be thwarted by the locked drawer. Donald refuses to believe his sister, who retrieves the Token and recounts that 'I held out the Token to him on the palm of my hand, as if it were proof that I had seen her' (p. 74). As Cicely is looking for proof of love, so Donald requires proof of Cicely's presence. Donald assumes that his sister's account is the product of an illness because none of this makes sense to him. However, she tells him that ' "I'm not so ill that I don't know what you put it away for [. . .] It was because she thought you cared for it more than you did for her" ' (p. 74). In effect she produces evidence to Donald that he did indeed love Cicely. However, the problem is that it needs to be made visible as evidence to the spectral Cicely. The narrator achieves this by asking Donald whether he cared for her, and he responds, ' "I was mad with caring for her! And she knew it!" '. His sister retorts, ' "She didn't. She wouldn't be here now if she knew" ' (p. 77). Donald holds the Token responsible for her death as it was their argument over it which had agitated Cicely and, in his view, contributed to her dying. He claims, ' "The damned thing killed her!" ' (p. 77), before breaking it by hurling it into the fireplace.

The tale operates at a symbolic level in which the Token represents Donald's attachment to a male, public world of validation, one which confirms his status as a writer. It is noticeable that when alive Cicely would join Donald in his library whilst he worked but would sit quietly and try not to disturb him. This symbolic exclusion of women from the process of intellectual production is what Donald is forced to repudiate when he destroys the Token. In doing so he is briefly reunited with Cicely – 'He stepped forward, opening his arms, and I saw the phantasm slide between them. For a second it stood there, folded to his breast' (pp. 77–8) – before disappearing. Later the narrator tells Donald that Cicely does not come back any more because ' "She knows what she wanted to know" ' (p. 78). This view leaves Donald feeling 'queer, submissive, wistful' (p. 78) as he contemplates that it might have been preferable to communicate his love to Cicely whilst she was alive.

At one level 'The Token' is a love story in which love becomes the mechanism that guarantees personal validation. At another level the tale develops a mode of symbolism that dematerialises objects, such as the Token, by revealing their true significance. Such issues are clearly gender inflected, as the associations with writing and economics suggest. Central to these disparate processes is the construction of evidence which leads to knowledge. Cicely may gain knowledge of Donald's love, but Donald also gains knowledge of a benign spiritual domain which exists beyond, and so challenges, his attachment to material realities – an attachment which is broken in his destruction of the Token. These otherwise disparate narrative strands are pulled together by an implicit model of philosophical idealism in which spectrality, evidence, and knowledge are closely aligned. Sinclair's formal interest in such issues is clear from 'The Finding of the Absolute', which also enables, through comparison, a reconsideration of the type of historicising that characterised the tales of Vernon Lee.

In Lee's tales we observed how she positions art as the medium through which to conjure historical narratives. Sinclair's interest in history is elaborated in her re-working of Kantian Idealism in 'The Finding of the Absolute', where Spalding, a metaphysical philosopher, discusses history with Kant. As in 'The Token' the tale centres on the pursuit of verifiable knowledge. Spalding 'had flung over the God he had been taught to believe in because, besides being an outrage to Mr. Spalding's moral sense, he wasn't metaphysical enough. The poor man was always worrying about metaphysics; he wandered from system to system, seeking truth, seeking reality, seeking some supreme intellectual satisfaction that never came'.[43] Spalding only gains answers to such grand metaphysical concerns after death when Kant shows him a vision of all history which encompasses 'the French Revolution, the Napoleonic wars, the Franco-Prussian war, the establishment of the French Republic, the Boer war, the death of Queen Victoria [. . .] the Great War, the Russian and German Revolutions' (p. 359) and a projected future in which there is 'the Indian Republic, the British Revolution, the British Republic, the conquest of Japan by America, and the federation of the United States of Europe and America' (pp. 359–60). He is also made aware of an earlier history consisting of 'the mammoth and the cavemen' and a future in which 'he saw the Atlantic flood-ing the North Sea and submerging the flats of Lincolnshire, Cambridgeshire, Norfolk, Suffolk, Essex and Kent' (p. 360), a future characterised by a melting polar ice cap that 'saw men and animals driven before it to the belt of the equator' (p. 360). The scene then shifts to a model of cosmic time in which 'He was pre-sent at the beginning and the end. He saw the earth flung off, an incandescent ball, from the wheeling sun. He saw it hang like a dead white moon in a sky strewn with the corpses of spent worlds' (p. 361).

Such images are replayed endlessly and Spalding becomes united with these cyc-lical movements: 'The whole universe stood up on end round him, doubling all its future back upon all its past' (p. 361). Spalding 'was drawn in with it. He passed from God's immanent to his transcendent life, into the Absolute' (p. 362). Finally Spalding finds the type of experience that he has been looking for. It is confirmed by a metaphysical system generated from within a version of Kant's idealism, in which the subject becomes merged with a form of collective experience. The type of history at stake here is clearly wider than that entertained in Lee's specific rework-ings of the Renaissance. Also, it is staged at a necessarily abstract level and appears, on the surface, to lack the gender implications that underpin Lee's recovery of seemingly occluded female voices. The answer as to why Sinclair structures history in this way cannot be explained just through the tale's references to Kant and Hegel; it is also an issue that can be explained by locating this history within a modernist epistemology.

David Glover has noted that visions of the future and their connections to the past are features of H.G. Wells's *The Time Machine* (1895) and T.S. Eliot's *The Waste Land* (1922). Both Wells and Eliot represent such tensions in a pessimistic way by suggesting the unavoidability of a particularly tragic view of history. Glover, via a discussion of Marshall Berman and Jacques Derrida, identifies two post-Enlightenment movements which inaugurate Modernity and which become reformulated as acute forms of anxiety within modernism: a new form of 'speculative historicism' and 'a melding of psychoanalysis and philosophy'.[44] Glover's discussion of modernism moves beyond Wells and Eliot to include Conrad's *Heart of Darkness* (1902) and Ford Madox Ford's *The Inheritors* (1901). He argues that in these novels a new modernist Gothic can be observed in which:

> we see the Gothic starting to change its meaning: no longer associated with an irruption of unreason or an inexplicable violence directed against the symbols of individual and social cohesion, it now begins to adumbrate the fear of a generalised breakdown in the narrative of progress itself, producing a vision of the future as a new calamity that would recapitulate, yet also dramatically reconfigure, the worst features of the past. (pp. 41–2)

In 'The Finding of the Absolute' Spalding's momentary qualm about this access to history is overcome by a reassuring sense of belonging. He notes that 'For one moment he thought that this was death; the next his whole being swelled and went on swelling in an unspeakable, an unthinkable bliss' (p. 362). The tale suggests that this 'death' is overcome by an affirmation of God's presence. Glover has also claimed of this conclusion that 'clearly the inclusiveness of Sinclair's dramatisation of her preferred version of Idealism is meant to ameliorate the lovelessness and waste that motivate the apparitions who stalk the pages of the other stories in her book' (p. 30). Indeed, Spalding's sense of 'ecstasy' when united with history is because it is an abstract and universal form of it rather than an intimate and personal one. Earlier, as Spalding lies dying, he recalls a brief and unhappy relationship with one Connie Larkins after his wife, Elizabeth, had left him for the Imagist poet Paul Jeffreson: 'Fancy going on with Connie Larkins for ever and ever, never being able to get away from her, doomed to repeat [. . .] That was hell' (p. 334). To that degree the tale functions as a corrective to the doomed lovers who are fated to repeat their unhappy affair for eternity in 'Where Their Fire Is Not Quenched', the story with which *Uncanny Stories* begins. However, 'The Finding of the Absolute' is ultimately unclear about whether Spalding's apparent happiness can be construed as an endorsement of a transcendent and alternative *zeitgeist*. After all, the history mapped in the tale includes images of an environmental apocalypse which implies the type of concerns about the inescapability of history that Glover saw in Wells, Eliot, Conrad, and Ford. According to this view, 'the Gothicisation of the past stands as a sign of the radical unavailability of a definitive break with what has gone before' (p. 32). In 'The Finding of the Absolute' there is a

Gothicisation of the future within a model of history which endlessly recycles itself and so feels more like a non-transcendent version of hell.[45] If in Lee the past is important, in Sinclair it is the present or the future. Sinclair's endorsement of love complicates this picture of a world heading towards its end and it is an issue which reinstates the type of speculation about gender which characterised 'The Token'.

Spalding loses Elizabeth to Paul Jeffreson, who is described as an 'immortal genius; but he had no morals; he drank; he drugged [. . .] he did everything he shouldn't do' (p. 330). Elizabeth also leaves Spalding just as 'he had discovered a fatal flaw in his own system of metaphysics' (p. 329), which means that 'His belief in Elizabeth was gone. So was his belief in the Absolute' (p. 329). Spalding mulls over whether the two losses are related and concludes that 'if he had not been wrapped up in his system of metaphysics, Elizabeth might still have been wrapped up in him. He had nobody but himself to thank for her behaviour' (p. 330). The loss of love and the loss of a model of truth were also apparent in 'The Token'. However, when Spalding dies a reconciliation of sorts is staged as he finds himself in a heaven that embraces both Elizabeth and Jeffreson. Spalding asks Jeffreson how he got into heaven, given his dissolute past, and Jeffreson explains that it was due to his love of beauty and that Elizabeth had been admitted due to her love of him. (In Spalding's case it is a passion for truth that gains him entry.) Abstract values relating to beauty and love thus grant access to heaven – itself an abstract entity which is tinged with a peculiarly impersonal notion of the eternal. Heaven thus becomes the space where Spalding finds his pursuit of abstractions developed to their logical conclusion, even whilst it was the pursuit of such abstractions which led him to neglect Elizabeth when they were married. This is an amoral version of heaven which symbolically relocates the amoral (image-focused) abstractions that coloured a particular strand of Imagist poetry. This situation leads the Imagist Jeffreson to summarise his failings and merits: 'if I *was* what they call a bad man, that's to say a bad terrestrial organism, I was a thundering good poet' (p. 337). A certain type of art triumphs over ethics so that Sinclair's radical reconceptualisation of heaven is one which associates it with pure abstractions rather than moral choices. For that reason the spectral Spalding now enters a dimension which appears to be joyous because it is beyond such prosaic issues as personal moral commitments. However, the tale also affirms the notion of a puzzle at the end as the final line indicates that God 'was going to make another jig-saw puzzle of a universe' (p. 362). Gender issues are thus seemingly elided, but ultimately they inform how love is turned into something abstract in this version of heaven in which the neglectful Spalding and the dissolute Jeffreson are exonerated. Spectres in this tale form sanitised and depoliticised abstractions and heaven does not seem quite so utopian after all as the final pursuit of evidence is thwarted by a cosmic 'jig-saw puzzle' which suggests that abstractions are ultimately not a coherent means through which to produce knowledge about morality, art, or metaphysics.

According to Bleiler, 'The Finding of the Absolute' should be read as a radical challenge to social convention – one in which the love between Jeffreson and Elizabeth questions 'the established social norms by arguing that laws concerning love and marriage can be completely inappropriate' (p. 132). However, nowhere does the tale explicitly state that Jeffreson loves Elizabeth, and it is his passion for poetry which has got him into heaven rather than his love of her. Women are thus in danger of fading into the background as the intellectual and artistic enthusiasms of Jeffreson, Spalding, and Kant take over. At one level a social world with its 'parochial morality' (p. 337) is radically erased but the tale also questions what replaces it. It is tempting to see the tale as a conceit for the throwing off of older Victorian mores in order to embrace Imagist abstractions. But the purpose of such abstractions is ultimately challenged by the concluding lack of certainty. Sinclair's ghosts are thus specifically modernist in emphasis – forward looking and experimental, but ultimately unable to assert what it is that replaces the older literary and intellectual culture. This impulse in Sinclair's writing is captured in the title of Suzanne Raitt's biography, *May Sinclair: A Modern Victorian* (2000), which indicates Sinclair's culturally transitional position.[46] Paul March-Russell also acknowledges this in the introduction to the 2006 Wordsworth edition of *Uncanny Stories*, where he concludes that the post First World War ghost story 'was definitely in transition, becoming a seedbed for that other rich and strange phenomenon known as Modernism'.[47]

Sinclair's engagement with history is thus tempered by how she engages with abstractions. Art and writing are closely linked to a modernist aesthetic which also shapes her elaboration of a model of history that is at odds with Lee's reclamation of the past. Also, because such deliberations are abstract they seem to be far removed from the issues about money and art which are to be found in Riddell. Nevertheless, the relations between art, history, and gender which are addressed by Lee are reworked in ways that illustrate how a modernist context operates on a language of spectrality during the period. In this way Sinclair's modernist ghosts indicate an unease about knowledge which is generated within a context that works towards obliterating the social and political narratives which both Riddell and Lee, at different levels of explicitness, had addressed in their ghost stories.

This chapter has focused on three quite different writers in order to give a sense of the diversity of British women's writing in the ghost story tradition and to observe how issues about love, money, and history were articulated within a sample of female-authored ghost stories between the 1870s and the 1920s. The tales examine the place of women in economic, artistic, historical, and philosophically formulated contexts. Vanessa D. Dickerson has noted that in such tales 'the ghost corresponded' to images of 'visibility and invisibility [. . .] power and powerlessness, the contradictions and extremes that shaped female culture' (p. 5). The identification of women with images of liminality opens up that context for critical evaluation. Although the interests of Riddell, Lee, and Sinclair are diverse (and diversely expressed, the intellectual ambitions of Lee and Sinclair distancing them somewhat from Riddell's more populist tales), they nevertheless share a concern about cultural visibility which is key to understanding their configurations of the spectral and their specific engagements with ideas about love and its associations with money (Riddell) and history (Lee and Sinclair).

We also saw how issues relating to spiritualism underpin the interests of Sinclair in 'The Token' as they inform the idea of evidencing the presence of a spirit world. The spiritualist movement was also interested in the relationship between psychology and notions of a sublimated world. This relationship also appealed to modernists such as T.S. Eliot and Virginia Woolf, and it is the culture of spiritualism and the issues that it raises about narrative decoding which is the subject of the following chapter.[48]

Notes

1 A notable omission here, because of space, is the work of Margaret Oliphant. In particular see her 'The Library Window' (1896) in *A Beleaguered City and Other Tales of the Seen and the Unseen* (Edinburgh: Canongate, 2000) pp. 363–402. The tale addresses issues about reading and writing within a gendered context.

2 Vanessa D. Dickerson, *Victorian Ghosts in the Noontide: Women Writers and the Supernatural* (Columbia and London: University of Missouri Press, 1996) p. 133. All subsequent references are to this edition and are given in the text.

3 Diana Wallace, 'Uncanny Stories: The Ghost Story as Female Gothic', *Gothic Studies*, 6.1 (May 2004), special issue on the 'Female Gothic', ed. Andrew Smith and Diana Wallace, 57–68, 57.

4 Benjamin F. Fisher, 'Mrs. J.H. Riddell and Late Victorian Literary Gothicism' in Felice A. Coles (ed.), *In Memory of Richard B. Klein: Essays in Contemporary Philology* (Oxford: University of Mississippi Press, 2005) pp. 175–93, p. 175. All subsequent references are to this edition and are given in the text.

5 Vanessa Dickerson has also noted that Riddell, and indeed Margaret Oliphant and Florence Marryat, were engaged with issues about money and female autonomy which constituted a new trend in female-authored ghost stories. See *Ghosts in the Noontide*, p. 138.

6 J.H. Riddell, *The Uninhabited House*, in *Five Victorian Ghost Novels*, ed. and introd. E.F. Bleiler (New York: Dover, 1971) pp. 1–118, p. 107. All subsequent references are to this edition and are given in the text.

7 J.H. Riddell, *The Haunted River* in *The Haunted River and Three Other Ghostly Novellas by Mrs. J.H. Riddell*, ed. and introd. Richard Dalby (Mountain Ash: Sarob Press, 2001) pp. 1–84, p. 6. All subsequent references are to this edition and are given in the text.

8 This may seem like a contentious point, but it is noteworthy that Riddell's use of impoverished male narrators places them in conventional positions of femininity.

9 It could be argued that Collins's *No Name* (1862) also comes around to an unproblematic romance plot. However, as discussed in Chapter 3, the culmination of that plot implies a critique of a form of male control (or can be read as such).

10 In that regard the novella problematises the social context in which women only come to money through marriage (or possibly prostitution).

11 See also Melissa Edmundson's 'The "Uncomfortable Houses" of Charlotte Riddell and Margaret Oliphant' forthcoming in *Gothic Studies*, 10 (2010), where she also acknowledges this link to *A Christmas Carol*.

12 J.H. Riddell, 'The Old House in Vauxhall Walk' in *The Collected Ghost Stories of Mrs. J.H. Riddell*, ed. E.F. Bleiler (New York: Dover, 1977) pp. 85–101, p. 85. All subsequent references are to this edition and are given in the text.

13 Linda H. Peterson, 'Charlotte Riddell's *A Struggle for Fame*: Myths of Authorship, Facts of the Market', *Women's Writing*, 11.1 (2004), 99–115.

14 Lee had a falling out with Henry James due to her thinly disguised satirical portrayal of him in 'Lady Tal' (1892); although James claimed not to have the read the tale, he was clearly aware of its content. Money is the theme of her first publication, 'Les aventures d'une pièce de monnaie', published in the periodical *La Famille* in June 1870 when she was thirteen.

15 Kathy Alexis Psomiades, ' "Still Burning from This Strangling Embrace": Vernon Lee on Desire and Aesthetics' in Richard Dellamora (ed.), *Victorian Sexual Dissidence* (Chicago: University of Chicago Press, 1999) pp. 21–41, p. 21. See also Burdett Gardner, *The Lesbian Imagination (Victorian Style): A Psychological and Critical Study of 'Vernon Lee'* (Ph.D. dissertation, Harvard University, 1954) (New York: Garland, 1987) and Martha Vicinus, 'The Adolescent Boy: Fin-de-Siècle Femme Fatale' in Dellamora (ed.), *Victorian Sexual Dissidence*, pp. 83–106.

16 Vernon Lee, preface to *Hauntings: Fantastic Stories* in *Hauntings and Other Tales*, ed. Catherine Maxwell and Patricia Pulham (Ontario: Broadview, 2006) pp. 37–40, p. 37. All subsequent references are to this edition and are given in the text.

17 This is a view that she shared with her one-time friend Henry James.

18 Vernon Lee, 'Amour Dure' in *Hauntings and Other Tales*, ed. Catherine Maxwell and Patricia Pulham (Ontario: Broadview, 2006) pp. 41–76, p. 41.

19 Mary Patricia Kane, *Spurious Ghosts: The Fantastic Tales of Vernon Lee* (Rome: Carocci, 2004) pp. 22–5. Angela Leighton, 'Resurrections of the Body: Women Writers and the Idea of the Renaissance' in Alison Chapman and Jane Stabler (eds), *Unfolding the South: Nineteenth-century British Women Writers and Artists in Italy* (Manchester: Manchester University Press, 2003) pp. 222–38, pp. 224–5. Christa Zorn, *Vernon Lee: Aesthetics, History and the Victorian Female Intellectual* (Athens, OH: Ohio University Press), pp. 157–68.

20 Walter Pater, *The Renaissance*, ed. and introd. Adam Phillips (Oxford: Oxford University Press, [1873] 1986) p. 80. All subsequent references are to this edition and are given in the text.

21 Mary Patricia Kane, *Spurious Ghosts: The Fantastic Tales of Vernon Lee* (Rome: Carocci, 2004) p. 23. All subsequent references are to this edition and are given in the text.

22 Leighton, 'Resurrections of the Body', p. 224.

23 Vernon Lee, *The Beautiful: An Introduction to Psychological Aesthetics* (Cambridge: Cambridge University Press, 1913) p. 1. Cited by Lois Agnew in 'Vernon Lee and the Victorian Aesthetic Movement: "Feminine Souls" and Shifting Sites of Contest', *Nineteenth-Century Prose*, 26.2 (1999), 127–42, 133.

24 Catherine Maxwell, 'Vernon Lee and the Ghosts of Italy' in Alison Chapman and Jane Stabler (eds), *Unfolding the South: Nineteenth-century British Women Writers and Artists in Italy* (Manchester: Manchester University Press, 2003) pp. 201–21, p. 215.

25 Diana Wallace, 'Haunted by History: Vernon Lee's "Fantastic Tales"', in Wallace, *Female Gothic Histories*, m.s. in progress (Cardiff: University of Wales Press, forthcoming 2012) p. 8.

26 Patricia Pulham, *Art and the Transitional Object in Vernon Lee's Supernatural Tales* (Aldershot: Ashgate, 2008) p. xvi.

27 The title evokes M.R. James's 'Canon Alberic's Scrapbook' (1895), which is discussed in Chapter 8. James's tale also focuses on the past and its resurrection and such references illuminate how issues about art and history are related by Lee to models of myth and gender.

28 Ruth Robbins, 'Vernon Lee: Decadent Woman?' in John Stokes (ed.), *Fin de Siècle Fin du Globe: Fears and Fantasies of the Late Nineteenth Century* (Basingstoke: Macmillan, 1992) pp. 139–61, p. 157.

29 Keats is at one level also exploring issues about gender but his gender scripts tend to be conventional as they relate femininity to art and masculinity to science.

30 Vernon Lee, 'Prince Alberic and the Snake Lady' in *Hauntings and Other Tales*, ed. Catherine Maxwell and Patricia Pulham (Ontario: Broadview, 2006) pp. 182–228, pp. 183, 184. All subsequent references are to this edition and are given in the text.

31 John Keats, *Lamia*, in *Keats: Complete Poetical Works*, ed. H.W. Gorrod (Oxford: Oxford University Press, 1970) pp. 161–78. All subsequent references are to this edition and are given in the text.

32 This is a point I am indebted to Diana Wallace for making in comments on a draft version of this chapter.

33 Martha Vicinus, 'The Adolescent Boy: Fin-de-Siècle Femme Fatale' in Richard Dellamora (ed.), *Victorian Sexual Dissidence* (Chicago: University of Chicago Press, 1999) pp. 83–106, pp. 96, 97.

34 Vernon Lee, *Miss Brown*, 3 vols (Edinburgh: W.M. Blackwood and Sons, 1884), vol. 3, p. 136. All subsequent references are to this edition and are given in the text. Cited in Psomiades, ' "Still Burning from This Strangling Embrace" ', pp. 21–41, p. 26.

35 Psomiades, ' "Still Burning from This Strangling Embrace" ', p. 26. Lee, *Miss Brown*, cited in Psomiades, p. 26.

36 Denis Denisoff, 'The Forest Beyond the Frame: Picturing Women's Desires in Vernon Lee and Virginia Woolf' in Talia Schaffer and Kathy Alexis Psomiades (eds), *Women and British Aestheticism* (Charlottesville: University of Virginia Press, 1999) pp. 251–69.

37 Suzanne Raitt has read the tale as an exploration of how the woman writer negotiates her position in terms of her precursors. See Suzanne Raitt, 'Literary History as Exorcism: May Sinclair Meets the Brontës', in Katherine Binhammer and Jeane Wood (eds), *Women and Literary History: 'For There She Was'* (Delaware: University of Delaware Press, 2003) pp. 187–200. This point is cited by Richard Bleiler, 'May Sinclair's Supernatural Fiction' in Andrew J. Kunka and Michele K. Troy (eds), *May Sinclair: Moving Towards the Modern* (Aldershot: Ashgate, 2006) pp. 123–38, p. 125. All subsequent references are to this edition and are given in the text.

38 Laurel Forster, '"Imagism . . . Is a State of Soul": May Sinclair's Imagist Writing and *Life and Death of Harriett Frean*' in Andrew J. Kunka and Michele K. Troy (eds), *May Sinclair: Moving Towards the Modern* (Aldershot: Ashgate, 2006) pp. 99–122, p. 112.

39 F.W.H. Meyers in *Human Personality and Its Survival of Bodily Death* (London: Longmans, [1903] 1907) attempted to develop a theory of sublimation which bridged the world of the mind and the world of the spirit.

40 David Seed, '"Psychical" Cases: Transformations of the Supernatural in Virginia Woolf and May Sinclair' in Andrew Smith and Jeff Wallace (eds), *Gothic Modernisms* (Basingstoke: Palgrave, 2001) pp. 44–61, p. 44.

41 However, as an exception to this see 'The Villa Désirée', which was first published in 1926. Diana Wallace in 'Uncanny Stories: The Ghost Story as Female Gothic' has explored in depth the gender and sexual implications of the tale.

42 May Sinclair, 'The Token' in *Uncanny Stories* (New York: Macmillan, 1923) pp. 51–78, p. 54. All subsequent references are to this edition and are given in the text.

43 May Sinclair, 'The Finding of the Absolute' in *Uncanny Stories* (New York: Macmillan, 1923) pp. 329–62, p. 331. All subsequent references are to this edition and are given in the text.

44 David Glover, 'The "Spectrality Effect" in Early Modernism' in Andrew Smith and Jeff Wallace (eds), *Gothic Modernisms* (Basingstoke: Palgrave, 2001) pp. 29–43, p. 32. All subsequent references are to this edition and are given in the text.

45 I also discuss this tale in similar terms in my *Gothic Literature* (Edinburgh: Edinburgh University Press, 2007) p. 130.

46 Suzanne Raitt, *May Sinclair: A Modern Victorian* (Oxford: Clarendon Press, 2000).

47 Paul March-Russell, introduction to *Uncanny Stories* (Ware, Herts: Wordsworth, 2006) pp. 7–21, p. 21.

48 For a discussion of Woolf's interest in the ghost story see David Seed, '"Psychical" Cases: Transformations of the Supernatural in Virginia Woolf and May Sinclair' in Andrew Smith and Jeff Wallace (eds), *Gothic Modernisms* (Basingstoke: Palgrave, 2001) pp. 44–61.

5

Reading ghosts and reading texts: spiritualism

So far we have focused on images of spectrality as they are manifested in literary narratives. However, the relationship between literature and the spectral can be given an additional critical turn through an exploration of spiritualism. The broad cultural context of spiritualism has been extensively explored but there is an under-examined strand within that culture concerning the literary imagination and textual interpretation.[1] The culture of spiritualism played an important part in shaping a language of spectrality which in turn informed literary representations of ghosts. However, this was not a one-way process and this chapter explores the interactive relationship between spiritualism and the literary culture during the late nineteenth to early twentieth century, and so provides an alternative exploration of the ghostly.

Literature's association with spiritualism is indicated by how various deceased writers became (allegedly) channelled through mediums during the period. There are spirit writings which purport to be from Shakespeare, Charlotte Brontë, Oscar Wilde, Joseph Conrad, and George Eliot, amongst many others.[2] In addition W.T. Stead, the investigative journalist and editor of The *Pall Mall Gazette*, also included in his *Review of Reviews* a special issue on 'Real Ghost Stories' which was published in book form in 1897. The appendix consists of a list of prominent individuals who had apparently been touched by contact with spirits and it includes a section on 'Men of Letters' which refers to the supposed spirit encounters of Petrarch, Dante, Goethe, Donne, Byron, Shelley, Thackeray, Elizabeth Barrett Browning, Maria Edgeworth, and Madame De Staël.[3] As we shall see, spirit messages were often decoded as if they were complex literary texts which required sophisticated critical exegesis. In this sense they can be read as literary rather than metaphysical encounters.

This chapter focuses on how reading spectrality was developed within the context of spiritualism and how this was covertly informed by a literary culture which includes George Eliot, Robert Browning, Henry James, and A.C. Benson.[4] A 'novel', *The Book of the Golden Key* (1909), which was purportedly dictated by spirits, will also be discussed. Whilst models of the literary imagination shaped spiritualist conceptualisations of the spirit world the influence was not all in one direction. Ideas about spiritualist 'visions' bear a close relationship to notions of literary inspiration and many of the texts discussed here reveal the complex synergies which existed between literary and spiritualist cultures. This chapter also explores how reading as a literary critic is central to one of the classic accounts of after-death experience: Sir Oliver Lodge's *Raymond* (1916), which reflects on his post-death correspondences with his son Raymond, who was killed in the First World War. How to write, and interpret writing, plays an important role in accounts of the literary imagination and spiritualist ideas about the meaning of messages sent from the 'other world'. However, before elaborating these relationships it is necessary to explore in more detail the specific links which existed between accounts of spiritualism and models of reading at the time.

Interpreting spirits

A key leader of the spiritualist movement, F.W.H. Myers, promoted the view that one of the clearest ways of establishing the scientific veracity of spirit messages was through what became known as cross-correspondences. This involved having partial, or simultaneous, messages sent to a number of mediums who were work-ing independently of each other. Such messages could be reassembled to reveal a coherent narrative and the process depended upon the collaboration of spirits who were eager to prove the existence of the spirit world.[5] After his death in 1901, Myers obligingly sent such messages (in 1908 and 1909) in a form which, as Roger Luckhurst has noted, constituted a type of literary collage that evokes Roland Barthes's idea that 'the writerly text is nothing more than a tissue of quotations'.[6] Such texts require a complex reassembly, one that depends on advanced analytical skills which reveal how to correctly sequence the messages. One irony in this, noted by Luckhurst, is that these 'allusive fragments promise esoteric meaning, a coherence just beyond the threshold of readerly competence' (p. 268).

Arthur Conan Doyle in Volume II of his *The History of Spiritualism* (1926) sets out a few examples of these messages which indicate this problem with 'readerly competence' and also suggest that the brevity of some messages placed them beyond plausible literary analysis. Doyle recounts how between March and April 1907 three mediums, Mrs Piper, Mrs Verrall, and Mrs Holland, all seemed to channel a series of fragmented but related narratives. The first communication begins with a cryptic reference to 'violets' sent to Mrs Piper on the same day that Mrs Verrall received a message concerning 'Violet and olive leaf, purple and hoary'. Such a communication suggests that not all messages were intended to be coherent, merely that a reiterated message indicated a spirit communicating with more than one medium. A second communication occurred a month later and came from the spirit of Myers. His message to Mrs Piper was 'Do you remember Euripides? Do you remember Spirit and Angel?', which had earlier been received by Mrs Verrall as 'Hercules Furens' and 'Euripides'. In April Mrs Holland received the word 'Mors' and 'The shadow of death', whilst Mrs Piper received a misconstrued 'Tanatos' (Thanatos), and Mrs Verrall 'wrote a script wholly occupied with the idea of Death, with quotations from Lander, Shakespeare, Virgil and Horace, all involving the idea of Death'.[7] These fragments, although alluding to literature, have no obvious narrative structure and Doyle gives highly abbreviated examples from the cross-correspondences because 'it is impossible to exaggerate how wearisome they are to the reader in their entirety' (p. 41). Doyle also cites Oliver Lodge, who noted of such messages that their 'ingenuity and subtlety and literary allusiveness' make them 'difficult to read' (p. 42). For Doyle the only point of such messages is to convince unbelievers, whereas 'To the ordinary Spiritualist they seem an exceedingly roundabout method of demonstrating that which can be proved by easier and more convincing methods' (p. 42).

The problem posed by such messages is one of interpretation, which in some of the more elaborate examples of cross-correspondences seems to require highly specialised critical skills. Doyle, for example, notes disapprovingly of some of the more complex messages that 'So recondite were the classical allusions that even the best scholars were occasionally baffled' (p. 43). Myers, a classically educated Cambridge don, appears to have been closely associated with such allusive literary messages, leading Luckhurst to note that 'His surviving spirit seemed intent on turning the discipline towards a form of literary hermeneutics' (p. 265). However, although such a complex series of messages played a key role in shaping Lodge's *Raymond*, it is also necessary to account for how literary texts complicated the issue of spectrality. It is therefore important to explore how literature engaged with spiritualist ideas as this provides a way of understanding why the literary and the spectral became so closely aligned in the period. How to read spectral visions and their relationship to narrative form can be exemplified through a reading of Eliot's 'The Lifted Veil' (1859).

Writing spiritualism and the poetic imagination: 'The Lifted Veil'

George Eliot was hostile to spiritualism, although she did correspond with F.W.H. Myers and was a sceptical attendee at a séance in the 1870s.[8] In addition Jill Galvan has noted that Latimer, the novella's narrator, functions like a medium because he operates as a 'deliverer or conduit' for the story, which suggests that Eliot reworked the spiritualist emphasis on the transmission of messages.[9]

The tale opens with a medical diagnosis of impending death. The narrator, Latimer, notes that as a consequence of '*angina pectoris*' 'my life will not be protracted many months'.[10] This is a prognosis that Latimer has been aware of for some time because due to his special second sight 'I foresee when I shall die, and everything that will happen in my last moments' (p. 3). The tale therefore centres on a retelling of the moments that will lead up to this death, paradoxically related (for the reader) before the event. For Julian Wolfreys this structure represents a deconstructive turn because it means that the tale is told by the (soon to be) ghostly Latimer, which

has the effect of making writing itself spectral, or as Wolfreys puts it 'The apparition of this writing has arrived from the future'.[11] The narrative possesses a complex
temporality because it is about the future, but it is also strangely retrospective as
it dwells on the circumstances that lead up to Latimer's demise. For Wolfreys, the
tale's evocation of the relationship between the living and the soon to be dead Latimer
implicates a strictly textual production of the uncanny which is generated within
the reader's experience, meaning that 'we are witness to this uncanny instance [which]
unveils the spectral nature of all figurative language' (p. 87). However, it is important to note that this seemingly 'empty' literary language harbours within it quite
specific thwarted literary ambitions.[12]

The tale focuses on a father's ambitions and concerns for the future of his two
sons, Latimer and his elder brother, Alfred. Latimer is constitutionally timid and
anxious, with an interest in poetry, whereas Alfred is represented as masculine and
self-controlled, and has received an education in science. Both vie for the love of
Bertha Grant, to whom Alfred becomes engaged. However, Alfred is subsequently
killed in a riding accident and Latimer and Bertha are married, unhappily, for a
number of years before it is revealed that Bertha plans to poison Latimer, and
they separate. The tale emphasises Latimer's feelings of isolation as he is unable
to emotionally bond with either his father or brother, and his romantic fantasies
about Bertha turn out to have rested on the delusion that his feelings were recip-
rocated. The revelation that Bertha hates, rather than loves, Latimer comes as a
shock to him as although he is clairvoyant he has never been able to read Bertha's
mind.

At the end Latimer is left with only the certainty of his impending death, and
although the narrative contains within it, as Wolfreys notes, a sense of textual production before the fact, it is also a tale that is governed by secret feelings of poetic
ambition. For Latimer, his ambitions to write poetry are more important than the
prosaic memoir that he leaves behind. He notes, for example, that 'I wish to use
my last hours of ease and strength in telling the strange story of my experience',
which is belied by his sense that considered in artistic terms the document is
useless because it is 'a trivial schoolboy text; why do I dwell on it? It has little
reference to me, for I shall leave no works behind me for men to honour' (p. 4).
The narrative thus develops an explicit separation between poetry and prose. The
suggestion that poetry is a form that is more closely aligned with the imagination
than prose is arguably a false dichotomy, but it is one that dogs later spiritualist
writings where cryptic messages are often expressed, as we shall see in the discussion of *Raymond*, through complexly coded references to poetry.

Latimer is given a cranial assessment which suggests a troublingly fanciful
disposition that can only be corrected by an education in modern languages and
natural sciences. Nevertheless, 'I read Plutarch, and Shakespeare, and Don Quixote
by the sly, and supplied myself in that way with wandering thoughts' (pp. 6–7).
However, even this experience leads to an estrangement from writing:

You will think, perhaps, that I must have been a poet, from this early sensibility to Nature. But my lot was not so happy as that. A poet pours forth his song and *believes* in the listening ear and answering soul, to which his song will be floated sooner or later. But the poet's sensibility without his voice – the poet's sensibility that finds no vent but in silent tears on the sunny bank, when the noonday light sparkles on the water, or in the inward shudder at the sound of harsh human tones, the sight of a cold human eye – this dumb passion brings with it a fatal solitude of soul in the society of one's fellow-men. (p. 7, italics in original)

The passage includes a series of clues about how the issue of spectrality is developed in the text. Latimer's *cri-de-coeur* might appear to be a conventional account of feelings of isolation, but it is more complex than that. Latimer's alienation is closely related to his inability to develop a poetic voice through which to articulate his genuine emotions. In effect his alienation is overdetermined because he is alienated from nature, poetry, people, and himself. He is left, somewhat despondently, with only a lesser prose form through which he struggles to represent his inner life. The text implies that reality for Latimer can be intimated within a Romantic landscape which contains a hidden, possibly immanent, meaning. Latimer is searching for a moment of epiphany in which all will be revealed in the same way that 'the landscape' is when 'the sun lifts up the veil of the morning mist' (p. 10).

Initially, Latimer optimistically senses that his clairvoyant insights might represent such a lifting of the veil. His 'vision' of Prague, for example, seems to suggest an awakening of the poetic imagination. The vision 'was not a dream; was it – the thought was full of tremulous exultation – was it the poet's nature in me, hitherto only a troubled yearning sensibility, now manifesting itself suddenly as spontaneous creation?' (p. 10). However, as his retrospective feelings of alienation have made clear, the answer is no. Latimer's clairvoyance might be an ability but it is not in itself an imaginative one and does not carry off 'some dull obstruction' (p. 10) so as to free his poetic sensibility. The meaning of his second sight is different in kind to the poetic imagination but Latimer cannot help trying, somewhat desperately, to link them because both are tied to his inner, seemingly subconscious, mind. The revelation of meaning suggested in the clairvoyant vision is thus associated with the immanence of meaning that can only be developed through a poetic discourse, as prose itself functions as a 'dull obstruction' to this higher, subconscious, imaginative ideal.

At one level this debate about the poetic imagination suggests that 'The Lifted Veil' indulges a mystique about the relationship between poetry and the 'true' self. However, Latimer's pursuit of a poetic language functions as a gloss on the whole concept of revelation. Visions are revealed to Latimer and Latimer reveals the narrative to the reader before it concludes.

Latimer's link between literary revelation (poetry) and his vision breaks down when he consciously attempts to conjure a poetic vision of Venice in order to compare it with his vision of Prague: 'I stimulated my imagination with poetic memories, and strove to feel myself in Venice, as I had felt myself present in Prague. But in vain. I was only colouring the Canaletto engravings that hung in my old bedroom at home' (p. 10). This does not mean that the vision of Prague is non-poetic, only that Latimer cannot consciously stimulate a poetic imagination.

The narrative thus supports, through Latimer's thwarted literary ambitions, a view of poetic discourse as an inherently subconscious force, although ultimately one of a different order to clairvoyance. How to read poetry and how to read a spiritualist message became linked later in the period.

These considerations about poetry are also clearly gendered. The scientifically trained and masculine Alfred is contrasted with the effete Latimer, who notes of his lack of manliness that 'I thoroughly disliked my own *physique* and nothing but the belief that it was a condition of poetic genius would have reconciled me to it' (p. 14, italics in original). The representation of a mind/body dualism suggests that inspiration, creativity, and vision come from a feminised inner mental world. Critics such as Alex Owen, amongst others, have explored the gender implications of female mediumship and Latimer implicitly sees poetry as a fundamentally feminine activity which contrasts with mundane, masculine, prose.[13] Latimer wrestles with these forms of writing and he appears as an in-between being who can neither commit to one form or the other even as his visions often seem arbitrary or inconsequential. What is revealing is what is left out. Why, for example, is he unable to read Bertha's thoughts? And why is he given no premonition of Alfred's death in a riding accident?

These questions are never satisfactorily answered as Latimer develops a theory of poetry and prose which he extends to his view of the 'unimaginative' (p. 15) Bertha: 'The most prosaic woman likes to believe herself the object of a violent, a poetic passion' (p. 16). Later, Latimer's father will dismiss one of Latimer's ideas as 'my usual "poetic nonsense"' (p. 22). Latimer, worried that Bertha might be deceiving him about her true feelings, claims that she would not dupe him because, paradoxically, she says ' "The easiest way to deceive a poet is to tell him the truth"' (p. 26). Her comment acknowledges that Latimer inhabits a largely cryptic world which contrasts with prosaic truth. Latimer had initially conceived of Bertha in poetic terms, but is eventually horrified that her mind can only entertain 'a blank prosaic truth' (p. 32). Ultimately, for Latimer, the problem becomes reduced to a concern about language itself: 'We learn *words* by rote, but not their meaning; *that* must be paid for with our life-blood, and printed in the subtle fibres of our nerves' (p. 30, italics in original). The narrative thus finally addresses the impenetrability of meaning; not only the meaning of the visions themselves but also about the meaning of Latimer's life, and indeed his death. However, these key spiritualist questions are consistently constituted in literary terms that oppose poetry and prose and so implicate literature, and the problems of analysing the literary, as a central, indeed defining, concern of the narrative.

'The Lifted Veil' raises issues about textual production and interpretation which can be usefully illuminated by a discussion of Browning's view of spiritualism, and also by how Browning (the writer and the man) was perceived in contemporary literary circles.

Reading Browning

Adam Roberts has persuasively argued that Robert Browning in *The Ring and the Book* (1868–9) included an image of himself 'as a poetic Resurrectionist'.[14] Browning's attempt to give a voice to the dead through a version of himself as a 'medium' is for Roberts also addressed in the relationship between Browning's well-known anti-spiritualist poem 'Mr Sludge, "the Medium"' and his account of Christ's resurrection in 'A Death in the Desert', both published in *Dramatis Personae* (1864).[15] The poems provide a contrasting perspective on resurrection, the one 'real' (the resurrection of Christ), the other bogus (Mr Sludge's claims to give voice to the dead).[16] However, as Helen Sword notes, 'Mr Sludge' is a poem 'in which Browning, despite his obvious antipathy toward spiritualism, likens professional mediums to poets'.[17] The poem is intended as a lampoon of the well-known spiritualist medium Daniel Dunglas Home, and focuses on an exposed medium who pleads with an implied interlocutor not to make that exposure public. The poem is somewhat confessional in tone, although it is one in which the medium defends themself by suggesting that their services are merely called into being by the needs of others.

Sludge argues that the medium is like an artist, but one who exposes the tricks which the artist uses to beguile their readers or listeners.

> Suppose, the spirit of Beethoven wants to shed
> New music he's brimful of: why, he turns
> The handle of this organ, grinds with Sludge,
> And what he poured in at the mouth o' the mill
> As a Thirty-third Sonata. (ll. 355–9)[18]

Later he elaborates his technique in a specific reference to writing:

> The spinning out and drawing fine, you know –
> Really mere novel-writing of a sort,
> Acting, or improvising, make-believe. (ll. 445–7)

The medium thus represents a kind of bastardised version of artistic influence in which:

> Sludge would introduce
> Milton composing baby-rhymes, and Locke
> Reasoning in gibberish, Homer writing Greek. (ll. 612–14)

This leads Sludge to claim, 'Bless us, I'm turning poet!' (l. 1217).

The poem thus implicitly develops a link between the poetic imagination and mediumship, a link that Eliot explored in 'The Lifted Veil'. However, Browning's poem is self-conscious about such a link and suggests a connection between poetry and the potential for deception. Sludge convinces his accuser to keep the secret but intends to have revenge upon him by spreading a rumour that he murdered his mother in order to inherit her house. Sludge concludes that there are still opportunities for him because, as he says of his accuser, 'is he the only fool in the world?' (l. 1565). 'Sludge' suggests that the power of poetry lies in its ability to create bogus, rhetorical, possibilities and this implies a relationship between writing and deception which informed certain perceptions of Browning, as witnessed by Henry James's story 'The Private Life' (1893).

'The Private Life', published four years after Browning's death, is James's meditation on the seeming difference between Browning the man and Browning the writer. As we shall see, A.C. Benson also noted a curious disjunction between the complex man of letters and the quotidian bourgeois. James's tale is set in Switzerland and concerns a holiday taken by the anonymous narrator, Lord and Lady Mellifont, Clare (or Clarence) Vawdrey, described as 'the greatest (in the opinion of many) of our literary glories', and a prominent actress, Blanche Adney, who is emotionally attached to Vawdrey.[19] Vawdrey 'used to be called "subjective and introspective" in the weekly papers, but if that meant he was avid of tribute no distinguished man could in society have been less so. He never talked about himself' (pp. 219–20). Instead, Vawdrey the man seems to be about external appearances and the commonplace: 'His opinions were sound and second-rate, and of his perceptions it was too mystifying to think. I envied him his magnificent health' (p. 220). This surface version of Vawdrey (Browning) seemingly conceals, indeed entombs, the creative spirit. In this regard James's tale suggests links between writers and mediums, as if writing constituted a force which comes from the spirit world. The narrator notes, 'For myself, when he was talked about I always had an odd impression that we were speaking of the dead [. . .] His reputation was a kind of gilded obelisk, as if he had been buried beneath it' (p. 226). The public status of the writer stifles creativity. James thus argues that what is made invisible is the life of the mind, or the function of the creative imagination, whereas *Raymond* would foreground writing itself as the mystery. James, like George Eliot, associates the imagination with an inexplicable invisible inner world.

The tale refers to a play which Vawdrey is writing for Adney, and which he seemingly labours over during the day. However, Vawdrey appears to be unsure whether he has been writing the play or not, telling the narrator 'If there *is* anything, you'll find it on my table' (p. 232, italics in original). One evening the narrator leaves Vawdrey and Adney talking on the terrace and goes to fetch the manuscript of the play from Vawdrey's room. To his astonishment he discovers Vawdrey writing in the room and Vawdrey neither stops writing nor acknowledges the presence of the narrator, who leaves in some confusion.

The narrator discusses this with Adney and proposes a startling idea: ' "There are two of them [. . .] One goes out, the other stays at home. One's the genius, the other's the bourgeois, and it's only the bourgeois whom we personally know" ' (pp. 243–4). There is also the suggestion that Lord Mellifont is incomplete because he seems only to possess a public persona and seemingly has no inner life. Mellifont 'was all public and had no corresponding private life, just as Clare Vawdrey was all private and had no corresponding public' (p. 246). In 'The Private Life' these issues are specifically related to an account of the spectral life of the writer.

The narrator has a particular view of authorship in mind when he suggests that Vawdrey the writer has 'the Manfred attitude' (p. 264). The reference to Byron's 1816–17 play, set in Switzerland, implies that the author is an impetuous Romantic figure who is far removed from the bourgeois Vawdrey known by the narrator. He speculates that Adney may have greater access to Vawdrey's inner Byronic spirit, and the narrator notes in somewhat sexually ambivalent terms, 'I could only envy Mrs Adney her presumable enjoyment' of such Byronic 'responsive flashes' (p. 264).

'The Private Life' reads as a formal appraisal of the disjunction between public status and private, or solitary, creation. Vawdrey is a somewhat supernatural entity: a possible doppelgänger. Vawdrey is also ghosted by a spirit of creativity that cannot, in the end, be accounted for. These issues are addressed in quasi-spiritualist terms by George Eliot and underpin texts such as *The Book of the Golden Key* (discussed below) and *Raymond*. The view of Browning expressed through James's fictional version of him (Vawdrey) is significant because it reveals how a writer such as James evidenced an anxiety about the workings of the literary imagination. How the mind conceives of literary texts and how the mind receives spirit messages are closely related in the period and this can be illustrated by a close reading of a spirit novel.

Writing romance: writing otherness

An example of spirit writing in the Edwardian era, and one that is typical of its kind, is *The Book of the Golden Key* by Hugo Ames and Flora Hayter (aka Mrs Northesk Wilson), a book subtitled *An Idyll and a Revelation Being a Message from the So-called Dead*. Ames had produced, amongst other writings, a collection of essays entitled *Thirteen Thoughts* (1903) and a critique of socialism, *The Red God* (1908), as well as founding an esoteric order, the 'Order of Sir Galahad'. Flora Hayter had written a number of novels including *All Among the Barley* (1882), *Poppy! A Novel* (1883), *A Social Scandal* (1893), and a novel about the Boer war, *Satan's Courier* (1904), as well as a history titled *Belgrade, the White City of Death* (1903). That her more recent interests had leaned towards the mystical is evidenced by her *The Talk of the Hour: The Explanation of Human Rays, Character and Healing* (1905). Ames and Hayter had also worked together on a pamphlet titled 'The Position of Woman and the Problem of Sex'. *The Book of the Golden Key* is seemingly a novel, although it never quite admits to its literary status. It focuses on the relationship between Iris Delorme and Murray Compton, who meet at a fashionable London soirée and it is gradually revealed that they had been lovers in ancient Egypt.[20] Their love story carries a strong imprint of Rider Haggard's *She* (1887) in its echo of the relationship between Leo Vincey (as the resurrected Kallikrates) and Ayesha.

The Book of the Golden Key is explicitly spiritualist and recounts how a recently deceased friend of Compton's, Gerald Urquhart, helps to channel the spirit of 'Signor', who was linked to their earlier love affair in ancient Egypt. In the introduction Signor is described as a 'discarnate Spirit who, having passed over, has now returned to do his work here'.[21] In ancient Egypt Compton was a priest and Delorme a priestess. They (Ames and Hayter?) claim to be a conduit for Signor's story and in effect act as his medium. However, the complicated status of the narrative (is it a novel or not?) becomes an essential part of the story. Delorme notes that 'although the literary form of Signor may lack polish, we have left it' (p. x), and she also states that 'the travail of the souls of the Priest and the Priestess through chains of desire and matter, right up to everyday modern life, must be read as a symbol' (p. x). The symbol is a distinctly Haggardian one concerning the conflict between public duty and personal desire. The 'Editors' Preface' appears under the names of Ames and Hayter and notes that to people familiar with spirit messages 'there will be nothing particularly new or unusual in most of that which has been here set down' (pp. xi–xii). However, the preface reiterates the suggestions about literary symbolism which are referred to in the introduction and claims that 'we can state that the story and the facts are true' even though 'Herein lies enfolded a poem, a drama, and a revelation all in one' (p. xiii). This prefatory material is then followed by an 'Authors' Introduction' which further elaborates how the tale will be told.

How to relate the story is seemingly just as important as the story itself. One problem is that what might be of interest to spiritualists might not be so for readers of fiction, and vice versa:

> It seemed to the authors that if, in order to weave the facts with which it deals [. . .] into a harmonious whole they had resorted to the more conventional and pleasing form of fiction, they would have been sacrificing unintentionally a certain amount of interest that was paramount and important for what was unimportant, albeit perhaps interesting. (p. xxxii)

The example given is that of historical fiction, which is inevitably more fiction than fact. However, it is explicitly stated that the issue concerns how to develop the appropriate idiom through which to transmit Signor's messages. The ambition is to find a form which places the narrative outside of an anticipated 'crop of psychical novels, or plays' (p. xxxv). However, the narrative proper reworks the epistolary novel and in the main consists of letters exchanged between Delorme and Compton. One irony is that so many of these letters dwell upon the significance of fiction. Delorme, in what is a character-positioning opening letter, describes herself as 'By turns [. . .] actress, dramatist; poetess and painter' (p. 2). Indeed, it is her status as a dramatist which 'gives me a certain literary position'; currently, she says, 'I am trading on my literary reputation' (p. 2).

After Compton and Delorme meet the evocation of *She* becomes clear, and when Delorme refers to herself as 'the child of flame' (p. 22) she even goes so far as to imply the flame of life that Ayesha steps into in Haggard's novel. Compton's associations with literature are noted in a letter to Delorme where he claims that 'I have spent the greater part of my energetic life (in my spare time) in writing fiction of varied kinds' (p. 28). Also, although he claims a preference for the fact-based nature of the entries in his personal journal, he regards it as a place 'for notes and jottings for possible future fictions or writings' (p. 29). Later he laments that a play of his has yet to be produced. His account of his literary ambitions is interspersed with a series of rants about the state of Britain and its alleged imperial decline. Such outbursts associate him with a serious public (reactionary) politics which contrasts with Delorme's view of herself as fundamentally artistic and apolitical. Their shared interest in literature and literary production unites them. Her evaluation of one of his book manuscripts could stand as a representative view of *The Book of the Golden Key* and the cryptic nature of spirit messages: 'There are those who will read it with a pleased ear, not understanding; and those who do understand will see that the reality of joy is really the mystery of life. Is there not a science in the art of understanding which is not given to all?' (p. 72).

How to read critically is emphasised and how to read, interpret, and then reconstruct Signor's account of their past life is central to *The Book of the Golden Key*. Signor manifests himself through George Urquhart, a friend of Compton's who has recently died at a young age. The account of Urquhart's life evokes the Bohemian world of artists that du Maurier represented in *Trilby* (1894). Urquhart had 'a giant's frame [. . .] and a muscular body that would have done no injustice to a wrestler in the Olympic games' (p. 92). Intended for the army, he nevertheless 'flew to Art. For he was by nature a creator and a builder' even whilst he spent his leisure time 'riding, fencing, boxing, flirting, dancing' (p. 93). Urquhart's spirit suggests to Compton and Delorme that they attempt to create a salon which would 'include a Library and Lectures on Art, Literature and Occult Science' (p. 110).

Urquhart contacts Delorme directly, but Delorme is also given to automatic writing which she can produce when awake or asleep. Urquhart's intention is to illuminate Delorme about 'Art and its message', but he also informs her about the non-symbolic modes of communication which take place within the spirit world. Delorme tells Compton that 'on the Other Side (he told me) everyone *corresponds*' (p. 126, italics in original), which is not just a seemingly unintentional pun on communication but is meant to indicate that everything in the spirit world is directly expressed. This contrasts with communication on the earthly plain because Urquhart tells Delorme that in the spirit world 'we have deception by form, but not deception in regard to *expression* if it be carefully looked for' (p. 126, italics in original). How to interpret such messages is crucial and throughout the book

these messages are of a literary and symbolic kind. It is as if the spirit world generates the type of poetic visions that Latimer had been desperately searching for in
'The Lifted Veil'.

The Book of the Golden Key frequently links revelation with a quasi-biblical idiom.
One of Urquhart's more portentous statements is ' "And behold in the latter days
men shall dream dreams and women shall see visions" ' (p. 138), which is interpreted by Compton as a reference to St. Peter, Acts ii 17, a reference to 'last days'.
However, Urquhart's message also contains a synopsis about how the book
(passed on to him by Signor) is to be structured, stating that it is about:

> The Life and Love of three souls
>   The Artist
>   The Author
>   The Instrument – a mere woman! (p. 138)

Compton regards this as a 'harking back to the idea of the book' that Urquhart
has constantly been suggesting, although one apparent problem for Compton is
that 'It will be difficult to cast it *all* into the form of fiction without necessarily misleading the reader' (p. 138, italics in original). Therefore how to find the correct
narrative mode governs both the nature of spirit messages and the construction
of the book. Urquhart plays a key role in structuring the text, and he informs
Delorme, 'The "fiction" is what I'll tell you – and I tell it you as fiction' (p. 164),
and then reiterates 'You must remember that this is fiction' (p. 164), even if it is
a fiction which symbolically expresses the truth about their past lives.

The relationships and tensions between Signor, Urquhart, Compton, and
Delorme are framed by a debate about authority and authorship. Urquhart
emphasises the importance of fiction whereas Compton and Delorme, as their
prefaces indicate, are trying to find an idiom which will make the spirit experience
'real'. That Urquhart senses that he might be losing editorial control over the book
is indicated when he dictates to Delorme his intended structure of the book that
will become *The Book of the Golden Key*.

> Introduction to Murray's book.
>   Prologue – first.
>   The old story.
>   His view of it.
>   The trial of you both. (p. 172)

The conclusion refers to Delorme's response to the priestess's punishment of
an enforced suicide. Urquhart even goes so far as to explain what the symbolism
refers to: ' "The Priestess is the symbol of the Virgin heart of the world [. . .] The
Priest is Power" ' (p. 173). However, the more immediate problem confronted by
Delorme is about how to make sense of the messages (which refer to her past life)
as they are being dictated to her by Urquhart. He tells her, ' "You want to know
where you are going to find the story word for word. It's in indelible carving and

hieroglyphics"' (p. 177). Urquhart's (and Signor's) claims on authorship are emphasised when he tells Compton and Delorme: '"The story is for the world [. . .] I will give you careful instructions as to how it is to be done. But get on with it, for God's sake – for all our sakes. That can't be plainer. I haven't come to fool about it."' (p. 185). He goes on, '"Now, here you are, word for word"' (p. 185) and it is mooted that the manuscript follows the preface in the book.

Part of the self-reflexive nature of the narrative is therefore a consequence of how the 'book' is conveyed. The book is not so much about cryptic messages sent from the 'other world' as about the nature of literary production. In that regard Urquhart/Signor function as a metaphor for creativity in which the medium does not always understand the message, with Delorme noting that 'By what strange allegorical methods and in what oddly symbolical fashion he has always demonstrated his presence near and about me!' (p. 188). Read in these terms it is possible to see a parallel with Latimer's desire to identify the poetic imagination as the source of his seemingly cryptic visions. As Latimer cannot move beyond a consideration of the literary imagination, so *The Book of the Golden Key* never properly resolves an internal debate about the significance, and origin, of narrative form. The book claims that literature is divinely inspired because '"God is an artist in Divine creation"' (p. 204). However, the narrative is not quite the one conceived of by Urquhart/Signor as a number of omissions are made on the grounds of privacy (relating to the earlier relationship between Delorme and Compton). Also, Compton and Delorme repeatedly attempt to define the book as a curious mixture of the fanciful and the real, or 'like something between a fairy-tale and the commonplace' (p. 257), which emphasises the importance of textual (and metaphysical) revelation. Significantly, what is important is not just the idea of revelation (or 'vision' in 'The Lifted Veil'), but the ability to interpret it: 'God *paints* the world and *sings* the soul to ecstasy' whereas 'His *interpreters*, by pen and sometimes by the sword, with steam and electricity and gold and coal, create for him the Is-to-be' (p. 342, italics in original). This grouping of writers with other creative types argues for the existence of a divinely inspired excelsior plan. An emphasis is placed on being able to read the signs and symbols which evidence the presence of this plan and in order to do that the reader needs to possess some expertise in literary analysis. However, although spiritually inspired messages may have a divine providence they overwork the writer; the main narrative of *The Book of the Golden Key* concludes, 'With aching arm I flung the pen from me' (p. 346), an image which turns writing into manual, rather than intellectual, labour.

The ultimate ambitions for the book appear to have been to establish the type of salon ('The Salon of the Golden Key') suggested by Urquhart/Signor. The salon was intended as an upmarket forum for spiritualist explorations and therefore would not host séances or materialisations, but rather would 'focus [on] all that is most cultured' (p. 352), and so accord Art a privileged role in manifesting spirit communications.

The literary imagination and the spectral are fused in *The Book of the Golden Key* because it suggests that the writer and the artist are inspired by messages from the spirit world; in that regard the text can be contrasted with 'The Lifted Veil', where the literary and the spiritual are allocated to different mental faculties. Both texts, however, share the view that literary production and the ability to interpret literary narratives are key to understanding how a rarefied world (of the imagination, of the spirits) functions. These are issues which subtly inform Lodge's *Raymond*.

Messages from the dead: *Raymond*

Sir Oliver Lodge was president of the Society for Psychical Research between 1901 and 1903. He was also a fellow of the Royal Society and held a professorship in physics at Liverpool University before becoming the first principal of Birmingham University in 1900.[22] *Raymond* was reprinted numerous times between 1916 and 1919 and was a popular if somewhat controversial book.[23] Lodge's exploration of spirit phenomena was tempered by his scientific interests, which led him to account for such phenomena as part of a hitherto overlooked aspect of the natural world. In the preface to *Raymond* Lodge claims that the spirit world 'belongs to a coherent system of thought full of new facts of which continued study is necessary, that it is subject to a law and order of its own, and that though comparatively in its infancy it is a genuine branch of psychological science'.[24] However, such messages about Raymond's impending death (he was killed in September 1915) possess a decidedly literary turn.

The initial spirit messages come through before Raymond's death and begin with a reference to 'Faunus'. This was a message that involved a collaboration between the mediums Mrs Piper and Mrs Verrall, whose activities from 1907 Doyle was to refer to in *The History of Spiritualism*, and whom Myers had apparently contacted in 1908 and 1909. At a séance held at Mrs Piper's New Hampshire home in August 1915, the medium Mrs Robbins received a message from 'Richard Hodgson' which was in turn relayed to him by Myers (rather as Signor relayed messages via Urquhart). The following dialogue takes place:

> Hodgson: Myers says you take the part of the poet, and he will act as Faunus. FAUNUS.
> Robbins: Faunus?
> Hodgson: Yes. Myers. *Protect*. He will understand. What have you to say Lodge?
> Good work. Ask Verrall, she will also understand. Arthur says so. (p. 90)

Arthur is Mrs Verrall's husband, the deceased classical scholar Arthur W. Verrall.

Initially Robbins confuses the reference to Arthur and poetry by asking if this is a reference to 'Arthur Tennyson' (sic), and is quickly corrected by Hodgson: 'You got mixed, but Myers is straight about Poet and Faunus' (p. 91). Lodge notes that 'I venture to say that to non-classical people the [. . .] message conveys nothing.

It did not convey anything to me' (p. 91), however he is sure that 'it certainly meant something definite' (p. 91). To understand such messages required an elite specialist knowledge and skills in literary analysis. Lodge writes to Mrs Verrall requesting clarification and she informs him that it is a reference to Horace's *Odes*, specifically in Ode II.xvii, where Horace recounts how he was saved from being killed by a falling tree due to the intervention of Faunus, who as a consequence is described as 'the guardian of poets' (p. 91). Lodge reads this as 'meaning [. . .] that some blow was going to fall, or was likely to fall, though I didn't know of what kind, and that Myers would intervene, apparently to protect me from it' (p. 92). A few days later Raymond was killed, leading Lodge to contemplate whether Myers had intended to indicate that he would try and 'ward off' (p. 92) this blow.

In order to pursue the specialist line in textual exegesis begun by Mrs Verrall, Lodge corresponds with the Reverend M.A. Bayfield, the classical scholar and former headmaster of Christ College, Brecon, and Eastbourne College. Bayfield corrects Lodge's view that the message suggested that he might be protected from a blow. According to Bayfield, Horace 'says Faunus lightened the blow; he does not say "tuned aside". As bearing on your terrible loss, the meaning seems to be that the blow would fall but would not crush; it would be "lightened" by the assurance, conveyed afresh to you by a special message from the still living Myers, that your boy still lives' (p. 93). Bayfield thus exhibited a willingness to interpret the meaning of the passage in terms of how it could be adapted to Lodge's plight. Bayfield notes, 'I shall be interested to know what you think of this interpretation' (p. 93), which is followed by a note outlining the extant academic interpretations of the passage, all of which seem to confirm Bayfield's view of a blow 'lightened'.

The spirit of Myers is subsequently manifested at a series of séances where he is referred to as 'a writer of poetry' who 'is helping your son to communicate' (p. 133). Even Raymond's spirit becomes linked to a certain bookishness, with one medium noting that 'His home is associated with books – both reading and writing books. Wait a minute, he wants to give me a word, he is a little impatient with me. Manuscripts, he says manuscripts – that's the word' (p. 132). Later, Lodge experiments with mediums who practise table tilting, in which a spirit spells out messages by rapping on the table when certain letters of the alphabet are referred to. Lodge found these messages less satisfactory than the more literary form of the first message concerning Faunus. There is, for Lodge, a practical difficulty with such messages because 'when the sentence spelt out was a long one, we lost our way in it and could not tell whether it was sense or nonsense; for the words ran into each other' (p. 151). Isolated words are often received and the apparently random 'Argonauts' and 'Dartmoor', which are the focus of much family discussion, are regarded as a possibly oblique reference to a motoring mishap in their car near Dartmoor when Raymond was alive, although even for Lodge its significance is qualified as it is explained only through a 'semi-accidental reminiscence' (p. 157) by one of Raymond's brothers.

A later medium, Katherine Kennedy, tries to persuade Lodge of the important role that single-word messages have in helping to establish cross-correspondences, so that 'One word might be much more valuable than a long oration' (p. 160). The scale of messages therefore ranges from individual words to anticipated complete manuscripts. Raymond's brother, Alec, receives a message from their deceased mother via a medium which suggests that Oliver Lodge will at some point produce *the* book (*Raymond?*) which will prove the existence of spirits. She tells Alec: 'The book that is to be will be written from the heart, and not the head. But the book will not be written now. NOT NOW! NOT NOW! NOT NOW! (loud). Written later on. THE Book which is going to help and convert many' (p. 165). Her outburst aligns the ambitions of the project with those outlined in *The Book of the Golden Key*.

It is, however, the cross-correspondences which in particular seem to have taxed Lodge. His view foreshadows that of Doyle, who also saw them as somewhat confusing. However, Lodge explicitly states that such confusion is due to their hidden literary qualities. He acknowledges that the initial problem is that such messages seem to be fragmented and if viewed individually appear to be little more than 'meaningless jargon' (p. 173). However, 'ultimately when all the messages are put together by a skilled person the meaning is luminous enough. Moreover, we are assured that the puzzles and hidden allusions contained in these messages are not more difficult than literary scholars are accustomed to; that, indeed, they are precisely of similar order' (p. 173). Whilst Lodge is cautious with his language here ('precisely [. . .] similar'), such a comment makes explicit the view that spirit messages, in the form of cross-correspondences, require skills of literary analysis. Luckhurst notes of such communications that they align 'collage techniques with parallel kinds of "occult" hermeneutic – in the broad sense of practices dedicated to unveiling the hidden' (p. 267) and need to be reassembled into a coherent message. As Lodge notes, what is required is the expertise to structure these messages.

Such acts of reconstruction, this reassembling of fragments, should also be seen within the context of anxieties about the war. In one of his exchanges with a medium, for example, Lodge explores whether those who were blown up would be reconstituted as whole in the spirit world. The medium consults Raymond and they relay the response back to Lodge: 'I am told [. . .] that when anybody's blown to pieces, it takes some time for the spirit-body to complete itself, to gather itself all in, and to be complete [. . .] The *spirit* isn't blown apart, of course [. . .] but it has an effect upon it' (p. 195, italics in original). Corporeal bodies are thus conflated with fragmented textual bodies. They are recomposed, made 'healthy', and given meaning and legibility in this 'other world' in which 'they call for whisky sodas' (p. 198) in what resembles a pre-war society.

Raymond incorporates a view of writing and its production which echoes *The Book of the Golden Key* and its obsessions with the transmission of writing. Issues about writing are developed through a platonic idea of imaginative production.

Raymond, via a medium, passes this message to his brother Alec: 'There are books there not yet published on the earth plane. He is told [. . .] that these books will be produced, books like these that are there now; that the matter in them will be impressed on the brain of some man, he supposes an author' (p. 209). He concludes by indicating that 'Father is going to write one' (p. 209).

In the spirit world it seems as though communication is sub-linguistic. Raymond notes of one lecture he attends in the spirit world that 'he didn't get only the words of the speaker, words didn't seem to matter, he got the thought – whole sentences, instead of one word at a time' (p. 265). This view of the platonic transmission of messages accords with Latimer's model of artistic inspiration, even if Latimer might be in some doubt as to what his 'visions' are intended to signify. The issue of the relationship between language and literary inspiration was important in 'The Lifted Veil' and *The Book of the Golden Key*, as both concern writers or would-be writers. However, this is handled in an alternative way in *Raymond* because Lodge regards himself as a man of science whose approach to literary matters is quite different to that of writers or classically trained interpreters of literature. He states, 'The tendency of a simple word to have many glancing meanings – like shot silk, as Tennyson put it – is a character of high literary value; though it may be occasionally inconvenient for scientific purposes' (p. 289). However, in a short chapter (of five and a half pages) on 'Death and Decay' he quotes from Edwin Arnold, Coleridge, Shakespeare, Tennyson, Fitzgerald, and Longfellow, in order to suggest that it is, as Latimer claims, poetry which expresses a higher symbolic truth.

Raymond makes reference to many different forms of writing and Lodge reduces writing to its crudest possible form when he claims that 'Writing and Reading' takes place 'by aid of black marks on a piece of paper' (p. 339). For Lodge 'the symbols are ultimately to be interpreted as if heard' (because dictated by the medium), but they 'hardly need elaboration in order to exhibit their curiously artificial and complicated indirectness' (p. 339). Science, in other words, is unable to identify the precise grounds on which meaning is generated because spirit messages are shaped by antecedent literary forms. However, Lodge does not leave the debate there, because elsewhere in *Raymond* he philosophises on whether any writing can truly represent mental processes as writing is also, in part, the consequence of *physical* activity. In a chapter on 'Mind and Brain', he claims:

Sometimes in order to remember a thing, one writes it in a note-book; and the memory may be said to be in the note-book about as accurately as it may be said to be in the brain. A physical process has put it in the note-book; there is a physical configuration persisting there; and when a sort of reverse physical process is repeated, it can be got back into consciousness by simply what we call 'looking' at the book and reading. But surely the real memory is in the *mind* all the time, and the deposit in the note-book is a mere detent for calling it out or for making it easy of recovery. In order to communicate any information we must focus attention on it; and whether we focus attention on a part of the brain or on a page of a note-book matters very little; the attention itself is a mental process, not a physiological one, though it has a physiological concomitant. (p. 326)

This passage has been quoted at length because it provides a synopsis of the type of challenge confronted by a scientist such as Lodge. Writing, in this discussion of the mind, is potentially rendered meaningless because the processes of physical production compromise the idea of writing as an inherently, or purely, mental function. Writing thus inscripts the body and therefore cannot rework the same type of sub-linguistic understanding that Raymond sees as governing communication in the disembodied spirit world. Ultimately, Lodge implies that writing may evoke a form of emptiness because it is thoughtless and soulless (a series of notations that might prompt a recollection of an idea but which is not captured in writing) and thus an imperfect vehicle through which to apprehend the mind.

Raymond represents a complex attempt to explore the relationship between literary analysis and textual production. These ideas can also be related to conceptions of identity to the extent that they beg questions about the 'reality' of the spirit that is communicated with. Literary inspiration and a view of the subject that is associated with such inspiration can, however, break down and this suggests that the issue of authenticity is more complex than it first appears.

An exploration of how Lodge's contemporary, A.C. Benson, responded to Browning provides an illuminating closing contextualisation for the debate about the literary imagination and its relationship with spiritualism.

Benson's Browning

A.C. Benson had an interest in the ghost story (among other forms of writing) and was the author of *The Hill of Trouble and Other Stories* (1903), as well as the lyricist for Elgar's 'Land of Hope and Glory' (1902). His brother, E.F. Benson, wrote ghost stories and his father, E.W. Benson, was the archbishop of Canterbury. His uncle was the Cambridge philosopher Henry Sidgwick, who was one of the founding members (with F.W.H. Myers) and first president of the Society for Psychical Research.[25] A.C. Benson had a long interest in spiritualism and with E.F. Benson he became familiar with M.R. James's ghost stories, discussed in Chapter 8, whilst at Cambridge.

In the introduction to his 1915 collection, *Escape and other Essays*, he explicitly situates the volume within the context of the war. He argues for the necessity of escaping from 'a certain poison in the air, a tendency towards suspicion and contentiousness and vague hostility'.[26] He argues for an exorcism of this 'evil spirit [. . .] by letting our minds go back to the old peace for a little' (p. xix) and privileges literature as the means of enabling this escape. In the opening essay, 'Escape', he argues that 'All the best stories in the world are but one story in reality – the story of an escape' (p. 1). However, the reality of the war ghosts the book and subtly shapes the essays about spirit visions ('The Visitant'), fears of psychological doubling ('That Other One'), and an analysis of dreams ('Behold, This Dreamer Cometh'). There are also numerous references to the process of writing and the work of selected authors. His discussion of Browning, like James's, addresses what he saw as an essential dichotomy. In 'Literature and Life' he notes of Browning, 'He was as reticent about his occupation as a well-bred stockbroker, and did his best in society to give the impression of a perfectly decorous and conventional gentleman, telling strings of not very interesting anecdotes, and making a general point of being ordinary' (p. 27).

For Benson, as for James, this public affirmation of bourgeois conviviality conceals the intellectual and emotional complexity of the literary imagination. Indeed Browning 'never seems to have given the smallest hint as to how he conceived a poem or worked it out' (p. 27). This view of Browning implies that writing is a secretive and so mysterious process. However, there is also a more unconsciously expressed anxiety suggested here because Benson and James share a concern that perhaps Browning's carefully manufactured public persona might indicate that poetry is also 'manufactured'. As 'Mr Sludge' implies, poetry might constitute a form of mediumship, but if mediumship is fundamentally performative then so is poetry and this explains Benson and James's attempt to preserve the mystique of the literary imagination. In 'Herb Moly and Heartease' Benson outlines, in allegorical mode, his view of poetry, concluding that 'the poet sees things in a flash, and describes his visions, without knowing what they mean, or indeed if they have any meaning at all' (p. 244). This might seem to accord with Latimer's view of poetic visions in 'The Lifted Veil' but it is also, paradoxically, evoked in Lodge's concern that writing itself might be meaningless because ultimately texts are formal and physical productions rather than the product of a scientifically adduced imagination. Lodge, of course, is a scientist who is sceptical about the nature of texts, even if *Raymond* claims that some messages do come from the spirit world.

There is also an implied horror in Benson's class-bound account of Browning when he claims of him that:

> Inside the sacred enclosure, the winds of heaven blow, the thunder rolls; he proclaims the supreme worth of human passion, he dives into the disgraceful secrets of the soul: and then he comes out of his study a courteous and very proper gentleman, looking like a retired diplomatist, and talks like an intelligent commercial traveller. (p. 28)

This is an image of deception which is also associated with Sludge. Sludge, like Browning, is a kind of 'commercial traveller', plying his services in various places. He is also, of course, at one level, a poet.

The relationship between this view of Browning and spiritualism is a complex one because whilst both Benson and James affirm the mystique of the poetic imagination, they implicitly evidence a concern that in reality there might exist links between textual performance and social identity. To read their account of Browning in this way is to suggest, paradoxically in relation to 'Mr Sludge, "The Medium"', that Browning is sceptical about idealist accounts of the literary imagination and by association, his poem also debunks spiritualist ideas of otherworldly influence – especially those that ape models of literary production.

Spirit messages posed particular problems for their interpreters. Part of their complexity lies in the fact that such messages, at least in part, were imbricated by concerns about literary production which were central to debates about creativity. This aligns the pursuit of agency in *Raymond* with the anxieties of James and Benson. The questions of how to account for the 'ghost' and the creative 'spirit' oddly coincide, which indicates just how far literature became implicated in spiritualist practice, and spiritualism was conditioned by the literary.

The examples discussed here indicate how links can be made between 'The Lifted Veil' and later spiritualist writings. They share the preoccupations of how to account for the origin of literary inspiration and the 'authenticity' of spirit messages. Such issues, as Eliot maps them, are separate, but they become oddly linked by a pursuit for origins in which the 'imaginative' and the 'visionary' become elided. The spirit, as Myers saw it in *The Human Personality and Its Survival of Bodily Death* (1903), represents our inner 'ghost' and as such *is* our creative spirit, although one now set free from bodily constraints.[27] Creativity and the ghost are thus closely linked during the period and have their shared roots in a literary culture (such as that exemplified here by Eliot, James, and Benson), which raised issues that permeate spiritualist texts such as *The Book of the Golden Key* and *Raymond*. Also, as the example of Browning indicates, authenticity is central to a view of the emotional veracity of poetry (which is also true of 'The Lifted Veil'). Spirit messages also require authentication and this in part implicates literary analysis in bringing out the hidden meaning of otherwise cryptic messages. As *The Book of the Golden Key* makes clear, how to write and how to read can become strangely conflated. Reading the ghost and writing the ghost are ultimately difficult to disentangle, but this indicates how certain forms of literature helped to establish a context for later spiritualist deliberations which would then feed back into this literary culture.

This chapter has addressed issues of artistic construction and the role of the imagination. These issues, and how they relate to conceptualisations of history, are a central theme in the ghost stories of Henry James, which will be discussed in Chapter 6.

Notes

1 The history of nineteenth-century spiritualism has been well documented. Some notable studies (to mention a very few) include Janet Oppenheim's *The Other World: Spiritualism and Psychical Research in England 1850–1914* (Cambridge: Cambridge University Press, 1985), which provides a comprehensive examination of the variety

of contexts (scientific, religious, socio-historical) that shaped spiritualist ideas. Alex Owen in *The Darkened Room: Women, Power, and Spiritualism in Late Victorian England* (Chicago: University of Chicago Press, 1989) explores the gender implications of female mediumship and more recently Roger Luckhurst in *The Invention of Telepathy* (Oxford: Oxford University Press, 2002) has argued that Victorian conceptions of telepathy can be read in literary and cultural contexts that are influenced by, amongst other factors, ideas of imperialism. In addition, Sarah A. Willburn in *Possessed Victorians: Extra Spheres in Nineteenth-Century Mystical Writings* (Aldershot: Ashgate, 2006) examines how the 'possessed' self can be related to formulations of the political economy. An article which addresses the issue of reading and spiritualism in general terms is 'Psychic Reading' by Lisa Brocklebank in *Victorian Studies*, 48. 2 (Winter 2006), 233–9.

2 See Helen Sword's *Ghostwriting Modernism* (Ithaca and London: Cornell University Press, 2002) p. 44.

3 W.T. Stead (ed.), *Real Ghost Stories* (New York: George H. Doran, [1897] 1921) pp. 246–8.

4 In *Ghostwriting Modernism* Helen Sword examines how the Edwardian experience of spirit writing, including automatic writing in which spirits seemingly dictate their ideas, influenced modernists such as T.S. Eliot, Ezra Pound, W.B. Yeats and H.D. Sword notes a parallel between a modernist writerly self-consciousness and the medium, because mediums, like writers, 'have typically regarded themselves as privileged recipients and interpreters of the written word'. The specific links with modernism are because such texts 'engage with many of the dominant tropes of literary modernism – linguistic playfulness, decenterings of consciousness, fracturings of conventional gender roles – and betray a characteristically modernist obsession with all things textual: reading, writing, literature, authorship, publication, libraries, and even the discourses and methodologies of literary criticism' (p. 11). Despite Sword's acknowledgement that such narratives are 'largely devoid of formal experimentation' (p. 11) she does argue that they rework potentially radical ideas about literary production that are central to modernism. Roger Luckhurst, however, notes of such writings that 'automatic texts from Spiritualist contexts are conservative in their social and religious visions of the afterlife' as well as being 'formally unadventurous' (*The Invention of Telepathy*, p. 256). This chapter examines how such ideas about literary production can be located within the nineteenth century and so explores how these issues were addressed before the advent of modernism.

5 F.W.H. Myers was the author of the influential work *The Human Personality and Its Survival of Bodily Death* (New York and Bombay: Longmans, [1903] 1907), in which he elaborated a theory of the subliminal self that argued that the unconscious mind was effectively our spirit self, one which is released after death.

6 Roger Luckhurst, *The Invention of Telepathy* (Oxford: Oxford University Press, 2002) p. 267. All subsequent references are to this edition and are given in the text.

7 Arthur Conan Doyle, *The History of Spiritualism*, vol. II (Teddington: The Echo Library, [1926] 2006) p. 41. All subsequent references are to this edition and are given in the text.

8 See Brocklebank 'Psychic Reading', 236. See also Vanessa Dickerson's *Victorian Ghosts in the Noontide: Women Writers and the Supernatural* (Columbia: University of Missouri Press, 1996), ch. 4 'A Ghost in the Noontide: George Eliot's Lifting of the Veil', pp. 80–102, p. 82.

9 Jill Galvan, 'The Narrator as Medium in George Eliot's "The Lifted Veil"', *Victorian Studies*, 48. 2 (Winter 2006), 240–8, 240.

10 George Eliot, *The Lifted Veil and Brother Jacob*, ed. and introd. Helen Small (Oxford: Oxford University Press, [1859] 1999) p. 3, italics in original. All subsequent references are to this edition and are given in the text.

11 Julian Wolfreys, *Victorian Hauntings* (Basingstoke: Macmillan, 2002) p. 75. All subsequent references are to this edition and are given in the text.

12 At one level the novella can be read in relation to literary and financial anxieties. Martin Willis in 'Clairvoyance, Economics and Authorship in George Eliot's "The Lifted Veil"', *Journal of Victorian Culture*, 10.2 (2005), 184–209, has explored how during the writing of the novella Eliot was influenced by a series of literary concerns (about her identity as a writer, something that she had been eager to conceal given her relationship with the married G.H. Lewes) and financial concerns (relating to discussions about how her work could be more remuneratively marketed). Willis notes that the potential theft of her authorial identity by the clergyman Joseph Liggins (who had made a claim on the authorship of *Scenes of Clerical Life* [1857–8]), combined with financial anxieties, became displaced into the narrative as a concern about the nature of writing and worries over the 'future'. Latimer's father has made his wealth by investing in 'futures' on the Stock Exchange and this glosses Latimer's concern with the future which is evidenced through his clairvoyance. Willis notes: 'Financial speculation, like clairvoyance, involves partial recognition of future possibilities contingent upon a number of unknown present and future events. Both speculative practices, therefore, involve an element of risk; one with capital the other with one's own security in the self' (186). This financial plot can be related to the kinds of economic speculation that we witnessed in Dickens and Collins. However, it is the specific issue of literary ambition and the problem with developing a properly literary language that helps to open the text to a reading which enables us to see why issues of interpretation and spectrality become so important in the period.

13 See Galvan, 'The Narrator as Medium in George Eliot's "The Lifted Veil"', 241. See also Martin Willis's discussion of this in 'Clairvoyance, Economics and Authorship in George Eliot's "The Lifted Veil"', p. 199, where he refers to Alex Winter's *Mesmerized: Powers of Mind in Victorian Britain* (Chicago: Chicago University Press, 1998).

14 Adam Roberts, 'Browning, the Dramatic Monologue and the Resuscitation of the Dead' in Nicola Brown, Carolyn Burdett, and Pamela Thurschwell (eds), *The Victorian Supernatural* (Cambridge: Cambridge University Press, 2004) pp. 109–27, p. 109.

15 See Roberts, 'Browning, the Dramatic Monologue and the Resuscitation of the Dead', p. 120.

16 See Roberts, 'Browning, the Dramatic Monologue and the Resuscitation of the Dead', p. 120.

17 Sword, *Ghostwriting Modernism*, p. 152.

18 Robert Browning, 'Mr Sludge, "Medium"' in *The Poems of Robert Browning* (Ware, Herts: Wordsworth, 1994) pp. 499–518. All subsequent references are to this edition and are given in the text.

19 Henry James, 'The Private Life' in *The Altar of the Dead, The Beast in the Jungle, The Birthplace, and Other Tales*, vol. 17 of the *New York Edition of Henry James* (New York: Charles Scribner's Sons, [1909] 1937), pp. 215–66, p. 217. All subsequent references are to this edition and are given in the text.

20 As an interesting aside to this, Ames and Hayter seemed to have been bigamously married in 1910 in Idaho, and again in London in 1911. The *New York Times* of 27 April 1912 indicates that on the previous day Ames and Hayter were found guilty in a London court and sentenced to six months in prison. The report records that Hayter was the author of *The Book of Divorce: Its Use and Abuse*, which she had dedicated to Ames.

21 Hugo Ames and Flora Hayter, *The Book of the Golden Key: An Idyll and a Revelation Being a Message from the So-called Dead* (London: Kegan Paul, 1909) p. ix. All subsequent references are to this edition and are given in the text.

22 His scientific inventions included pioneering work on the wireless.

23 See Jay Winter's *Sites of Memory, Sites of Mourning: The Great War in European Cultural History* (Cambridge: Cambridge University Press, 1995); ch. 3, 'Spiritualism and the "Lost Generation"', pp. 54–77, includes an account of *Raymond* and some of the controversies with which it was associated. For an interesting account of *Raymond* and its place in war memoirs see Victoria Stewart, ' "War Memoirs of the Dead": Writing and Remembrance in the First World War', *Literature and History*, 14.2 (Autumn 2005), 37–52.

24 Sir Oliver Lodge, *Raymond* (London: Methuen, [1916] 1917) p. viii. All subsequent references are to this edition and are given in the text.

25 The Society for Psychical Research was founded in 1882.

26 A.C. Benson, *Escape and other Essays* (London: Murray, 1915) p. xix. All subsequent references are to this edition and are given in the text.

27 Myers, *The Human Personality and Its Survival of Bodily Death*, p. 215.

6

Haunted houses and history:
Henry James's Anglo-American ghosts

Henry James, by virtue of his American birth, might seem an odd inclusion in a study of the British ghost story. However, James's strong links with Britain (he became a British citizen in 1915) underpin a peculiarly Anglo-American spectrality in his writings. Crucially it is a sense of place which articulates an Anglo-American experience and this chapter explores how, in part, images of the haunted house reflect that. As long ago as 1961 R.W. Stallman referred to James and his 'edifice complex'. Other critics have noted that this jocular reference to Freud suggests the house as an uncanny generator of secrets that shape James's representation of traumatic childhood, as in *The Turn of the Screw* (1898).[1] The house is also closely related to the Jamesian house of fiction. Carren Osna Kaston has associated this with a type of Freudian role play in which 'houses are [. . .] parental structures in which family dramas show us what it means to be a child and what it means to grow up, structures in which versions – fictions – of life are imposed on personality or "character by parents", in what becomes "the house of fiction" ' (27).

Fiction plays a central role in this process and this chapter explores the role of the house in James's writings on spectrality; writings which encompass ghost stories, his ostensibly realist writing, and non-fiction. As we shall see, James's houses are successively inhabited by different sets of people in different epochs, and each set leave their traces to haunt the next.[2]

Leon Edel in *The Ghostly Tales of Henry James* (1948) argues that James's contribution to the ghost story should not be restricted to the tales which simply include ghosts. For Edel there are tales which elaborate a language of spectrality that transcends the formal limits of the ghost story and yet also helps the critic to contextualise James's spectres. This argues the case that an early tale such as 'De Grey: A Romance' (1868), which concerns ancestral secrets that spectrally influence the present and the future, should be read alongside more conventional ghost stories such as 'The Romance of Certain Old Clothes' (1868), which concerns a sister's ghostly revenge. For Edel both tales indicate that psychology is the key to understanding their specific representations of the spectral. Indeed, Edel argues that this constitutes James's particular contribution to literature about ghosts and ghostliness in which his ghosts 'possess an unusual degree of reality because we see them invariably through the people who see or "feel" them'.[3] T.J. Lustig in *Henry James and the Ghostly* (1994) develops this view to encompass James's putatively non-supernatural writings. For Lustig, 'At a very general level a great deal of James's fiction is ghostly in its enigmatic impalpability, its vague precision, its subtle allusiveness, its hovering uncertainty, its fascination with awe, wonder and dread'.[4]

Whilst this chapter will explore ghostly tales it will also examine the broader discourse of spectrality mapped by Edel and Lustig. However, the specific focus here on art, history, and place provides an alternative way of mapping James's use of the spectral. What is also noteworthy is that James also addresses issues of spectrality and money which we observed in the writing of Dickens, Collins, and Riddell. How James links the idea of spectral money to notions of art, history, and place indicates how he moves beyond, yet develops, some of those earlier investigations.

James wrote eighteen tales between 1868 and 1908 which either explicitly or implicitly rely upon images of the ghostly. However, fourteen of these were published between 1891 and 1908, with twelve of them produced between 1891 and 1900. The writing of ghost stories thus coincided with a period in which his work was characterised by innovation and experiment. However, ghosts also play an important role in *The Portrait of a Lady* (1881, revised 1907), which is discussed here with *The Turn of the Screw*, *The American Scene* (1907), 'The Jolly Corner' (1908), and his uncompleted novel *The Sense of the Past* (published posthumously in 1917). These texts have been selected on the basis of their representation of haunted houses, which are linked to notions of art, history, place, money, and national identity. James's 'The Ghostly Rental' (1876) helps establish some of these links and evokes a model of Nathaniel Hawthorne's romance that informs James's debate about art – a debate which he returned to in some of the later writings discussed here.

'The Ghostly Rental': Hawthornian romance and counterfeit ghosts

'The Ghostly Rental' centres on Captain Diamond's feelings of guilt that he is responsible for his daughter's death after he sought to interfere in what he regarded as an inappropriate love match. The narrator, a vacationing theology student, discovers that the captain's daughter's ghost inhabits a property which belongs to the captain and that she pays him a quarterly rental for lodging there. The captain only sees her on the day appointed for collecting the rent. This seemingly outlandish tale addresses issues about the relationship between material and immaterial worlds, one in which the narrator's status as a theology student suggests possible associations with spirituality.

It is also clear that the daughter has not died but is securing her father's financial well-being as he enters his dotage, even whilst there is an element of punishment in her disguising this from him. Significantly, the idea of the house takes on historical importance in the tale:

... it was of very large proportions, and it had a striking look of solidity and stout-
ness of timber. It had lived to a good old age, too, for the woodwork on its
doorway and under its eaves, carefully and abundantly carved, referred it to the
middle, at the latest, of the last century.[5]

The materiality and historical weight of the building is a counterpoint to the narrator's feeling that ' "The house is simply haunted!" ' (p. 40), because he senses
that 'it had been spiritually blighted' (p. 40). The house is real but also unreal because
of the figure of the ghost. However, the ghost is not even a 'real' ghost, which means
that the issue of what constitutes reality is foregrounded. According to Lustig this
liminality indicates that James is consciously engaging with a Hawthornian model
of the romance. For Lustig, 'The haunted house [. . .] represents something like
the American house of fiction, the house of romance, the house of James's early
career' (p. 71). Lustig claims that Captain Diamond's associations with the material
and immaterial illustrate this engagement with Hawthorne, so that ' "The Ghostly
Rental" sets out to assess the nature of Hawthorne's captaincy, his ownership of
the house of romance, the status of his ghosts and the validity of his fears' (p. 71).
The tale thus, at one level, represents a battle over literary authority.

Hawthorne's famous conceptualisation of the romance in the 'Custom House'
episode of *The Scarlet Letter* (1850) emphasises the necessity of using the unreal
(the fictional) to animate reality (history). Hawthorne envisions a form of romance
which exists 'somewhere between the real world and fairyland, where the Actual
and the Imaginary may meet, and each imbue itself with the nature of the other.
Ghosts might enter here without affrighting us'.[6] In that regard the romance is a
textually spectral entity and so one which appealed to James, who acknowledges
in the preface to *The Turn of the Screw* that he too is seeking to blur the fanciful
with the concrete: 'The thing was to aim at absolute singleness, clearness and round-
ness, and yet to depend on an imagination working freely, working (call it)
with extravagance'.[7] It is a view of the romance which importantly contrasts with
allegory. For James, unlike for Dickens (as we saw in Chapter 2), the ghost story
is not allegorical. In *Hawthorne* (1879) James claims that allegory 'is apt to spoil
two good things – a story and a moral, a meaning and a form; and the taste for it
is responsible for a large part of the forcible-feeble writing that has been inflicted
upon the world'.[8] Thus whilst James approved of the romance as a form he distanced himself from some of its allegorical expressions (such as a scarlet A) which
could come to inhabit and so compromise it.[9] Lustig has noted James's debt to
Hawthorne as indicated in his review of Braddon's *Aurora Floyd* from 1865,
where he states that 'a good ghost-story . . . must be connected at a hundred points
with the common objects of life'.[10] This, according to Lustig, represents support
for a romantic aesthetic which strategically enables James to give the issue of inde-
terminacy (but also modes of cultural attachment) a crucial role in his consideration
of the relationship between America and Europe. He blurs the relationship between
'the Old World and the New' so that 'in no aspect of his fiction was James seeking

to establish fixed and absolute borders. The thresholds which did exist were the effects of intersecting fields of energy; they did not make meaning possible: they *were* meaning' (p. 62). This relates to James's concern that allegory can 'spoil' the idea of 'meaning' by making it formal and stylised. It also suggests that 'meaning' and its production were central to James's aesthetic. Such a view could seem to be a purely abstract, or solely artistically considered one, but as we shall see it reworks a more politicisable, if implicit, narrative relating to Anglo-American identity.

The emphasis on a counterfeit ghost also suggests the idea of an estrangement from history – one in which signs can no longer be trusted. What the narrator of 'The Ghostly Rental' pursues, however, is a version of experience in which signs properly signify. The captain's house creates unease in the narrator because, somewhat tautologically, he cannot account for why it generates such unease. A subsequent house, at which he makes enquiries about the apparently haunted house, is described as 'the model of the house which is in no sense haunted – which has no sinister secrets, and knows nothing but blooming prosperity' (p. 41). Wealth, and the signs of wealth, are therefore in accord in a tale which is not a ghost story but which (to a certain point) claims to be one. According to Pericles Lewis, in the tale 'The visible, conscious world, with its familiar motives such as desire, ambition, and greed, interacts in subtle ways with an unseen realm, inaccessible to consciousness, where desire, ambition, and greed have more deep-seated, even uncanny equivalents'.[11] The reference to the uncanny is telling as it is relevant to how the home also becomes the place where secrets are generated and concealed. Throughout, however, emphasis is given to how the narrator will rationalise what he sees. This is difficult for him because the house 'seemed to keep observers at a distance' (p. 44). The problem with perception is also related to the wider sense of the perverse in which a ghost seemingly rents a house from their father. Miss Deborah, who tells the narrator the story of the ghost, says before embarking on it that ' "It was strange, but it was ridiculous too. It is a thing to make you shudder and to make you laugh" ' (p. 50). However, because the narrator has witnessed Captain Diamond receive the money from what at that stage he believes to be a ghost he 'laughed at the recital' but also 'shuddered' because although apparently 'ridiculous' the tale is seemingly true (p. 51).

Fictions become realities as identities become blurred or merge. Miss Deborah tells the narrator that the daughter pays the captain ' "In good American gold and silver" ' and that ' "the pieces are all dated before the young girl's death. It's a strange mixture of matter and spirit!" ' (p. 51). Her observation could be extended to include James's wider use of the spectral, one in which, as Lewis notes, 'the "unseen" [. . .] involves the unconscious sexual, material, and social desires of his characters but cannot be reduced to any one of these' (p. 59). Even the narrator, when loitering near the house in an attempt to catch a glimpse of the ghost, notes that he felt 'like a restless ghost myself' (p. 52). The question of the reality of the ghost is secondary, however, to the effect that it has on the observer.

The narrator notes that whether the ghost is real or unreal does not, on a psychological level, matter because 'a sham ghost [. . .] might do as much execution as a real ghost' (p. 59). Ghosts might be counterfeit but they have a psychological effect. However, the ghost in James is closely related to place. His ghosts do not wander but inhabit places because they represent the secret historical identities of their locale.

'The Ghostly Rental' foreshadows concerns about money, identity, and place that James would develop in *The Portrait of a Lady*. The emphasis on money as something material and tangible (coins not banknotes) does not, however, stop identities collapsing in moments of insight or revelation. The narrator attempts to secure the final quarter's funding on behalf of the now dying captain (who wants the money to secure a good doctor and a decent burial) and in the process seeks to expose the ghost. He notes that 'what I saw before me was not a disembodied spirit, but a beautiful women, an audacious actress' (p. 63), a view which would later be echoed in *The Turn of the Screw* in the governess's perception of Quint as an 'actor'. That the 'ghost' is in some way in character is clear once he finally removes her veil to reveal 'a large fair person, of about five-and-thirty' and notes 'her pale, sorrow-worn face, painted to look paler' (p. 63). Finally, the counterfeit ghost is exposed. The narrator tells her about her dying father and she exclaims, ' "I have seen his ghost!" ' (p. 64), which she regards as a reprisal for her performance as a spectre.

'The Ghostly Rental' foregrounds ideas about artificiality and spectrality which would be developed in both *The Turn of the Screw* and *The Portrait of a Lady*. The tale, revealingly, closes on the destruction of the 'haunted' house, caused by the captain's daughter dropping a candle. With the end of the ghost, the house, as an emblem of the past, is destroyed.

For Peter Buitenhuis the house represents America and James's anxious attempt to assert some form of ownership over it.[12] In Lustig's terms its destruction could be read as a laying to rest or a surpassing of Hawthorne's romance (one in which 'reality' is emphasised). Either way there is the suggestion that implicit to 'The Ghostly Rental' is a debate about nationality and national writing. These ideas are given further treatment in *The Portrait of a Lady*.

The Portrait of a Lady: history, money, and art

In the novel's preface James recalls that he wrote much of the text in Florence and Venice. It was whilst in Venice that he felt that the sights and the noises of the city constituted a distraction. He notes 'the ceaseless human chatter of Venice' and sees the city as producing what is to him an alien vision of art.[13] He had originally anticipated that Venice would inspire his imagination, only to come to the conclusion that the city's 'historic sites':

> are too rich in their own life and too charged with their own meanings merely to
> help him [the author] out with a lame phrase; they draw him away from his small

question to their greater ones; so that, after a little, he feels, while thus yearning toward them in his difficulty, as if he were asking an army of glorious veterans to help him to arrest a peddler who has given him the wrong change. (p. 3)[14]

James is overwhelmed by history and this informs his view of a building as the locus of history. He notes that 'I would rather, I think, have too little architecture than too much – when there's a danger of its interfering with my measure of the truth' (p. 5). The problem of balance is, metaphorically speaking, the problem of how to be accommodated within history. As his reference to Venice implies, it is not his history that he observes and these subtle, but nevertheless powerful, feelings of alienation become translated into a more generalised sense of Italy.[15] James emphasises, as he would do in *The Turn of the Screw*, the significance of the observer with their possible partial vision. The conceit of the building thus becomes a conceit for the vision of the artist because 'The house of fiction has [. . .] not one window, but a million – a number of possible windows not to be reckoned, rather; every one of which has been pierced, or is still pierceable, in its vast front, by the need of the individual vision and by the pressure of the individual will' (p. 8).

James then develops this conceit in specific terms which elaborate on the role of the artist: 'The spreading field, the human scene, is the "choice of subject"; the pierced aperture, either broad or balconied or slit-like and low-browed, is the "literary form"; but they are, singly or together, as nothing without the posted presence of the watcher – without, in other words, the consciousness of the artist' (p. 8). James proceeds to refer to Isabel Archer as an 'apparition' that could only be made sense of if one were 'to write the history of the growth of one's imagination' (p. 9). Ghostly figures and watchers are thus imaginative constructs that inhabit buildings and historical contexts which do not quite belong to them – so turning them into doubly ghostly figures. James notes that Isabel is an alienated figure who is not naturally at home even within the structure of the novel, which is again likened to a building. The novel 'came to be a square and spacious house – or at least seemed so to me in this going over it again; but, such as it is, it had to be put up round my young woman while she stood there in perfect isolation' (p. 10). She comes to inhabit 'a literary monument' which entombs her in its 'fine embossed vaults' (p. 13). The house of fiction refutes the history of Venice even whilst through the figure of Isabel the novel relocates anxieties about alienation which are conditioned by an exclusion from history.

The opening lines of *The Portrait of a Lady* refer to Gardencourt, 'an old country house' (p. 19) whose history, from Edward VI to the present, appears to animate the house with its 'magisterial physiognomy' (p. 21). The descriptions of the house's history replicate the types of history that James dwells on in *English Hours* (1905). However, the current owner, Touchett, is introduced as 'a shrewd American banker, who had bought it originally because [. . .] it was offered at a great bargain' (p. 20). History is effectively bought but cannot be intellectually owned.

Instead it exists as a form of dead history from which the Touchetts are inevitably estranged. As the elderly Mr Touchett notes of his time in England, he had been 'assimilated yet unconverted' (p. 55), although his Harvard and Oxford educated son, Ralph, 'became at last English enough' (p. 55). The themes of the novel relating to American and English (or more broadly, European) relations are familiar from James's other writings. However, the new emphasis on art, buildings, and history incorporates within it a language of spectrality which suggests the continuing presence of alienation. For Isabel the possibility that Gardencourt might be haunted grants it a type of local colour. She asks Ralph if there is a ghost; however he indicates that if there is one it is not a romantic vision because it is conjured by suffering: 'I might show it to you, but you'd never see it. The privilege isn't given to every one; it's not enviable. It has never been seen by a young, happy, innocent person like you. You must have suffered first, have suffered greatly, have gained some miserable knowledge' (p. 65). At the end of the novel her sight of Ralph's ghost indicates, as Lustig has noted, that she has indeed suffered.[16]

To see the ghost, however, superficially appears to suggest a perception which is beyond the material, and financially focused, world of so many of the characters in the novel. Nevertheless, the novel links these issues at a more sophisticated level. Ralph's ghost might be seen by Isabel but there is also an emphasis on Mrs Touchett's view that Ralph 'had left all the commodities of life behind' (p. 628) as the novel focuses on the details of the deposition of his will. The appearance of Ralph's ghost and the details of his 'commodities' are given a proximity that suggests a relationship between the two and this is an issue developed elsewhere in the novel.

In the preface James argues that the writer should write as their sense of the novel's structure dictates and that any pleasure that the reader might gain should be considered 'as a gratuity "thrown in," a mere miraculous windfall' (p. 15) or an 'occasional charming "tip"' (p. 15). James thus elaborates a language of money that is associated with the idea of the novel's possible positive reception. Money, of course, is a central theme of the novel. Money is used to buy freedom for Isabel, but she loses this freedom on her marriage to Gilbert Osmond, who marries her *for* her money. However, there is a sustained focus on the issue of money which is also related to art and emotion. Isabel, after Gilbert's protestation of love, responds with feelings of dread:

> What made her dread great was precisely the force which, as it would seem, ought to have banished all dread – the sense of something within herself, deep down, that she supposed to be inspired and trustful passion. It was there like a large sum in a bank – which there was a terror in having to spend. If she touched it, it would all come out. (p. 336)

For Peggy McCormack, 'What could be described here as Isabel's frigidity may better be understood as her unconscious apprehension (feminine intuition?) of virginity as a unique commodity'.[17] However, although there are a series of financial transactions in the novel it is also clear that metaphors of money control how characters feel about each other. James appears to be arguing the case, as Dickens does in *A Christmas Carol* (1843), that in a money-based society consciousness becomes shaped as if it were like money.

These issues are subsequently related to art, as when Gilbert, for example, is described as 'seated at the table near the window with a folio volume before him, propped against a pile of books. The volume was open at a page of small coloured plates, and Isabel presently saw that he had been copying from it the drawing of an antique coin' (p. 569). Gilbert's obsession with money is registered here but it is also significant that the focus is on the representation of a representation of a coin. McCormack has noted that Gilbert's counterfeit aristocratic demeanour can be accounted for in Baudrillardian terms as part of a Renaissance discourse of social and economic competition which became transferred to signifying practices, so rendering signs ambivalent and open to interpretation.[18] Gilbert is thus unreal to the degree that he acts the role of an aristocrat and this unreality marks him out as especially spectral. As the painting of the coin is a representation of history so Gilbert represents a history which does not belong to him. It is an impulse which Jerrold E. Hogle sees as central to understanding how the Gothic represents history. Hogle has noted that Walpole's *The Castle of Otranto* (1764) masquerades as a medieval narrative written by a Renaissance priest. The whole idea of faking history subsequently appears through characters in the novel who 'are not just counterfeits but ghosts of counterfeits' as none of them properly belongs to the historical narratives with which they are ostensibly associated because the novel represents a mid-eighteenth-century, Whig, view of history.[19] Hogle goes on to summarise that 'the Gothic is inherently connected to an exploitation of the emptied-out past to symbolise and disguise present concerns' (p. 16). Gilbert's fabricated character, one which associates him with a history to which he does not belong, emphasises this and it makes him a ghostlike figure. The counterfeit self constructed on money that he has falsely acquired (because he does not really love Isabel) also suggests that money itself has a spectral, or counterfeit, dimension.

Money and its associations with alienation are implied in *The Portrait of a Lady* when Henrietta Stackpole notes of Ralph to Isabel that ' "There's a great demand just now for the alienated American, and your cousin's a beautiful specimen" ' (p. 105). Later Madame Merle complains to Isabel that ' "If we're not good Americans we're certainly poor Europeans; we've no natural place here. We're mere parasites, crawling over the surface; we haven't our feet in the soil" ' (p. 217). Issues about place, history, money, and counterfeiting had earlier been elaborated by James in 'The Ghostly Rental'. They are given a powerful reworking in *The Turn of the Screw*.

The Turn of the Screw: house, nation, and writing

Before discussing issues about history and place it is important to acknowledge that James's novella has, as Shoshana Felman has noted, posed particular demands on readers, who find themselves subtly occupying the positions of some of the key characters in the text. For Felman:

> The reader [. . .] can choose either to *believe* the governess, and thus to behave like Mrs. Grose, or *not to believe the governess*, and thus to behave precisely *like the governess*. Since it is the governess who, within the text, plays the role of the suspicious reader, occupies the place of the interpreter, to suspect that place and that position is, thereby, to take it.[20]

In that regard it becomes problematic to locate a position outside of the text where a detached critical view of it can be elaborated. At one level it seems as though the issue of how to read the text supplants the idea of textual production. Writing the text and reading the text thus appear to be assigned to mutually exclusive realms.

However, James's prefaces provide some insight into how the text (and the governess) can be approached. The idea of an outside of the text was clearly an issue that James was working to exclude: 'The thing had for me the immense merit of allowing the imagination absolute freedom of hand, of inviting it to act on a perfectly clear field, with no "outside" control involved, no pattern of the usual or the true or the terrible "pleasant" [. . .] to consort with' (p. 4). As Edel has noted, James routes this through the psychology of the governess so that it becomes difficult to move the events beyond her comprehension of them. However, this does not mean that the tale argues that ghosts are the products of a solipsistic imagination; rather it is the question of the reality that they threaten to compromise which intrigues James. He registers an ambition to write within a fairytale format but one which springs from 'a conscious and cultivated credulity' (p. 4), in which events are seemingly innocently observed rather than neurotically generated. James outlined this view of the governess in what has become a well-known letter to H.G. Wells:

> The grotesque business I had to make her picture and the childish psychology I had to make her trace and present, were, for me at least, a very difficult job, in which absolute lucidity and logic, a singleness of effect, were imperative. Therefore I had to rule out subjective complications of her own – play of tone etc.; and keep her impersonal save for the most obvious and indispensable little note of neatness, firmness and courage – without which she wouldn't have had her data.[21]

This passage is frequently quoted by critics intent on asserting the objective presence of the ghosts. However, it is clear that James intended the governess to be perceived as an impersonal conduit for a certain kind of psychic knowledge. Critics such as Martha Banta and Peter G. Beidler have explored possible connections between the governess and mediumship despite James's explicit rejection of 'the mere modern "psychical" case, washed clean of all queerness' (p. 3).[22] However, what James develops in the preface, and touches on in his letter to Wells, relates to knowledge and how it is produced and for whom. Whilst Felman emphasises the importance of interpretation, James emphasises the significance of knowing. How to generate meaning lies at the heart of both approaches but James's acknowledgement that this is all a construct ('conscious and cultivated') points towards the process of writing, which is closely related, as Lustig has noted, to the idea of the spectral.[23] James also acknowledges this in the preface when he states, 'Otherwise expressed, the study is of a conceived "tone", the tone of suspected and felt trouble, of an inordinate and incalculable sort – the tone of tragic, yet exquisite, mystification' (pp. 5–6). How to move beyond this mystique and read the spectre is what the tale both invites and challenges. However, one possible solution is associated with the notion of place.

Whilst the drama of the spectral Quint and Miss Jessel is explicitly ghostly, the building of Bly which stages their drama (or registers its ghostly return) also functions as an implicitly spectral form. James's *English Hours* includes a description of a visit to Haddon Hall in the Wye Valley in the Derbyshire Peak District which was originally published in 1872 (and reprinted in 1875 and 1883). Edel identifies this as clearly the model for Bly.[24] James describes how:

> The twilight deepened, the ragged battlements and the low broad oriels glanced duskily from the foliage, the rooks wheeled and clamoured in the glowing sky; and if there had been a ghost on the premises I certainly ought to have seen it. In fact I did see it, as we see ghosts nowadays. I felt the incommunicable spirit of the essence of the scene with the last, the right intensity. The old life, the old manners, the old figures seemed present again.[25]

In *The Turn of the Screw* the governess's first view of Quint is on a tower but the description, revealingly, focuses not on the spectral Quint but on the building. The tower is one of a pair: 'They flanked opposite ends of the house and were probably architectural absurdities, redeemed in a measure indeed by not being wholly disengaged nor of a height too pretentious, dating, in their gingerbread antiquity, from a romantic revival that was already past'.[26] In particular the governess is impressed 'by the grandeur of their actual battlements' (p. 136) and the history that is implied by them.

Before seeing Quint she anticipates that 'Someone would appear [. . .] at the turn of the path and would stand before me and smile and approve' (p. 135), although this clearly does not conjure the subsequently sinister image of Quint on the tower. Indeed there is an emphasis on a disjunction between the imaginary and the real which is attributed to Bly: 'Wasn't it just a story-book over which I had fallen a-doze and a-dream? No; it was a big ugly antique but convenient house, embodying a few features of a building still older, half-displaced and half utilised' (p. 127). The governess's imagination veers between fancy and fact in a way which corresponds to James's idea of how 'we see ghosts nowadays', in which the historical essence of the place becomes evoked through a prevailing mood. That James wanted to position the governess as just this kind of historian is indicated by a number of changes, noted by Edel, that he made to the text when it was published in a single volume (the narrative having earlier been serialised in weekly instalments in

Collier's magazine from 27 January to 16 April 1898).[27] Edel comments that 'per-ceived' has in the main be altered to 'felt', and that there are other instances where 'I now recollect . . .' has become 'I now feel . . .', and where 'Mrs. Grose appeared to me' has been changed to 'Mrs. Grose affected me' (Edel, p. 434). All of this emphasises that the world is experienced through the governess's largely uncon-scious feeling for it. However, it is the notion of place which is significant. Her view of the towers suggests that she cannot help but see the place as partially unreal because despite earlier registering it as 'ugly' and 'antique' she refers to it as a fairy-tale 'gingerbread' house. It is not quite real as it becomes spectrally freighted with possibilities that suggest that the house itself is subject to violation. When she returns to the main part of the house the governess ponders whether 'We had been, collectively, subject to an intrusion; some unscrupulous traveller, curious in old houses, had made his way in unobserved' (p. 139). Ownership over the house is key to understanding James's view of how British history is represented through such stately homes. For Bly to be inhabited by the dead (Quint and Jessel) is to effectively turn the place into a morgue which cannot be revivified by the governess's evocative use of the fairytale.

James in *English Hours* pursues a similar line in his account of Haddon Hall. He makes references to a comic Shakespearian spirit which seems to inhabit the place, but the overall mood is one of despondency and death: 'It is very dead, of a fine June morning, the genius of Haddon Hall; and the silent courts and cham-bers, with their hues of ashen grey and faded brown, seem as time-bleached as the dry bones of any mouldering mortality' (p. 52). To disturb the house is thus to awaken the dead and this is implied by the governess when she pursues Miles in the grounds one evening and observes, 'I had gone down to bring him in; choos-ing then, at the window, with a concentrated need of not alarming the house' (p. 177). Ambiguity about the house as an entity that should not be disturbed had been suggested earlier, in an exchange between the governess and Mrs. Grose concerning whether the governess intended going to church:

'Oh I'm not fit for church!'
'Won't it do you good?'
'It won't do *them* – !' I nodded at the house. (p. 145)

This confuses Mrs. Grose, who replies, 'The children?' (p. 145). At one level this '*them*' could refer to Quint and Jessel (or possibly Miles and Flora), but it is significant that it is the house which is gestured towards because ownership over it anchors a coherent sense of identity. Quint had been regarded as a possibly 'unscrupulous traveller', an invasive presence, but in a later encounter with Jessel the governess remarks, 'I had the extraordinary chill of a feeling that it was I who was the intruder' (p. 196). The ghosts of the house, Quint and Jessel, should be seen as a product of it: imaginatively constructed entities who hover around it and animate its secret past.

It is noteworthy that throughout *The Turn of the Screw* the 'ghosts' of Quint and Jessel are associated with an artificiality that suggests a reworking of the theme of counterfeiting in 'The Ghostly Rental' and *The Portrait of a Lady*. From the start Douglas's narrative operates as a fireside ghost story with the narrator recounting how he prepares to deliver the story 'with quiet art' (p. 116). How it is told as a construction is thus central to the tale. The governess's manuscript ' "in faded old ink and in the most beautiful hand" ' (p. 117) emphasises the materiality of the text's production. The governess first sees Flora as 'a rosy sprite' in 'a castle of romance' (p. 127). Whilst this implies her tendency to romantically project it also establishes a relationship between fictionality and the spectral that is later linked to Quint when she describes him to Mrs. Grose as ' "looking like an actor" ' (p. 146). The text refers to acting, music, art, and writing and these help to develop a narrative relating to artistic production which runs implicitly throughout the text. The governess notes in her first encounter with Quint that 'The gold was still in the sky, the clearness in the air, and the man who looked at me over the battlements was as definite as a picture in a frame' (p. 136). The ghost is as real as a representation and this shapes the imagination of the governess, who refers to Bly as a possible 'Udolpho' (p. 138) even whilst her language is shaped by the artificial in order to embrace the unreal. After her first sight of Quint she returns to Bly and recollects meeting Mrs. Grose in the hall: 'This picture comes back to me in the general train – the impression, as I received it on my return, of the wide white panelled space, bright in the lamplight and with its portraits and red carpet' (p. 138). The memory (a 'picture') is merged with the gallery and its portraits. Puns or locutions take on physical forms, which because they are representations (paintings) are inherently unreal. There is therefore a process in which experience is repeatedly accommodated to the artificial. Later the governess challenges Mrs. Grose when she claims that perhaps she concocted the ghosts, a view which the governess refutes by relating how she had produced 'a picture disclosing, to the last detail, their special marks – a portrait on the exhibition of which she had instantly recognised and named them' (pp. 160–1). Their very 'reality' is thus dependent upon a notion of the artistic, which is why Mrs. Grose had accused her of having ' "made it up" ' (p. 160) in the first place.

Haddon Hall might have been the model for Bly, as critics such as Edel have pointed out, but it is also the case that James's discussion of Warwick Castle, which immediately follows his account of Haddon Hall in *English Hours*, can be discerned in Bly. Warwick too has two towers, 'a Caesar's tower and a Guy's tower' (p. 55), and has historical associations. Significantly, James dwells on the Vandycks that he finds in the castle. One is 'from the Briganole palace at Genoa; a beautiful matron in black, with her son and heir [. . .] as I looked at her I thought of her mighty change of circumstance. Here she sits in the mild light of mid-most England: there you could almost fancy her blinking in the great glare sent up from the Mediterranean' (p. 56). The governess, recounting a sighting of Jessel to Mrs. Grose, describes ' "a figure of quite unmistakable horror and evil: a woman in black, pale and dreadful" ' (p. 156). This emotional response relocates James's view of the portrait of the exiled women in *English Hours*, where he notes the presence of an 'Intensity for intensity – intensity of situation constituted – I hardly know which to choose' (p. 56). This confused position represents in projected form James's own sense of exile and alienation.

Art in *English Hours* is closely related to notions of place, which are in turn associated with the history that they spectrally evoke. Art in James takes on the form of a projected entity which, like the ghosts of Quint and Jessel, informs us about the history, or the 'spirit', of the place. James thus plots a relationship between the imagination (ghosts, art, writing) and the historical contexts which give rise to it. Houses are places which play a role in shaping the imagination because for James they are the source of historical and artistic inspiration.

Issues about place, the role of the romance, and buildings (especially hotels) were reworked by James through a language of spectrality in *The American Scene*.

The American Scene: hotels and money

The American Scene recounts James's return to America after an absence of twenty-one years. If his earlier ghostly narratives suggest an alienation from European mores, his return suggests feelings of alienation from America. For James this new America, especially in the instance of New York, is driven by economic imperatives that have generated strict social codes and manners that have stifled free expression. New York is thus too prosaic as he discovers a society intent on 'reaching out into the apparent void for [. . .] amenities'.[28] This 'void' constantly renews itself so that nothing of permanence can be established: 'One was in [the] presence, every-where, of the refusal to consent to history' (p. 19). The danger is that all one encounters is an 'exquisite emptiness' (p. 30) so that the problem is how to find a language which can animate a place which appears to be inherently spectral.

The American Scene employs spectrality in two ways. One refers to historical or 'ghostly echoes' (p. 42), which James attempts to bring back to life. The other is related to how money depersonalises because it turns the financially obsessed into spectres (although this is not, of course, to argue that James was advocating socialism). The latter model of spectrality is one which enables James, at least poten-tially, to evoke the romance as the most appropriate means of representing, and indeed filling, this apparent 'void'. James recounts that 'every fact was convertible into a fancy' (p. 52), and in keeping with his earlier epistemological strategies it is a building which comes to represent how 'fancy' articulates a wider reality.

James's description of the Waldorf Astoria in New York attempts to capture the essence of America because 'one is verily tempted to ask if the hotel-spirit may not just *be* the American spirit most seeking and most finding itself' (p. 79, italics in original). What is new in James's text is a language of sexuality. For example, he glosses John Donne's 'Elergy XX: To His Mistress Going to Bed' (published in 1656) when he says that he is pursuing 'what may be behind, what beneath, what within' (p. 37).[29] This sexualisation of a language of exploration is matched by a sense of being in the presence of 'wanton provocation' (p. 83) on the streets of New York. He also notes this ambient presence in the hotel, where there is 'adventure in the florid sense of the word, the sense in which it remains a euphemism' for an 'immense promiscuity' (p. 79). James states that this 'American spirit' inhabits the hotel and represents this 'promiscuity' in human form:

> It sat there, it walked and talked, and ate and drank, and listened and danced to music, and otherwise revelled and roamed, and bought and sold, and came and went there, all on its own splendid terms and with an encompassing material splendour, a wealth and variety of constituted picture and background, that might well feed it with the finest illusions about itself. (p. 79)

James thus suggests that people have prostituted themselves in the pursuit of wealth. The problem is that this creates 'illusions', like Gilbert's aristocratic mores in *The Portrait of a Lady*, which are taken for realities. All one finds in these chic 'halls and saloons' is 'art and history, in masquerading dress' (p. 80). People become depersonalised in this desire for 'social sameness' (p. 80), not only because they have become a social 'type' but because in doing so they have become estranged from art and history.

He returns to the concept of the hotel in his account of Florida, where he refers to the residents of the hotel Poinciana as 'these idols and monsters of the market' (p. 332). A stay at another hotel, the Ponce de Leon, elicits a slightly different response as the hotel incorporates a Spanish style which is in keeping with the earlier Spanish occupation of the area, although even traces of that history are merely 'the ghost of a ghost' (p. 338). James sees hotels as having considerable cultural significance because they 'stand for so much more' (p. 323) than what they seem to represent. For James they signify the presence of a deracinated, dehistoricised, money-obsessed, spectral America. He therefore refers to 'The hotel-spirit' as 'an omniscient genius' (p. 323) which organises American life because 'The hotel was leading [. . .] not following – imposing the standard, not submitting to it' (p. 327); as it forms a version of the good life, a type of 'heaven' which the 'the Blest' may eventually enter 'or perhaps actually retire' to (p. 329).

The battle over the romance seems, ultimately, to have been lost in America because it requires an act of will by the analyst to create meaning (which echoes the role of the governess in *The Turn of the Screw*). James claims that the 'observer has early to perceive [. . .] that there will be little for him in the American scene unless he be ready, anywhere, everywhere, to read "into" it as much as he reads out' (p. 215). James searches for a pure, literary, language which exists beyond the sexualised '*grope* of money' (p. 123, italics in original). However, the problem is that the analyst can find themselves seduced by money, as when James notes that 'The observer, like a fond investor, must spend on it [America], boldly, ingeniously, to make it pay' (p. 274). In the end James cannot therefore find, like the governess in *The Turn of the Screw*, a place from which to make an objective evaluation. All he is left with is the 'void' created by money and the spectral presences of the past, as when he finds 'Charles Street ghosts' in Boston (p. 181). However, James does seek out the possibility of the romance on a journey to Salem to revisit Hawthorne's house.

In *Hawthorne* James had quoted approvingly a passage from Hawthorne's Note-Books of 1840, where Hawthorne states that 'Here I sit in my old accustomed chamber [. . .] This claims to be called a haunted chamber, for thousands upon thousands of visions have appeared to me in it' (p. 53).[30] In *Hawthorne* place becomes romantic because of its oblique attachment to the real world. James describes Salem as 'a provincial, rural community; it had few perceptible points of contact with what is called the world' (p. 1). However, during his visit to Salem in 1904–5 he claims that if there is romance here then it is a sanitised version: 'It's as if the old witches had been suffered to live again, penally, as public housemaids' (p. 199). The houses were open to the public but James avoids them, 'fearing nothing so much as reconstituted antiquity' (p. 199), which would compromise his vestigial romantic vision of the place.

The Salem that James recounts in *The American Scene* is quite different to the one described in *Hawthorne* as it is fringed by a 'large untidy industrial quarter' (p. 200). James separates the two worlds through an act of imaginative revisioning: 'I took the neighbourhood, at all events, for the small original Hawthornesque world, keeping the other, the smoky modernism, at a distance' (p. 200). This echoes his earlier view of the new America 'as a huge Rappacini-garden, rank with each variety of the poison-plant of the money-passion' (p. 46).[31] However, Salem proves to be more prosaic and on being directed to a house that is claimed as the model for the House of Seven Gables he notes a 'shapeless object by the waterside' (p. 201). Ultimately for James, romance, at least of the Hawthornian kind, no longer seems to exist. His view of the house echoes his critique of *The Blithedale Romance* (1852) in *Hawthorne* when he claims that 'we get too much out of reality, and cease to feel beneath our feet the firm ground of an appeal to our own vision of the world, our observation' (p. 137). This sense of intellectual and imaginative alienation is developed in implicit nationalistic terms in *The American Scene*, as James repeatedly employs a language of spectrality which emphasises his feelings of estrangement. These ideas were given explicit treatment in his ghost story 'The Jolly Corner' which was published shortly after *The American Scene*, and was informed by it.

' "Oh ghosts – of course the place must swarm with them! I should be ashamed of it if it didn't" ' – 'The Jolly Corner'[32]

In *The American Scene* James recounts his return to a now demolished house in Boston where he had once lived for two years: 'I found but a gaping void, the

brutal effacement, at a stroke, of every related object, of the whole precious past';
the house 'had been levelled and the space to the corner cleared' (p. 170). James
relates this as a personal tragedy in which 'It was as if the bottom had fallen out
of one's own biography, and one plunged backward into space without meeting
anything' (p. 170). In 'The Jolly Corner' the American protagonist, Spencer
Brydon, also goes back into the past and encounters a version of himself as he would
have been had he stayed in America, rather than emigrated to Europe. Like James,
Spencer's return to America is 'strangely belated', as he left New York thirty-three
years before. His life in Europe, however, has been supported by American money
as the rent on two properties has paid for his stay. Like James, he too encounters
'the monstrous' (p. 307) in this new America. However, the tale emphasises his
connection to money, even if he seemingly finds such a connection distasteful.
Spencer stays in one of his empty properties and it is whilst there that, like the
governess who anticipates her meeting with Quint, he intimates a ghostly presence
before confronting his alter ego. He imagines meeting 'some strange figure, some
unexpected occupant, at a turn of the dim passages of an empty house. The quaint
analogy quite hauntingly remained with him' (p. 309). The house, however, also
retains a family history when he notes 'the old silver-plated knobs of the several
mahogany doors, which suggested the pressure of the palms of the dead' (p. 312),
including 'the impalpable ashes of his long-extinct youth, afloat in the air like micro-
scopic motes' (p. 312).

He tells his friend Alice Staverton that he wonders whether, if he had stayed,
he too would have become ' "one of these types" ' whose lives are centred around
money: ' "It isn't that I admire them so much – the question of any charm in them,
or of any charm, beyond that of the rank money-passion, exerted by their conditions *for* them, has nothing to do with the matter: it's only a question of what
fantastic, yet perfectly possible, development of my own nature I mayn't have missed" '
(p. 314, italics in original).

Typically in James ownership of a house represents control over history. In 'The
Jolly Corner' this is represented as a form of social and economic control as
Spencer 'let himself in and let himself out with the assurance of calm proprietor-
ship' (p. 316). However, in entering into a new social world, one which is focused
through materialism, he begins to subtly develop a social identity which is at odds
with his self-perception: 'He was a dim social success – and all with people who
had truly not an idea of him' (p. 317). However, the context in which this takes
place is represented as superficial and peculiarly abstract: 'It was all mere surface
sound, this murmur of their welcome, this popping of their corks' (p. 317). His
response to them is just as unreal: 'his gestures of response were [. . .] extravagant
shadows' (p. 317). He cannot help but feel that the people he now associates with
are aspects of a 'ghostly life' although one which is not 'really sinister' (p. 318).
However, it is the psychological and emotional pressures of this world which
conjure into being an alternative version of him, one which is closely associated
with money: 'He knew what he meant and what he wanted; it was clear as the figure

on a cheque presented in demand for cash. His *alter ego* "walked" – that was the note of his image of him, while his image of his motive for his own odd pastime was the desire to waylay him and meet him' (p. 318, italics in original).

The self becomes split, and depending upon the context in which it is seen it could either 'be in peril of fear' or 'actively inspire that fear' (p. 321). For Lustig the house incorporates two spectral versions of Spencer, one of whom is a figure of 'the artist' who shuts themself away in the upper rooms of the house.[33] The artist is thus secluded from the world whereas the other spectre, who represents the possibility of worldly, wealthy success, lacks this passivity and poses a threat to Spencer. Spencer encounters 'Rigid and conscious, spectral yet human, a man of his own substance and stature waited there to measure himself with his power to dismay' (p. 329). The figure is attired in all the accoutrements of social and economic success. Spencer notes 'His planted stillness, his vivid truth, his grizzled bent head and white masking hands, his queer actuality of evening-dress, of dangling double eyeglass, of gleaming silk lappet and white linen, of pearl button and gold watchguard and polished shoe' (p. 329). He recounts that 'He had been "sold"' (p. 330) as this 'presence, the horror within him a horror' (p. 330) advances to meet him 'as for aggression' (p. 330). Spencer faints as this 'stranger' who is 'evil, odious, blatant, vulgar' walks towards him. His observation that the figure 'fitted his at *no* point' only invests that figure with an 'alternative' sense of the 'monstrous' (p. 330, italics in original).

When he regains consciousness Spencer seeks solace in the idea that the figure was not really him, but Alice points out that ' "Isn't the whole point that you'd have been different?" ' (p. 333). For Spencer the horror is that the being that he could have become represents the social abstraction that James had witnessed in *The American Scene*. The sense of having become a social type, or having been generalised as such, is for James to have become depersonalised and therefore an aspect of the urban 'void'. Spencer notes of the houses in New York that they constitute 'Great builded voids, great crowded stillnesses [which] put on, often in the heart of cities, for the small hours, a sort of sinister mask, and it was of this large collective negation that Brydon presently became conscious' (p. 326). Houses, again, articulate identities and also, as here, they suggest a threat to identity. It is Spencer's ambivalence about his house which indicates a growing awareness of the need for a renunciation of the material world: 'He tried to think of something noble, as that his property was really grand, a splendid possession; but this nobleness took the form too of the clear delight with which he was finally to sacrifice it' (pp. 327–8).

'The Jolly Corner' reworks the anxieties of *The American Scene* and makes explicit use of a language of spectrality. Spencer's problem is the same as that confronted by James in *The American Scene* because it centres on finding an identifiable home. The alienation that is implicit to *The Turn of the Screw*, which reconstructs James's position as a national outsider in *English Hours*, is reworked for an American context, one which is alienating for the now anglicised James. What seems to disconcert him is the loss of romance and the erasure of the past. How one might address the romance in relation to the past, and articulate such links through images of the ghostly, is one of the main themes of *The Sense of the Past*.

Historical ghosts

Throughout, what unites an otherwise disparate range of James's texts is a fascination with place and history. How to account for and interpret the pressure of the past is a theme touched upon in many of James's ghost stories. In 'Owen Wingrave' (1892) the notion of family duty is addressed; family duties depersonalise the subject by making them conform to specific familial expectations. In 'Sir Edmund Orme' (1891) a ghost monitors the behaviour of a lover who has jilted him and seeks to influence the present. In 'The Romance of Certain Old Clothes' a ghost has her revenge on a sister who tries to replace her. The past is thus inherently spectral in James. It is an issue which is given explicit treatment in *The Sense of the Past*.

The novel centres on the American Ralph Pendrel, who inherits some property from a branch of his family in London. Ralph is in love with a widow, Aurora Coyne, and believes that he might win her over if he displays a spirit of adventure by going to London to claim the property. The house appears to be haunted and Ralph finds himself transported back to 1820 and involved with the Midmores, who for financial reasons are eager for Ralph to marry into their family. Meanwhile the version of Ralph that properly belongs to 1820 lives in 1910 and has thus effectively exchanged places with him.

The complex time-travelling in the novel plays out a number of issues relating to history and the spectral. The opening scenes are centred on Ralph and Aurora. Initially Aurora attempts to dissuade Ralph from going to Europe, but Ralph wants to see the history that he anticipates finding there. Aurora sees his ' "historic passion" ' as indicating that ' "The sense of the past *is* your sense" ' and predicts that Ralph will merely encounter some projected version of himself, as indeed he does.[34] However, she also suggests that this might lead to a process of self-discovery: ' "Isn't an old property for you the very finger of fortune, the very 'lead' of providence? Profit for heaven's sake by your old property. It will open your eyes" ' (p. 33).

Ralph is the author of 'An Essay in Aid of the Reading of History', which had been read by the relative who bequeathed him the house, as an interesting historical relic. Ralph does not consider the acquisition, as Spencer does in 'The Jolly Corner', in terms of financial gain: 'The material advantage might be uncertain; but it was blessedly not for the economic question, it was for the historic, the aesthetic, fairly in fact for the cryptic, that he cared' (p. 43). What is important to Ralph is how one can interpret, or 'read', history. He has a semi-professional competence in this which focalises the tendencies that have hitherto been distributed across the numerous 'watchers' in James's ghost stories. However, as Aurora observed, Ralph's passionate investment in history also suggests the presence of a psychological need: 'If his idea in fine was to recover the lost moment, to feel the stopped pulse, it was to do so as experience, in order to be again consciously the creature that *had* been, to breathe as he had breathed and feel the pressure that he had felt' (p. 48, italics in original).

As James states in his prefaces, the question is how one can imaginatively reconstruct this process. Ralph also sees that 'art was capable of an energy to this end' (p. 48) as it is produced by 'the insistent ardour of the artist' (p. 48), a passion that can bring the past to life. However, the process of historical recovery is potentially dangerous: 'Recovering the lost was at all events [. . .] much like entering the enemy's lines to get back one's dead for burial' (p. 49). In part this is because Ralph understands that his exploration of English history represents an incursion into a history which, nationally speaking, does not properly belong to him. However, he believes that he can infiltrate such enemy lines because 'It was for the old ghosts to take him for one of themselves' (p. 50). The problem confronted by Ralph is one of historical methodology.

Ralph is described as an innocent (like the governess) although one with an acute sense of interpretation. However, 'Experience had lagged with him behind interpretation, and the worst that could have been said was that his gift for the latter might do well to pause awhile till an increase of the former could catch up' (p. 53). The development of Ralph as an historian is therefore paralleled by his development as a person. His sense of the past is determined by his sense of who he is.

The house bequeathed to Ralph was built around 1710. On awaking one morning he feels a presence in the house. He encounters a figure who seems to have stepped out of one of the portraits (James's notes to the novel acknowledge a debt to Walpole's *The Castle of Otranto*) and whom he perceives as an earlier version of himself. This encounter is crucial for Ralph, who senses that 'He was staring at the answer to the riddle that had been his obsession' (p. 87) – a view that neatly stands as a synopsis of James's historical enquiries. Ralph sees himself as isolated within history, within a painting which has come to life. However, this animation of the past and his links to it suggests to Ralph a possible historical continuity which can overcome feelings of alienation.

The next day, on a visit to the American ambassador, Ralph proudly tells him, ' "I'm somebody else" ' (p. 97). Later he confidently asserts, ' "I'm still an American [. . .] and not a Briton" ' (p. 100) because what he shares with the spectre is a feeling of being ' "but freshly disembarked" ' (p. 100). The meeting with the ambassador is important because, paradoxically, it enables a context in which Ralph can claim a coherent sense of identity, one which can acknowledge all of the psychological and historical complexity that has gone into its making. At one level this is also explained in terms of the family history which indicates a connection between America and England. One branch of the family had returned to England during the American Revolution, 'restoring themselves to England for a ten years' stay and not a little indebted under the stress to the countenance and even the charity of their English kindred' (p. 126). The family history thus reflects wider historical events and in the novel this is associated with the possibility of effective historical agency.

Ralph, now living in the 1820s, has to settle into a life which had been inhabited by his alter ego. The novel suggests that this past has a reality for Ralph so that what initially appears as 'an apparition' (p. 144) takes on a real historical presence. He notes of Mrs Midmore that 'she represented by the aid of dress the absolute value and use of presence as presence' (p. 145). This is not a sign or a symbol; it represents the material reality of the situation in which signs represent what they signify. Ralph, who is in love with Aurora, then discovers that it is intended that he will marry one of Mrs Midmore's daughters. However, Ralph's cautious approach to the Midmores brings back into focus a theme of money which, as we have seen, had conditioned earlier representations of the ghostly. Molly Midmore says to him, ' "You don't suspect us, I hope, of hugging you to rifle your pockets!" ' (p. 203). However, Ralph sees money as power and in a later encounter with her brother, Perry, he is happy to give him some money. Ralph plays with coins in his pocket: 'The guineas, or whatever they were, literally chinked to his ear, and he saw, the next thing, that they chinked to his companion's as well – which circumstance somehow made them on the instant a perfect mine of wealth' (p. 275).

Money is not turned into symbol as it in *The Portrait of a Lady*, however it does relate to a certain mode of characterisation. The tellingly named Aurora Coyne captures in her surname what Ralph sees as precious. The past takes on a reality for Ralph even as money becomes his means of exercising authority within it. His passion for history is in some way challenged by his passion for Aurora (as an associated passion for the present), but at a narrative level a notion of valuable coins/ Coyne develops a link between them. How James might have elaborated these issues is suggested in his working notes on what is an unfinished novel.

In the notes James explicitly addressed a number of issues about places and buildings which, as we have seen, characterise James's construction of history. He indicates that Ralph, the self-conscious historian, '*knows* now perfectly that on opening the door of the house with his latchkey he lets himself into the Past' (p. 292, italics in original). James describes looking for a 'kind of quasi-Turn-of-Screw effect' (p. 294), one in which the principal protagonist has to interpret the circumstances in which they find themself. The Gothic element that James intended to pursue was the idea that Ralph would have a much worse time in the past than his alter ego is having in the present. Ralph has therefore lost out in the trade and, like the horror experienced by Spencer in 'The Jolly Corner' on seeing his alter ego, feels that he has been ' "sold," horribly sold' (p. 312). Ralph, the ideal historian, comes to inhabit a history which he lays claim to but it is at the price of his love for Aurora. Also, the purity of Ralph's quest is put into question: 'In plain terms mayn't one put it that he buys, pays for, in hard cash, the pursuance of his opportunity?' (p. 317). Again, it is money which for James tarnishes the ambitions of what otherwise appears to be an idealistic protagonist.

The Sense of the Past brings together in a necessarily incomplete form a number of narratives relating to history, nation, and money which underpinned James's earlier models of spectrality. By focalising these issues through an historian James emphasises that the reclamation of the past requires an act of self-negation even whilst, for Ralph, it appears to be about a new possible self-assertion. The conclusion that Ralph has been 'sold' suggests that he has merely bought a version of the past. As Quint and Jessel play out a tragedy from the past so Ralph becomes locked into a history, one which he too is ultimately unable to transcend. In many respects this captures the essential paradox of James's ghosts: that they articulate a history from which they cannot escape because they are condemned to repeat it, so that history cannot be reclaimed, but rather like James's houses, only provisionally inhabited.

Haunted houses in James become places which enable points of contact between history, art, and nation. Models of identity, especially national identity, are closely related to a sense of place and their associated images of spectrality indicate the liminality of his complexly formed Anglo-American identity. James's interest in Hawthorne's version of the romance as a mode which bridges the real and the unreal, relocates the issue of liminality to the realm of art. James effectively collapses, certainly in *The Sense of the Past*, the historian with the artist in order, like Hawthorne, to explore how the past can be brought back to life.

The texts discussed here are all concerned with attempting to find a new language in which to account for how the subject can be located in terms of place and the past, and such issues obliquely reflect an anxiety about national identity. How ghosts can be related to national contexts which foreground this liminality is the subject of the following chapter on Dickens, Le Fanu, and Kiplng.

Notes

1 R.W. Stallman, *The Houses that James Built, and Other Literary Essays* (East Lansing: Michigan State University, 1961) p. 7. Quoted by Carren Osna Kaston in 'Houses of Fiction in *What Maisie Knew*', *Criticism: A Quarterly for Literature and the Arts*, 18 (1976), 27–42, 27. Kaston also notes the link between the uncanny and childhood, 27. All subsequent references are to this edition and are given in the text.

2 This is an observation that I am indebted to Tessa Hadley for making in her commentary on an early draft of this chapter. For James's wider view on writing see 'The Art of Fiction' (1884) in Morris Shapira (ed.), *Henry James: Selected Literary Criticism* (Harmondsworth: Penguin, 1968) pp. 78–97.

3 Leon Edel, *The Ghostly Tales of Henry James*, ed. and introd. Leon Edel (New Brunswick: Rutgers University Press, 1948) p. xvii.

4 T.J. Lustig, *Henry James and the Ghostly* (Cambridge: Cambridge University Press, 1994) p. 2. All subsequent references are to this edition and are given in the text.

5 Henry James, 'The Ghostly Rental' in *Ghost Stories of Henry James*, introd. Martin Scofield (Ware, Herts: Wordsworth, 2001) pp. 38–66, p. 40. All subsequent references are to this edition and are given in the text.

6 Nathaniel Hawthorne, *The Scarlet Letter* (New York: Signet, [1850] 1959) p. 45.

7 Henry James, 'The Author's Preface to *The Turn of the Screw*', in *Ghost Stories of Henry James*, introd. Martin Scofield (Ware, Herts: Wordsworth, 2001) p. 5. All subsequent references are to this edition and are given in the text.

8 Henry James, *Hawthorne* (London: Macmillan, [1879] 1883) p. 63. All subsequent references are to this edition and are given in the text.

9 See Lustig, *Henry James and the Ghostly*, p. 72.

10 Quoted in Lustig, *Henry James and the Ghostly*, p. 50.

11 Pericles Lewis, '"The Reality of the Unseen": Shared Fictions and Religious Experience in the Ghost Stories of Henry James', *Arizona Quarterly*, 61.2 (2005), 33–66, 34. All subsequent references are to this edition and are given in the text.

12 Peter Buitenhuis, *The Grasping Imagination* (Toronto: University of Toronto Press, 1970) p. 233. The reference is made in Lustig, *Henry James and the Ghostly*, p. 223.

13 Henry James, *The Portrait of a Lady*, introd. and notes Nicola Bradbury (Oxford: Oxford University Press, [1907] 1998) p. 3. All subsequent references are to this edition and are given in the text.

14 See also Henry James's account of Venice in *Italian Hours*, ed. and introd. John Auchard (Harmondsworth: Penguin [1909] 1995) pp. 7–76.

15 I am indebted to Tessa Hadley for this observation.

16 Lustig, *Henry James and the Ghostly*, pp. 80–1.

17 Peggy McCormack, *The Rule of Money: Gender, Class, and Exchange Economics in the Fiction of Henry James* (Ann Arbor: UMI Research Press, 1990) p. 16.

18 McCormack's reference is to Jean Baudrillard's *The Mirror of Production*, trans. Mark Poster (New York: Telos Press, [1973] 1975) p. 61, quoted in McCormack, *The Rule of Money*, p. 24.

19 Jerrold E. Hogle in Jerrold E. Hogle (ed.), *The Cambridge Companion to Gothic Fiction* (Cambridge: Cambridge University Press, 2002) p. 15. All subsequent references are to this edition and are given in the text.

20 Shoshana Felman, 'Turning the Screw of Interpretation', *Yale French Studies*, 55/56 (1977), 94–207, 190. All subsequent references are to this edition and are given in the text.

21 Henry James, *Selected Letters*, ed. and introd. Leon Edel (London: Rupert Hart-Davis, 1956) p. 182.

22 Martha Banta, *Henry James and the Occult: The Great Extension* (Bloomington: Indiana University Press, 1972) and Peter G. Beidler, *Ghosts, Demons and Henry James 'Turn of the Screw' at the Turn of the Century* (Columbia: University of Missouri Press, 1989).

23 Lustig, *Henry James and the Ghostly*, p. 1.

24 See Edel (ed.), *The Ghostly Tales of Henry James*, p. 433. Lustig also notes the connection to Haddon Hall, p. 105.

25 Henry James, *English Hours*, ed. and introd. Alma Louise Lowe (London: Heinemann, [1905] 1960) p. 51. All subsequent references are to this edition and are given in the text.

26 Henry James, *The Turn of the Screw and Other Stories*, ed. and introd. T.J. Lustig (Oxford: Oxford University Press, 1992) pp. 113–236, pp. 135–6. All subsequent references are to this edition and are given in the text.

27 See Edel (ed.), *The Ghostly Tales of Henry James*, p. 435.

28 Henry James, *The American Scene* (Harmondsworth: Penguin, [1907] 1994), ed. and introd. John F. Sears, p. 13. All subsequent references are to this edition and are given in the text.

29 The relevant lines are 25–7: 'Licence my roving hands, and let them go / Before, behind, between, above, below. / O, my America, my Newfoundland'.

30 In some respects James followed in Hawthorne's footsteps with the earlier *English Hours*, as Hawthorne had written a book about his impressions of England in 1864 titled *Our Old Home*. For James, 'It is the work of an outsider, of a stranger, of a man who remains to the end a mere spectator' (p. 152), a position which is also troublingly occupied by James.

31 This is also a point developed by Lustig, *Henry James and the Ghostly*, pp. 223–4.

32 Henry James, 'The Jolly Corner', in *Ghost Stories of Henry James*, introd. Martin Scofield, (Ware, Herts: Wordsworth, 2001) pp. 306–34, p. 312. All subsequent references are to this edition and are given in the text.

33 Lustig, *Henry James and the Ghostly*, p. 224.

34 Henry James, *The Sense of the Past* (Fairfield, CT: Augustus M. Kelley, 1976) p. 33, italics in original. All subsequent references are to this edition and are given in the text.

7

Colonial ghosts: mimicry, history, and laughter

We saw in the previous chapter how images of spectrality in Henry James's Anglo-American Gothic encode images of national identity. How ghosts can be discussed in a colonial context helps to illuminate the complex relationship which existed in the period between the colonial gaze and the apparently subaltern subject.

This chapter proposes a reading of spectrality which encompasses non-fiction such as Dickens's *American Notes* (1842) and selected tales by Sheridan Le Fanu and Rudyard Kipling. An examination of Dickens, Le Fanu, and Kipling helpfully illustrates how the respective national contexts of America, Ireland, and India were reconstituted through a language of spectrality which (certainly in the case of Le Fanu and Kipling) parodies and covertly compromises images of ostensible colonial authority. Dickens's account of America, Le Fanu's Anglo-Irish version of Irish history, and Kipling's Anglo-Indian analysis of the Raj all work through, at different levels of explicitness, images of power that are challenged by subtle representations of resistance. However, there are also significant differences between them. Dickens's *American Notes* moves from optimism to despair and revealingly pivots on an encounter with a ghost, after which Dickens becomes increasingly confident of asserting his colonial authority. Le Fanu's ghost stories explore a highly politicised version of the past and Kipling uses the ghost story to examine alienation. One critical view which unites these disparate writings is Homi K. Bhabha's idea of colonial mimicry as outlined in *The Location of Culture* (1994).

For Bhabha 'The discourse of post-Enlightenment English colonialism often speaks in a tongue that is forked, not false' (p. 85).[1] This bifurcation is a consequence of the ambivalence with which the coloniser regards the apparently successful colonial project. For Bhabha such ambivalence is generated by a process of 'colonial mimicry' in which 'the desire [is] for a reformed, recognizable Other, *as a subject of a difference that is almost the same, but not quite*' (p. 86, italics in original). The colonialising subject is confronted by a mimic version of themselves because the model of colonial subjectivity imposed upon the subaltern subject is one which mimics their own authority. Such a moment is also uncanny for the coloniser because they are confronted by a version of themselves which appears to lampoon their very authority. For Bhabha:

Mimicry is thus the sign of a double articulation; a complex strategy of reform, regulation and discipline, which 'appropriates' the Other as it visualizes power. Mimicry is also the sign of the inappropriate; however, a difference or recalcitrance which coheres the dominant strategic function of colonial power, intensifies surveillance, and poses an immanent threat to both 'normalized' knowledges and disciplinary powers. (p. 86)

This creates an 'area between mimicry and mockery' (p. 86), in which the sub-altern subject parodies its colonial 'master'. As we shall see, this idea of parody and mimicry characterises the otherwise quite different images of spectrality in Dickens, Le Fanu, and Kipling. However, there is an additional element that is linked to this idea of parody, which is comedy.

Avril Horner and Sue Zlosnik in *Gothic and the Comic Turn* (2005) have noted the Gothic's tendency towards narrative parody and comic excess. They have also noted that such comedy is an essential aspect of the Gothic as it is inherent to the form's instabilities and transgressions. Importantly this comedy, and the laughter which it may provoke, is non-cathartic because it provides a genuinely radical counterpoint to the sanctioned transgressions of the Bakhtinian Carnivalesque. In that regard the comic Gothic has a political agenda, one which 'is [. . .] dialogic, opening up new possibilities', as it radically questions formulations of narrative convention and socio-political reality; and it is these 'new possibilities' for reading the Gothic which enable an exploration of the relationship between the comic, the (post)colonial, and the spectral.[2] The issue of a colonial laughter (and whether that laughter can be read as the sign of an emerging postcolonial, or antecolonial, identity) plays an important role in the discussion of Kipling and edges my reading of Le Fanu's images of hysteria. Dickens, of course, was also to some significant degree a comic writer, although his *American Notes* for the most part taps a distinctly sombre Gothic vein.

Colonial ghosts: mimicking Dickens

Dickens's account of his first travels in America, published in 1842 as *American Notes for General Circulation*, includes a moment, in his description of solitary confinement at the State Penitentiary in Philadelphia, where he employs a ghost in order to critique the penal system. This moment represents a turning point in the narrative, one in which Dickens's attempt at understanding the institutions of democratic America (its schools, hospitals, and prisons) is replaced by an asser-tion of a supposedly superior British difference.[3]

In Dickens's account of the prison in Philadelphia he uses the image of the ghost to illustrate the feelings of self-haunting which characterise the experience of solitary confinement (in which prisoners are locked up with only a version of them-selves for company). Self-haunting thus provides Dickens with a vehicle through which to explore feelings of psychological and cultural alienation. Why this indicates a colonial interjection on Dickens's part will be explored later, but before discussing the prison episode it is important to acknowledge that the roots of what becomes an argument about visibility and invisibility (which were also discussed in Chapter 2 of this book) are to be found in earlier parts of the *American Notes*, in encounters which go some way to explain why Dickens introduces a ghost into his travelogue.

Throughout the *American Notes* Dickens responds to a perceived language of mimicry. Such moments represent feelings of uncanniness, but they also correspond to Bhabha's conceptualisation of colonial ambivalence. For Bhabha mimicry indicates just how far the colonised 'other' has internalised ideas that are foreign to them and which are intended as forms of regulation (political, educational, and bureaucratic). However, such moments of mimicry can also appear to the colonial gaze as unsettling parodies of colonisation that subtly subvert colonial power (or at least are seen as such by the colonial gazer). The uncanny also plays a role in this. Uncanniness, according to Freud, occurs when images of the past intrude into the present, so that such images are strangely familiar although repressed. This applies to a language of colonial gazing which asserts that the difference between self and other is, paradoxically, prone to collapse (as they become doubled, or linked through mimicry).[4] Thus Dickens's assertion of difference haunts his narrative through doubled, uncanny, versions of exclusion – of blind children who can read, incarcerated ghosts, and a quack doctor. In other words, Dickens receives back an image of himself as an unconsciously inflected, but politically loaded, parody, so that throughout there is a pervasive undertow of alienation and estrangement which inheres within images that reflect on Dickens as a national outsider.

Dickens's sense of alienation can be witnessed in his account of the Perkins Institution and Massachusetts Asylum for the Blind in Boston. Initially Dickens extols the virtues of what he regards as a just regime in which forms of employment (making brushes and mattresses) create alliances between the children in the school. For Dickens, this takes them out of their otherwise inner private and psychologically locked worlds.

At first he is impressed by the apparent candour of the pupils at the school: 'It is strange to watch the faces of the blind, and see how free they are from all concealment of what is passing in their thoughts; observing which, a man with eyes may blush to contemplate the masks he wears' (p. 81). However, this spirit of openness disappears when Dickens finds himself confronted by behaviour which, for him, is unfathomable. He encounters Laura Bridgman, a twelve-year-old pupil who is deaf, blind, and mute. He notes of her: 'Like other inmates of that house, she had a green ribbon bound round her eyelids. A doll she had dressed lay near by upon the ground. I took it up, and saw that she had made a green fillet such as she wore herself, and fastened it about its mimic eyes' (p. 82). The doll is a mimic representation of the pupil and this challenges the notion of immediacy and authenticity which had earlier characterised the seemingly open expressions of the children. The girl possesses an image of herself (the doll) which baffles Dickens and suggests to him that she is trapped in a self-referential world that is generated by her blindness (by her inability to see out to others). For Dickens she has become entombed 'in a marble cell, impervious to any ray of light' (p. 81). Dickens discovers a written history of the girl and he quotes approvingly from it the claim that 'her mind dwells in darkness and stillness, as profound as that of a closed tomb at midnight' (p. 86). This image of mental solitary confinement foreshadows the more literal solitary confinement in his later account of the prison.

Struck as he is by Laura Bridgman's doll, Dickens focuses on a passage in the history which emphasises her propensity for mimicry: 'Her tendency to imitation is so strong, that it leads her to actions which must be entirely incomprehensible to her [. . .] She has been known to sit for half an hour, holding a book before her sightless eyes, and moving her lips' (p. 89). For Dickens this mimicry poses a problem for interpretation. Laura appears to represent a familiar world, a child playing with a doll or reading a book, but her blindness defamiliarises this and functions as an unconscious conceit for Dickens's wider inability to rationally account for the perceived peculiarities of America. For Dickens, America is familiar, possessing similar institutions and a shared history, but is also culturally unfamiliar and strange because of how those institutions are organised. Also, the scene turns Dickens into an oddly liminal, or spectral, presence who is both there (observing) and not there (unobserved), which is closely bound up with the ideas of colonial mimicry suggested by Bhabha. For Bhabha, mimicry becomes identifiable, or visible, when it appears as implied mockery. Crucially, it is an experience in which colonial regimes of power (and the instances which Dickens discusses – schools, hospitals, and prisons, concern institutionalised power) marginalise, or spectralise, the colonial gazer because they no longer represent the older authority upon which those regimes once depended.

Dickens's sense of exclusion is further dramatised in his account of the 'State Hospital for the Insane' in South Boston, where Dickens is full of admiration for a benign regime which develops self-restraint in the inmates. However, he also discovers mimic forms of behaviour which appear to be actively encouraged. One inmate, for example, is supported in her belief that she owns the institution, and at this point images of European difference appear as she is described as having pretensions to European aristocratic lineage. Dickens notes that 'she was radiant with imaginary jewels' (p. 95) and that on introduction she puts down a newspaper 'in which I dare say she had been reading an account of her own presentation at some Foreign Court' (p. 95). He also discovers that the hospital holds a series of dances and marches which are much discussed by the inmates who practise dance routines for them. In effect a version of polite European society is used to regulate behaviour.

Dickens is thus confronted by another type of acting, here a performance of polite European society which is both familiar and unfamiliar. However, in Bhabha's terms we can see that the means of controlling 'insanity' appear to involve a lampoon of

European mores and Dickens cannot help but be struck by the mimicry (and mockery) of it all, and by the presence of a covert national narrative within it. These issues of visibility and invisibility (of what is being shown and why) are given a particularly dramatic turn in his account of ghosts.

Dickens's discussion of the blind school and the hospital suggest the presence of spectrality as they imply that there exist occulted, or hidden, realities concerning power – realities which Dickens cannot quite see. This idea of a hidden presence is readdressed in his account of solitary confinement. He writes of the emotional anguish suffered by such prisoners: 'there is a depth of terrible endurance [. . .] which none but the sufferers themselves can fathom' (p. 147). Like Laura Bridgman, the inmates are there but not there, physically present but mentally entombed: 'He is a man buried alive; to be dug out in the slow round of years; and in the mean time dead to everything but torturing anxieties and horrible despair' (p. 148). He describes an inmate's bed which 'looked [. . .] like a grave' (p. 150). Another inmate is summoned from his cell and stood in the corridor 'looking as wan and unearthly as if he had been summoned from the grave' (p. 150). Dickens, who had been unable to comprehend the actions of Laura Bridgman or the inhabitants of the hospital, makes a supreme effort to understand the psychological effects of solitary confinement. He imagines that such an inmate would be aware of inmates in adjacent cells and would create narratives concerning their possible lives and personalities and this leads him to employ an explicit language of ghosting. He imagines of his imaginary neighbour, 'How was he dressed? Has he been here long? Is he much worn away? Is he very white and spectre-like?' (p. 154).

These disembodied figures represent Dickens's attempt at explaining otherness – as a desire to account for the emotional life of the marginalised, the excluded, and the culturally disempowered. This moment also constitutes a crisis in the narrative because the figures are also fairly obvious instances of projection and transference. Dickens is a national outsider who cannot make sense of what he sees, and his emotionally fraught account of solitary confinement reflects his feelings of isolation and exclusion.[5] His attempt to imagine imaginary people illustrates the presence of this projection and importantly it is one in which haunting becomes self-haunting, as the self is unable to transcend its own boundaries (national and cultural) in order to properly embrace otherness.

Dickens argues that an inmate would see 'an ugly phantom face' (p. 154) peering in at them through the cell window, a phantom which is not externalised because it participates in the mental life of the prisoner. What is horrifying is the feeling that the phantom 'gave birth in his brain to something of corresponding shape, which ought not to be there, and racked his head with pains' (p. 154). The phantom haunts the prisoner wherever he goes because he is his own ghost, created by his living burial in solitary confinement:

When he is in his cell by day, he fears the little yard without. When he is in the yard, he dreads to re-enter the cell. When night comes, there stands the phantom in the corner. If he have the courage to stand in its place, and drive it out (he had once being desperate) it broods upon his bed. In the twilight, and always at the same hour, a voice calls to him by name. (p. 155)

Dickens here uses the Gothic as a means to interpret the depth of feeling of a prisoner locked in solitary confinement. To that degree the Gothic is employed to read this plight, rather than simply being used to capture the mood of the experience. In this moment Dickens asserts a peculiarly European mode of the Gothic (concerning the plight of the non-American othered, i.e. himself), which is an outsider's way of reading what otherwise appears to be unthinkable, or beyond representation. It is also, as in the earlier encounters, an experience in which Dickens becomes the strange, othered, spectral presence. This doubling suggests the uncanny, although in Bhabha's terms the presence of an implied mimicry also unsettles such encounters because it is this 'repetition of *partial presence* [. . .] that reverses "in part" the colonial appropriation by [. . .] producing a partial vision of the colonizer's presence; a gaze of otherness' (italics in original, pp. 88–9). The problem confronted by Dickens is to find a trope which can adequately capture such an experience.

Significantly any sense of horror is generated by Dickens rather than simply observed by him because in reality he has to imagine the whole thing. As an imaginative construction it illustrates the position of the outsider looking in, and enables Dickens to articulate the first moment in which he explicitly condemns an American institution (the penal system). The Gothic therefore functions in this instance as a political critique. This might appear to be overstating the matter were it not the case that after Dickens's moment of unconscious textual insight (in which he reads Gothically), he increasingly deploys a more confident narrative concerning national and cultural difference, rather than attempts to pursue an analysis of America through comparisons and implied similarities.

This is evidenced by the change of tone in the *American Notes*, in which the optimism of his arrival in Boston is tempered by his inability to 'read' the apparently inexplicable behaviour at the blind school and the hospital, a mood further soured in his account of solitary confinement. The growing sense of disillusionment and pessimism culminates in his final major chapter on the Gothic horrors of slavery. In slavery he reads the mutilated and branded bodies of the slaves as signs of a culture which has generated horror from within and created the potential for national self-destruction. Dickens's use of the ghost therefore functions as a colonial interjection into the narrative, one in which the sympathetic attempt at reading America is replaced by a more belligerent assertion of difference.

To not belong enables Dickens to, at last, stand back and 'read', in highly nationalistic terms, what for him is being staged within American institutions. Another example of this is in his account of a visit to the American frontier in the chapter 'A Jaunt to the Looking-Glass Prairie and Back', where the idea of mimicry is reasserted. At the frontier he encounters a Scotsman who is selling fake medicines in the guise of 'Dr Crocus'. The shantytown that Dickens visits is in a pestilential swamp in which disease is rife, so creating opportunities for quack doctors and conmen like Crocus. Dickens is introduced to him and they embark on a highly stylised, and very public, verbal exchange in which Crocus extols the virtues of American freedom in a bid to attract more customers to his show. Dickens implies a subtext, which is that Crocus's concern about a lack of freedom in Britain is because he is probably wanted there on criminal charges, something which is broadly implied by Crocus and understood by Dickens but which the gathering crowd do not register. Dickens colludes with Crocus in a display of public banter in which Dickens ask him whether he intends to return to ' "the old country" ' and Crocus replies, ' "You won't catch me at that just yet, sir. I am a little too fond of freedom for *that*, sir. Ha ha!" ' (p. 225, italics in original). The suggestion is that frauds like Crocus can flourish in such places because gullibility has, for Dickens, become a political feature of America. The attempt to build a town, to construct a model of civilisation, in a pestilential swamp represents for Dickens clear evidence that its inhabitants have been duped into believing that such things are possible and desirable. There is therefore a difference between the ideal and the real, between lived experience and political fraud. As he noted in a letter to W.C. Macready written around this time, 'This is not the republic I came to see; this is not the republic of my imagination', because instead of democracy he perceives a political con trick.[6]

The idea of political deception underlines Dickens's investment in his European credentials. These are emphasised in his account of the prairie, which is discussed in terms of national difference: 'Great as the picture was, its very flatness and extent, which left nothing to the imagination, tamed it down and cramped its interest. I felt little of that sense of freedom and exhilaration which a Scottish heath inspires, or even our English downs awaken' (p. 226). Here he relocates ideas used in his account of the prison; there too was an experience which was about taming and cramping the imagination, an experience articulated through the use of the ghost, one which had enabled him to exorcise such anxieties and assert the alleged freedoms of Britain.

However, there is an additional issue which relates to language. Dickens uses the image of the ghost as a conceit for how he perceives, and senses that he is perceived by, America. The ghost is part of the rhetoric of the Gothic and indicates Dickens's attempt to find a language through which to represent his ambivalent feelings about America.[7] The Gothic argot to which the ghost belongs is performative, and this idea of a performative language is developed at some length in the protracted bantering between Dickens and Crocus in which false realities are created for the benefit of the credulous observers.

It is the unreal nature of America which disturbs Dickens and this is why he uses the Gothic to account for this disturbance. Steven Marcus argues that

Dickens concurred with Tocqueville in arguing that American reality was governed by economic forces of mass production that also created mass-produced selves characterised by 'a certain mechanical type of human being'.[8] This was combined with the absence of older, European, social hierarchies so that for Dickens, according to Marcus, 'Having almost nothing finally but themselves to refer to, Americans tended to develop narrowly and unimaginatively, their characters and personalities to become thin and superficial' (p. 248).

However, in a neat reversal of Henry James's position discussed in Chapter 6, Dickens ultimately cannot either stand outside of his national context or properly embrace, or understand, an American one. Also the more or less overt images of mimicry that he frustratingly encounters in the early part of the book become disabling covert presences as the narrative progresses, which adds to the growing mood of pessimism.

However, if Dickens is uneasy in America it is significant that his presence also generated unease in others. Towards the end of the *American Notes* and whilst on a boat trip, Dickens recalls that 'There was a gentleman on board, to whom, as I unintentionally learned through the thin partition which divided our state-room from the cabin in which he and his wife conversed together, I was unwittingly the occasion of very great uneasiness' (p. 241). He later overhears the man say, ' "I suppose that Boz will be writing a book by-and-by, and putting all our names in it!" at which imaginary consequence of being on board with Boz, he groaned' (p. 242). The anonymous passenger's fears concern the possible content of an outsider's commentary – an anxiety which many conservatively minded Americans, disturbed by Dickens's condemnation of slavery and the media, felt strongly. However, the roots of this also exist within the subtle anxieties of Dickens, who cannot produce the celebration of democracy that he had hoped to write as America becomes constituted as an unreal space inhabited by unconsciously projected colonial ghosts. How Dickens, an outsider, reads America can be usefully contrasted with how Le Fanu, a member of the Anglo-Irish Protestant Ascendancy (although one with a mixed Catholic and Protestant background), reconstructs Ireland's past through a language of spectrality.

Reading Ireland, writing the past: Le Fanu's ghosts

Sheridan Le Fanu's place within a Gothic tradition has raised some complex issues for scholars working on Irish literary history, the cultural context of the Anglo-Irish, and the ideological location of an Irish Gothic. His position within a Gothic tradition would appear to be assured given his *Ghost Stories and Tales of Mystery* (1851) and *In a Glass Darkly* (1872). However, how to situate Le Fanu within a coherent Irish Gothic tradition has proved problematic. W.J. McCormack, for example, has argued that Le Fanu's writings were influenced by, amongst others, Balzac (rather than Maturin) and therefore he should be seen within the context of a European Gothic tradition.[9] Such a view in part repositions Le Fanu through reference to his background (Irish and French Huguenot). Jarlath Killeen has complicated McCormack's further claim that Le Fanu's Protestant (and therefore colonial) credentials compromise any attempt at reading his Gothic as a discourse of the oppressed. Killen notes that the period was characterised by successful agitation for Catholic emancipation, combined with economic, political, and territorial gains for Catholics which challenged the once dominant Protestant culture. Killeen claims that in this context, 'Gothic, in truth, may not belong to the dispossessed but to the paranoid possessors, the out-of-control controllers, the descending Ascendancy'.[10] For Killeen this means that 'a "colonial" history, Protestantism, and the fear of marginalisation – rather than marginalisation itself – are central features of the Irish Gothic tradition' (p. 2). He further claims that an anti-realist Irish Protestant literary tradition reflects these wider political anxieties, so that 'This sense of cultural hesitancy between the future and the past, the real and the supernatural, the Anglo and the Irish, runs through much of the literature of the Protestant Irish and helps to explain why the realist tradition was never very successful here' (p. 4). The key to understanding Le Fanu's representation of spectrality lies in his reconstruction of these issues about social and political authority – a reconstruction which informs his engagement with folklore.

Robert Tracy has argued that representations of folklore in Anglo-Irish literature were shaped by the changing political positions of Protestant and Catholic cultures from the late eighteenth to the mid nineteenth centuries. He argues that images of fairies, or *sidhé*, became associated with the Anglo-Irish because like them they represent a claim over the land which reflects issues about colonial power. For Tracy, 'Like the *sidhé*, the Anglo-Irish were powerful, unpredictable, sometimes malevolent, and different in their behaviour, religion, language and customs'.[11] However, with the advent of successful Catholic agitation for change the *sidhé* became associated, in the Protestant imagination, with Catholics, so that 'In the hands of Sheridan Le Fanu [. . .], the undead become the ancient Catholic masters of the land, eager to destroy those who now enjoy their former estates. The Irish past comes back, not to haunt the present but to destroy' (p. 18). McCormack has also noted that Le Fanu's fiction is characterised by a restless territoriality (with tales set in England, Ireland, and throughout mainland Europe) in which notions of a centralised, or centralisable, power become dispersed and fragmented because 'the displacements of Le Fanu's fiction are only part of its comprehensive rejection of all notions of fixed centrality, reliable identity and social stability' (p. 146). This disorientation and its relationship to the past marks out Le Fanu's use of spectrality as being quite different from either Dickens's or Kipling's. As Sally Harris has noted of Le Fanu's tales, 'The past, like a ghost, is a haunting force which works supernaturally in this world; it cannot be explained by science or materialism. Although it has no physical properties, the presence of the past is keenly felt in the events of the present'.[12]

However, also apparent is a covert humour which far from mitigating the implied anxieties of the Anglo-Irish complicates, but paradoxically supports, a suppressed hysteria that relocates this language of haunting. Victor Sage has noted the presence of comedy in Le Fanu's *Uncle Silas* (1864), whereby its comedic disorientations capture an aspect of the radical, non-cathartic elements of the Gothic. Revealingly Sage's article also refers to *Dracula* (1897) and this acknowledgement of a relationship between laughter, the Gothic and the Anglo-Irish can be developed via an analysis of how this relates to history.[13]

Luke Gibbons, in his analysis of the Irish Literary Revival, has argued that images of hysteria were closely associated with attempts at eluding the ghosts of the past; however, 'the figure of hysteria testified ultimately to the persistence of a troubled past, whether it be secreted in the body or in the petrified violence of the landscape'.[14] Significantly, Gibbons's model of hysteria is derived from Charcot, who notes that hysteria consists of stages in which the subject exhibits a propensity to either reveal intense emotional states, or *mimic* them, which is followed by laughter. This sequencing between a potential mimicry and laughter replicates the terms of Bhabha's theory of colonial mimicry, whilst positioning laughter as a stage just beyond such mimicry. Laughter and mimicry are thus, in this context, political acts and how this relates to Le Fanu's use of spectrality can be witnessed in a number of his tales.

'The Child that went with the Fairies' (1870) explicitly engages with ideas of the *sidhé* as outlined by Tracy. The opening of the tale locates it both in terms of place and history by referring to its proximity to Limerick and its connections with the Jacobite Patrick Sarsfield, who in 1690 had captured some English munitions intended to support the siege of the town. The area was 'famous as having afforded Sarsfield a shelter among the rock and hollows, when he crossed them in his gallant descent upon the cannon and ammunition of King William'.[15] The praise for such 'gallant' Jacobite resistance provides an ideological context for what follows.

The area of the community, and in particular the part of it inhabited by the Ryans, on whom the tale centres, is associated with a history that predates King William: 'Here certainly were defences and bulwarks against the intrusion of that unearthly and evil power, of whose vicinity this solitary family were constantly reminded by the outline of Lisnavoura, that lonely hill-haunt of the "Good people," as the fairies are called euphemistically' (p. 51). Sarsfield's successful Jacobite activity thus becomes associated with an older authority based on territorial rights, which asserts its claims on the present and the future by child abduction.

Mary Ryan, a widow, is concerned that her four children, Nell, Con, Bill, and Peg, may be susceptible to attack from the 'dreaded and subtle agents' (p. 52) of the *sidhé*. The account of Bill's abduction in a carriage centres on images of ancient splendour that are initially associated with 'the grand ladies' (p. 53) in their carriage: 'This carriage and all its appointments were old fashioned and gorgeous, and presented to the children [. . .] a spectacle perfectly dazzling' (p. 54). The tale goes on to note that 'Here was antique splendour' (p. 54). However, beneath such superficial glamour lurk more sinister presences. The servants on the coach 'were diminutive, and ludicrously out of proportion with the enormous horses of the equipage' (p. 54). They 'had sharp, sallow features, and small, restless fiery eyes, and faces of cunning and malice' (p. 54). In addition, 'The little coachman was scowling and showing his white fangs under his cocked hat, and his little blazing beads of eyes were quivering with fury in their sockets' (p. 54). An important-looking lady can be seen sitting beside another woman, 'a black woman, with a wonderfully long neck' who 'had a face as thin almost as a death's-head, with high cheek-bones, and great goggle eyes' (p. 55). As Tracy has noted, such imagery foreshadows that of the carriage and the black woman in *Carmilla* (1872), in a tale which also focuses on the attempted vampiric abduction of Laura (the tale's narrator).[16]

What is also significant in the tale is that throughout there are repeated references to laughter. The arrival of the coach interrupts 'the hilarity and eagerness' (p. 54) of the children's game. When they look into the carriage the children saw that 'A beautiful and "very grand-looking" lady was smiling from it on them, and they all felt pleased in the strange light of that smile' (p. 55). The lady selects Bill, who willingly gets into the carriage. The other children look on enviously but find the presence of the black woman disturbing. The description of her brings together the contrasting moods of the scenes which have culminated in Bill's abduction:

> She gathered a rich silk and gold handkerchief that was in her fingers up to her lips, and seemed to thrust ever so much of it, fold after fold, into her capacious mouth, as they thought to smother her laughter, with which she seemed convulsed, for she was shaking and quivering, as it seemed, with suppressed merriment; but her eyes, which remained uncovered, looked angrier than they had ever seen eyes look before. (p. 55)

Such a moment does not represent a comic Gothic in Horner and Zlosnik's terms. Nor does it reflect the type of Gothic excesses which Sage notes as being at the heart of an implied Gothic laughter. At one level it refers to competing languages of triumph: of hatred and a mocking derision. However, it also develops an image of a barely suppressed hysteria that Gibbons saw as one aspect of the Irish Literary Revival. At one level the tale mimics a folktale, and McCormack has noted the repeated uses of mimicry in Le Fanu's witing.[17]

The tale imitates a folktale in its reworking of a moral that functions as a precautionary warning to children. The tale also mocks this because it is clearly intended for an adult readership and it corresponds to Bhabha's notion that mimic writing attempts to deflect the political burdens of the past. For Bhabha, 'What emerges between mimesis and mimicry is *writing*, a mode of representation, that marginalizes the monumentality of history, quite simply mocks its power to be a model, that power which supposedly makes it imitable' (pp. 87–8, italics in original). This is the fundamental paradox of the tale; it resurrects a Protestant pre-history only to play out its presence through a demonised laughter that, paradoxically, mimics

the models of Protestant authority against which it rebels. Le Fanu is thus ambivalent here because the tale centres on this moment of suppressed laughter which
both damns the present and condemns the past and leaves the abducted Bill with
nowhere to go. Bill becomes a progressively spectral figure who, it is implied, haunts
the place as an invisible presence which, like a Catholic past and a marginalised
Protestant present, cannot be properly discerned or accommodated.

The suppressed laughter does not just capture the conflicting moods which lead
up to the abduction, but is also a consequence of its political context. The spectral vision of the coach emerges out of a politically troubled landscape (with its
Jacobite, but also Williamite associations) in order to attempt a reclamation of the
present. The laughter is non-cathartic and is used to represent the 'horror' of the
encounter. However, it does not invite the reader to participate in its humour, but
merely to note the close conjunction between laughter and anger. What is revealing is the horror that the stifling of the laughter engenders in the children; the black
woman is 'quivering [. . .] with suppressed merriment' (p. 55), which develops
the earlier image of the coachman whose 'eyes were quivering with fury' (p. 54).

The abducted Bill is subsequently associated with this ambivalent emotional state.
He periodically returns to his family as a spectral form, as if he now represents a
mood rather than a child. Sometimes the other children 'saw the pretty face of
little Billy peeping in archly at the door, and smiling silently at them' (p. 56). However,
if they attempt to touch him he shrinks from them, 'still smiling archly' (p. 56).
On later visits it is noted that 'always he was smiling with the same arch look
and wary silence' (p. 57). The emotional ambivalence that is associated with Bill's
ghost and the two women in the carriage relocates a mood of political ambivalence
that indirectly reflects on the idea of locale. The tale ends, 'So little Billy was dead
to mother, brother, and sisters; but no grave received him' (p. 57). Bill becomes
a spectral figure 'hidden from their loving eyes', whose suspected presence as something 'white and filmy in the moonlight' (p. 57) appears as a reminder of what has
been lost.

Not all of Le Fanu's ghost stories rework images from folklore, even though they
address similar themes as 'The Child that went with the Fairies'. One tale which
has received considerable critical attention because of its explicit referencing of history and the politics of Ireland is 'Ultor de Lacy' (1861). However, ghosts and their
relationship to political history are also addressed in a more critically neglected
narrative which is embedded within the earlier 'Ghost Stories of Chapelizod'
(published in *Dublin University Magazine* in 1851). The collection includes 'The
Spectre Lovers' and recounts how the young Peter Brien, after a drunken night
out, stumbles across what appears to be a ghostly army regiment encamped in
Chapelizod, an area of Dublin. Peter is drawn into a house where an officer and
a woman, who are with their child, attempt to enlist his support to help them
retrieve some treasure. He refuses and awakens within the ruins of the house. He
relates the events to his grandmother, who identifies the regiment as the Royal Irish
(a regiment established in 1689 from an irregular company that in December 1688

had defended Enniskillen against a Jacobite army). A subsequent meeting with the elderly Major Vandeleur and his wife helps to identify the spectral officer as one Captain Devereux, who had abandoned a pregnant woman and had subsequently been killed in a duel. Peter dies after falling from a building where the ghosts had indicated that the treasure was hidden.

When Peter firsts sees the spectral regiment he wonders whether they might be French and so part of a pro-Catholic force. The names of some of the officers also suggest this: Devereux, Vandeleur, and Vandeleur's wife who 'had French blood in her veins'.[18] When Peter asks the ghost of Captain Devereux if he was French he replies, ' "No; I am an Irishman" ' (p. 102) and utters in a tone of 'sorrowful sacrifice' (p. 102) ' "I serve the same King as you do" '. The implication is that they could just as easily have been fighting for the other side. This confusion over military authority is reflected in Peter's drunken disorientation. Peter is described as 'a good-natured slob of a fellow' (p. 97), and although 'Peter had of late years begun to apply his mind to politics' (p. 98), his knowledge of political history is very limited. Indeed the tale quickly moves from the political drama implied by the presence of the regiment to the more personal drama of Devereux, the woman, and the child.

Ghosts in 'The Spectre Lovers' are read through Peter's drunken haze, which suggests his inability to comprehend the reality of Dublin's militaristic past. The past, like the ghostly encampment which 'came into view, but all in [a] coy way, just appearing and gone again before he could well fix his gaze upon them' (p. 99), is there but not there. History is spectrally present, misinterpreted, and results in Peter's death. He is buried in the churchyard with 'the other heroes' that people the 'Ghost Stories of Chapelizod'. 'The Spectre Lovers' suggests that the past lacks clarity and that the legacies of that past are confusingly perceived and difficult to understand. For that reason history retains its presence because its significance and resolutions have yet to be fully realised.

W.J. McCormack, although sceptical of attempts to align Le Fanu with an Anglo-Irish culture, nevertheless echoes Killeen's assessment that the culture is characterised by a hesitancy that excludes realist forms of writing, rather as the focus on the spectral army in 'The Spectre Lovers' registers a confusion about political and military legacies. For McCormack there exists a need 'to address the persistent suspicion that something fundamentally unreal characterises Irish experience' (p. 247). Le Fanu's repeated emphasis on a spectral political history that induces a form of hysteria, or delirium (associated with 'drunkenness'), in the present suggests how this 'unreal' sense of experience is generated within the complexly hybrid (McCormack's term is 'mongrel', p. 246) culture of the time.

In 'The Child that went with the Fairies' ostensible images of laughter and of happiness bear a relationship to how Le Fanu plots the spectral return of an old pre-Protestant Irish culture, which in turn renders spectral, or makes liminal, the politically marginalised Anglo-Irish. These issues were also developed in an earlier non-folktale, 'An Account of Some Strange Disturbances in Aungier Street' (1853).

'Aungier Street' is narrated as if it were a fireside tale to be told 'on a winter's evening'. The narrator, Dick, recounts how he and his cousin, Tom Ludlow, came to inhabit a seemingly haunted house when they were medical students.[19] They discover that the house had belonged to one Judge Horrocks, a 'hanging judge' (p. 69), who had committed suicide in the house and whose ghost attempts to murder later tenants, some of whom have died with neck injuries. The house in Aungier Street in Dublin has a Jacobite provenance having once belonged to the Lord Mayor at the time of James II. The house directly refers to this past as the narrator notes that 'there was something queer and bygone in the very walls and ceilings [. . .] which hopelessly defied disguise, and would have emphatically proclaimed their antiquity through any conceivable amount of modern finery and varnish' (p. 69). The ghost appears to Dick in the guise of a nightmare vision of the judge's portrait and as a huge rat which laboriously descends the stairs at night. Dick discerns on this rat's face 'a perfectly human expression of malice' (p. 76) which echoes the portrait, where the judge appears 'sinister and full of malignant omen' (p. 71). Tom's visions are more precisely focused on the judge, whom he sees many times, once with a rope which the spectre intends for him.

The tale relocates images of an 'insane' notion of justice which is rooted in the past. However, as in 'The Child that went with the Fairies' there are references to laughter and comedy which complicate the way that the past relates to the present, and how the present relates to the past. First, Dick questions whether the apparition is real 'or the invention of my poor stomach?' (p. 71).[20] There is some consequent speculation about mesmeric and electro-biological explanations, although ultimately the spectre is granted an objective existence. However, Dick's response implicates a language of hysteria. Left alone for the first time in what he believes to be a haunted house, 'I walked up and down my room, whistling in turn martial and hilarious music, and listening ever and anon for the dreaded noise' (p. 75). The movements between 'hilarious music' and 'the dreaded noise' develop tensions between suggested hysteria and the Gothic which would be reworked in 'The Child that went with the Fairies'. Dick then recounts hearing what turns out to be the huge, strangely human, rat. Aware that he is telling this to an audience, he states, 'laugh at me as you may' (p. 76), but challenges any such laughter by claiming an inherent malignancy for the rat, even as it makes its way through the house on some obscure 'night lark' (p. 76). Later Dick tells Tom about this experience and he responds with his tale of the spectral judge.

Earlier in the tale, as we have seen, reference was made to the 'queer and bygone' architecture of the building and Tom admits to feeling 'quite queer' (p. 77) at the prospect of telling his tale in such a place. The language of queerness thus captures a mood of unease that is closely related to the notion of humour. Tom's statement registers his profound unease, although for Dick 'he spoke this like a joke' (p. 77). Tom's tale structurally echoes, although it inverts, Dick's earlier account in that it too relates how tension seems to be relieved by a comedic, musical, intervention.

Tom recounts how he awoke from ' "a horrible dream" ', and ' "I yet could hear a pleasant fellow singing, on his way home, the then popular comic ditty called 'Murphy Delany' " ' (p. 79). There follows an extract from the song that refers to the theme of drunkenness. As in 'The Spectre Lovers', this theme runs throughout the tale (Dick is a whisky drinker, and the house is eventually burnt down in an accident involving a drunk tenant). The perambulations of the drunk are subsequently replaced by the perambulations of the spectral judge in the house.

History in 'Aungier Street' becomes referenced through a comic mode which articulates a suppressed hysteria relating to the return of the past, staged within a Jacobite house which harbours the ghost of a 'hanging judge', who is metaphorically described as vermin. Laughter catches a mood of hysteria in which spectrality is risible, impossible, irrational, and yet persistent and palpable. How to make the past truly dead is a central issue in Le Fanu's tales, which repeatedly assert that the failure to do so will destroy the present.

This language of hysteria is given a rather different inflection in the ghost stories of Rudyard Kipling.

Kipling's India and Gothic laughter

This chapter has touched on how hysteria (which is manifested as suppressed 'laughter') plays an important role in shaping a language of spectrality; indeed this was a central feature of Le Fanu's ghost stories. In Dickens's *American Notes* the mood is more serious, although his account of Dr Crocus is not without its comic moments even if it is not a spectral encounter. The comic and its relationship to accounts of national identity are much clearer in Kipling, whose ghost stories run together images of hysteria and liminality and provide a helpful counterpoint to how similar images are formulated in Le Fanu.[21]

First, it is important to address the Anglo-Indian context of Kipling. Bart Moore-Gilbert in *Kipling and 'Orientalism'* (1986) has explored the contrasts between Anglo-Indian and British metropolitan versions of Orientalism, arguing that there existed a rupture between the Anglo-Indian view of India (largely as experienced by, for example, colonial administrators) and the British perception of the Raj. Moore-Gilbert notes a double form of alienation felt by those working in the colonial service as they were necessarily estranged from the indigenous Indian culture and did not share the British metropolitan conception of India. Moore-Gilbert also observes that at the time the 'gothic was [. . .] a well-established genre in Anglo-Indian fiction', and had been popularised by writers such as Morier, J.B. Fraser, Hockley, and Meadows Taylor.[22] For Moore-Gilbert the Gothic was popular because of the form's 'appropriateness as a medium to express the sense of estrangement' (p. 188). Such Gothic narratives also rework the type of doubling suggested by the uncanny because, as Moore-Gilbert summarises, 'Kipling manifests a double attitude towards the metropolitan homeland. On the one hand, it acts as an ideal which can inspire the exile – and at the same time it can exacerbate his sense of deprivation' (p. 44). Such a view provides an important context for understanding Kipling's Gothic. It is a context which has links to a model of laughter.

Lewis D. Wurgaft has claimed that 'deep brutal laughter rings throughout Kipling's stories on India. At times it seems forced or inappropriate; in other instances it approaches the transcendent stature of tragic insight. In either instance such laughter is a distancing device from the brutal and overstimulating realities of life as Kipling saw them'.[23]

In a piece titled 'A Free Hand' in the *Pioneer* of November 1888, Kipling stages an imagined conversation between Lord Dufferin, the outgoing viceroy, and Lord Landsdowne, his replacement. Dufferin tells Landsdowne, ' "You stand on the threshold of new experiences – most of which will distress you and a few amuse. You are [at] the centre of a gigantic *practical joke*. Strive to enter the spirit of it and jest temperately" '.[24] If there is comedy in the administration of India it is a bleak one as it informs Kipling's use of the Gothic. However, the laughter can, in many respects, be interpreted as a mode of mimicry that subtly unsettles notions of colonial power.

In 'The Strange Ride of Morrowbie Jukes' (1885) Kipling explores a language of liminality that is developed via images of the living and the dead, and the colonialist and the subaltern. These relationships are frequently punctuated by hysterical and demonic laughter which both resists colonial power and simultaneously compromises such resistance. Jukes loses consciousness after an accident and awakens in a strange isolated community which is geographically trapped in 'a horseshoe-shaped crater of sand with steeply graded sand walls about thirty-five feet high (the slope, I fancy, must have been about 65°)'.[25] This is situated next to a river that is patrolled by a warship which fires on anyone who attempts to escape. Jukes is initially struck by the pervasive aroma of death which characterises the trapped community. He notes the existence of a series of tunnels and the presence of 'a most sickening stench [that] pervaded the entire amphitheatre – a stench fouler than any which my wanderings in Indian villages have introduced me to' (p. 48). The people who emerge from the tunnels to greet Jukes 'were all scantily clothed in that salmon-coloured cloth one associates with Hindu mendicants, and, at first sight, gave one the impression of a band of loathsome *fakirs*' (p. 50). Jukes expects his colonial authority to be appropriately acknowledged because 'I have become accustomed to a certain amount of civility from my inferiors' (p. 50). However, 'The ragged crew actually laughed at me – such laughter I hope I may never hear again. They cackled, yelled, whistled, and howled as I walked into their midst; some of them literally throwing themselves down on the ground in convulsions of an unholy mirth' (p. 50).

Jukes quickly transforms their laughter into a fear by 'cuffing' a number of them: 'The wretches dropped under my blows like nine-pins, and the laughter gave place to wails for mercy; while those yet untouched clasped me round the knees, imploring me in all sorts of uncouth tongues to spare them' (p. 50). The scene might suggest Jukes's reassertion of his authority, but the encounter is constructed as a parody of subservience in which the imploring crowd (of sixty people) play out a mock obsequiousness. The tale also suggests links between mimicry and mockery when Jukes relates his encounter with Gunga Dass, a Brahmin who had worked for the government as the manager of a branch telegraph office. Dass, like Jukes, has been effectively stripped of his signs of authority: 'the man was changed beyond all recognition. Caste-mark, stomach, slate-coloured contumations, and unctuous speech were all gone. I looked at a withered skeleton, turban-less and almost naked, with long matted hair and deep-set codfish-eyes' (p. 51). Dass informs Jukes about the strange place he has found himself in. The community consists of people who had been falsely identified as dead, but who have merely been in a trance. The place is a form of limbo in which people are effectively dead, or at best only ambivalently alive. As Dass puts it, ' "Now I am dead man" ' (p. 53). To Jukes's suggestion that they might escape down the heavily guarded river, Dass, 'to my intense astonishment, gave vent to a low chuckle of derision – the laughter, be it understood, of a superior or at least of an equal' (p. 53). In this limbo social rank is no longer acknowledged, and it is laughter which constitutes a political critique of colonial authority. Dass's position effectively replicates that of Jukes because Jukes's lost sense of colonial authority is reflected in Dass, who has also been divested of his signs of authority.

Bhabha's notion of colonial mimicry, which was discussed at the beginning of the chapter, is particularly relevant here, especially his claim that such mimicry is always ambivalent because it is 'almost the same, *but not quite*' (p. 86, italics in original). Stripped of his emblems of rank, Dass glosses Jukes's position, but he is still at some fundamental level 'othered'. However, one consequence of this is that Jukes, trapped in this strange limbo, is in turn divested of much of his power. As Bhabha notes, such a moment of colonial mimicry 'does not merely "rupture" the [colonial] discourse, but becomes transformed into an uncertainty which fixes the colonial subject as a "partial" presence' (p. 86). Bhabha elaborates that 'By "partial" I mean both "incomplete" and "virtual" ' (p. 86). Jukes exemplifies this liminality in which his now lost colonial status is mimicked by Dass, whose laughter openly mocks Jukes's new 'incomplete' and 'virtual' existence. Jukes's lack of visibility is emphasised when he collapses with exhaustion near a well where 'Two of three men trod on my panting body as they drew water' (p. 54). Dass throws 'half a cupful of fetid water' over Jukes's head, 'an attention for which I could have fallen on my knees and thanked him, but he was laughing all the while in the same mirthless, wheezy key that greeted me' (p. 54). Dass agrees to look after Jukes but only if he gives him all of his money, warning him, ' "all you have, or I will get help, and we will kill you!" ' (p. 56). Dass's desire for money serves no practical purpose because in this limbo world there is nothing to buy. However, it has a symbolic significance because it is yet another means of stripping Jukes of his associations with authority. As Dass reminds him, ' "you are dead, my dear friend.

It is not your fault, of course, but none the less you are dead and buried"' (p. 56). This leads Dass to taunt him that this hellish place '"is like your European heaven"' (p. 57).

Jukes sees himself as 'a representative figure of the dominant race, helpless as a child and completely at the mercy of his native neighbours' (p. 57). Dass torments Jukes and mocks his attempts at escape; Jukes collapses, exhausted, after one such attempt only to be 'roused at last by the malevolent chuckle of Gunga Dass' (p. 62). Dass further taunts him by claiming that he now lives in a republic and Jukes finds Dass increasingly 'offensively jocular' (p. 63). Jukes re-establishes his authority by threatening Dass with violence until he clears out one of the huts that contains a corpse which 'The dry sand had turned [. . .] into a yellow-brown mummy' (p. 66). The body is that of a murdered westerner. A notebook found on the body contains in its binding a list of directions which indicate that he had nearly successfully plotted an escape route through the quicksand near the river bed. Dass admits shooting the man because he did not want him to leave and because '"it is not advisable that the men who once get in here should escape. Only I, and *I* am a Brahmin"' (p. 70, italics in original). As Jukes remarks, 'The prospect of escape had brought Gunga Dass's caste back to him' (p. 70). The limbo world of the tale erases social status and only the outside world can potentially reconjure it. Jukes is ultimately rescued by his servant, Dunnoo.

In 'The Strange Ride of Morrowbie Jukes' Jukes's ostensible authority is played out through a language of spectrality in which his social status is suspended. It is a particularly demonic laughter which affects this and this type of laughter, revealingly, can also be located within the Indian culture.

Baidik Bhattacharya has explored the relationship between colonial parody and mimicry. The principal question he addresses is 'why do we laugh at the texts that imagine reverse colonialism in spite of the fact that they so intimately mimic the narrative strategies, styles and often vocabularies of Orientalist discourse?' The short answer is because 'Orientalist knowledge is often absurd, or deeply flawed'.[26] However, Bhattacharya, like Horner and Zlosnik, sees laughter as non-cathartic and so not contained within the sanctioned transgressions of the Bakhtinian Carnivalesque, because such laughter 'is political and (post)colonial in nature' (p. 280). This laughter is associated, like Bhabha's account of mimicry, with how parody operates as a mode of uncanny doubling, one which undoes Freud's psychodrama in order to restage it as a political drama. As Horner and Zlosnik have noted, this Gothic laughter is 'dialogic', and as Moore-Gilbert has argued, Kipling's Anglo-Indian status puts him beyond the Orientalist model generated by the British metropolitan culture. Indeed, Kipling's dialogue with such laughter has its roots within Indian folklore, which is itself both comic and Gothic.

Maurice Bloomfield in 'On Recurring Psychic Motifs in Hindu Fiction, and the Laugh and Cry Motif', published in 1916, explored a number of ancient Hindu texts and concluded that they were characterised by an 'inability to discriminate between fact and fancy'.[27] They consist of narrative forms which resemble 'fairy-tales, apologs, riddles, acrostics, tricks and pranks' (p. 55). Such ancient narratives had in recent years taken 'the shape of folklore' (p. 56), which had spread beyond India 'to the greater part of Central and Eastern Asia' (p. 56) and, given their widespread cultural dissemination it is unlikely that Kipling would have been unaware of them. Bloomfield notes that one strand in these narratives relates to 'The Laugh and Cry Motif' in which frequently these 'two extreme emotions touch' and become 'a fixed item in the apparatus of narration' (p. 69); as in 'Morrowbie Jukes' the crowd's mocking laughter becomes replaced by a mimic cry of subservience that essentially unites the two. However, Bloomfield's account of Indian folkloric laughter accords it the kind of Gothic significance noted by Horner and Zlosnik: 'It expresses not only pure joy, but also triumph, scorn, impish mischief, irony, malice, fading out to uncanny, demonic mystery [. . .]. It is finally used to trick and befog' (p. 69). Bloomfield observes that the relationship between this complex, indeed Gothic, laughter and crying is played out as a 'gruesome mystery' in a number of ancient Indian vampire stories. He also notes in tales which employ this Gothic laughter that, as in 'Morrowbie Jukes', 'an enigmatic laugh serves as the pivotal point of a story, or is used with rhetorical or dramatic effect to mark its point' (p. 81). He discusses one tale where 'The laugh of [a] satanic corpse' (p. 84) leads to the demise of a prince; laughter is used to mock the powerful, a trope which often finds itself expressed in 'the laugh of the dead' (p. 86) that also characterises Gunga Dass.

Harish Trivedi has helpfully explored the issue of postcolonial intertextuality, arguing that it has its roots in translations of Sanskrit tales from the late eighteenth century which led to a European 'Oriental Renaissance'.[28] Trivedi notes that in India during the mid-nineteenth century, although universities promoted western literature, Sanskrit tales were also available in translation. The teaching of such literature helped to develop a culture which forged links between western and non-western forms of writing, so that 'the Western influence on Indian literature was nothing if not dialectical and dialogic'.[29] Kipling seems to absorb such native texts in his work which stage a dialogic relationship with (post, and paradoxically, ante) colonial laughter (one which has its roots in Indian folklore), in order to illustrate the seemingly Gothic encounters typically confronted by the Anglo-Indian.

Trivedi argues that western literature helped to shape an Indian tradition of writing in the late nineteenth century, and Sudipta Kaviraj has explored this issue of influence in depth, claiming that a tradition of irony that had once been excluded on the grounds of frivolity entered Bengali literature at that time. He notes of Bankim's novel *Kamalakanta* (1885) that it concerns 'the self, the collective of which the self is a part, and the civilization of colonial India which formed the theatre in which this darkly comic spectacle of the search for the self unfolds'.[30] The principal problem that Kaviraj notes was that traditional Indian narrative forms 'did not have a name for this new laughter' (p. 388). In relation to Kipling this suggests that issues about laughter are not solely an aspect of a potentially Gothicisable Anglo-Indian identity; it also implies that much of this is worked out at a fundamentally textual level.

These issues of narrative meaning are ones which Kipling addresses in a sombre key in 'My Own True Ghost Story' (1888). The tale opens with a repudiation
of a British ghost story tradition which is associated with Walter Besant (whose
The Case of Mr Lucraft: And Other Tales was published in 1876), who becomes a
representative figure of 'the Other World' of Britain. Besant treats 'his ghosts [. . .]
with levity', but in India 'You may treat anything, from a Viceroy to a Vernacular
Paper, with levity; but you must behave reverently toward a ghost, and particularly
an Indian one'.[31] The title of the tale indicates the narrator's claim of ownership
and it does not, as 'Morrowbie Jukes' does, seek to integrate an ostensibly othered
language of laughter. The tale attempts to distinguish between Indian and English
ghosts. Indian ghosts 'are only vernacular articles and do not attack Sahibs' (p. 36);
however, although 'No native ghost has yet been authentically reported to have
frightened an Englishman [. . .] many English ghosts have scared the life out of
both black and white' (p. 36). These are the ghosts of colonial administrators.

The tale notes that 'Nearly every other Station owns a ghost' and that 'The older
Provinces simply bristle with haunted houses, and march phantom armies along
their main thoroughfares' (p. 36). In particular it is the dâk-bungalows which seem
to harbour so many of the colonial dead: 'A ghost that would voluntarily hang
about a dâk-bungalow would be mad of course; but so many men have died in
dâk-bungalows that there must be a fair percentage of lunatic ghosts' (p. 37).
What concerns the narrator is how to develop the appropriate idiom in which to
tell his tale: 'In due time I found my ghost, ghosts rather, for there were two of
them. Up till that hour I had sympathized with Mr. Besant's method of handling
them [. . .] I am now in the Opposition' (p. 37).

The narrator stays at a dâk-bungalow which is ghosted by a lost imperial past.
The bungalow had once been occupied by an eminent administrator who had died
twenty-five years earlier: 'I had seen a steel engraving of him at the head of a double
volume of Memoirs a month before, and I felt ancient beyond telling' (p. 38). The
problem is that the *khansamah* who looks after the bungalow speaks as if the old
master were still alive. Whilst eating dinner the narrator records that he had 'a curious meal, half native and half English in composition – with the old *khansamah*
babbling behind my chair about dead and gone English people' (p. 39).

The tale, despite its sombre tone, is not without humour in its reading of this
colonial past. The narrator first becomes aware of a spectral presence in the bungalow when, 'Just as I was getting into bed [. . .] I heard, in the next room, the
sound that no man in his senses can possibly mistake – the whir of a billiard ball
down the length of the slates when the striker is stringing for break. No other sound
like it' (p. 40). The narrator is entranced but horrified by this noise and concludes
that this must be a ghostly game of billiards as the room is in reality a furnished
bedroom. He next hears 'the double click of a cannon' followed by 'another cannon,
a three-cushion one to judge by the whir' (p. 40). He reacts by saying, 'I had found
my ghost and would have given worlds to escape from that dâk-bungalow. I

listened, and with each listen the game grew clearer' (p. 40). He subsequently discovers that the room had been a billiard room some ten or twenty years before. The narrator records, in a comedic vein, that 'I had my ghost – a first-hand, authenticated article. I would write to the Society for Psychical Research – I would paralyze the Empire with the news!' (p. 43). The tale suggests that billiards represents a form of Britishness which playfully persists. However, ultimately the narrator advances a more prosaic explanation that the noises have been a consequence of the wind playing against the window bolts (possibly combined with the noise of a gnawing rat). With a change in the weather the sounds cease: 'Then the wind ran out and the billiards stopped, and I felt that I had ruined my one genuine, hall-marked ghost story' (p. 44). At this point the narrator laments, 'Had I only stopped at the proper time, I could have made *anything* out of it. That was the bitterest thought of all!' (p. 44, italics in original).

The truth of 'My Own True Ghost Story' is thus explained away in a moment of closure which appears to compromise the idea that the tale has actually been a ghost story at all. However, on a more complex level the tale represents the narrator's projection of a haunted past, one which suggests that the '*anything*' which could be made of it is related to the possible presence of metaphoric meaning. Such metaphors of meaning might appear to be undone by a 'meaningless' realism (in that it has all just been a trick of the weather), but at an abstract level the tale represents an attempt to discover a language for conceptual meaning (one which relates to the presence of the colonial past). 'Ghosts' in the tale are thus only realised at the level of 'rhetoric', in a narrative which is self-conscious about its possible place in a ghost story tradition that has been influenced by Besant.

What the ghost means therefore depends on how it can be decoded. 'My Own True Ghost Story' employs humour to debunk the possibility of discovering meaning, whilst it nevertheless registers this in a language which is dogged by pathos and disappointment. In this instance humour is held in a dialectical tension with fear. At the end, the narrator is paradoxically relieved and bitter at the explanation for the ghost.

An alternative use of the comic is staged in 'The Phantom 'Rickshaw' (1888). The tale begins by asserting the essential explicability of India:

> One of the few advantages that India has over England is a great Knowability. After five years' service a man is directly or indirectly acquainted with the two or three hundred Civilians in his Province, all the Messes of ten or twelve Regiments and Batteries, and some fifteen hundred other people of the non-official caste. In ten years his knowledge should be doubled, and at the end of twenty he knows, or knows something about, every Englishman in the Empire, and may travel anywhere and everywhere without paying hotel-bills.[32]

However, any such knowledge is inevitably partial, relating solely to an Englishman's experience of other Englishmen. This partial knowledge was also developed in 'My Own True Ghost Story' through a suggested language of self-generated haunting. Indeed 'The Phantom 'Rickshaw' is self-conscious about this 'Inner Circle' (p. 7) which keeps India at bay. Nevertheless, it is the pressures of this closed community which, so the tale suggests, develop emotional instabilities and psychological trauma. How to find the right language for this experience is also stressed, but in more playful tones than those found in 'My Own True Ghost Story': 'The weather in India is often sultry, and since the tale of bricks is always a fixed quantity, and the only liberty allowed is permission to work overtime and get no thanks, men occasionally break down and become as mixed as the metaphors in this sentence' (p. 8).

Moore-Gilbert has noted that at this time 'A great preoccupation of Anglo-Indian culture [was] the problem of demoralisation in the subcontinent' (p. 139), and 'The Phantom 'Rickshaw' suggests that such demoralisation is engendered within the Anglo-Indian community. Unlike the other tales explored here it is also, at one level, a love story – one in which the narrator retells the strange experiences of Theobald Pansay, who has an affair with a Mrs Wessington and then abandons her and she dies, seemingly of a broken heart. Pansay becomes engaged to Kitty Mannering, and their occasional horse rides are interrupted by the ghostly presence of Mrs Wessington in a rickshaw that only Pansay can see. The vision includes servants and this leads Pansay to speculate that he may have gone insane: 'One may see ghosts of men and women, but surely never of coolies and carriages' (p. 17). Pansay subsequently discovers that the four men who crew the rickshaw had died of cholera: '[I] laughed aloud at this point; and my laugh jarred on me as I uttered it. So there *were* ghosts of rickshaws after all, and ghostly employments in the other world! How much did Mrs. Wessington give her men? What were their hours? Where did they go?' (pp. 19–20). These comic deliberations are developed when Pansay stops to speak with the spectral Mrs Wessington. One observer notes of this scene that Pansay was ' "Mad as a hatter, poor devil – or drunk" ' (p. 20). After some medical treatment (the 'hallucinations' are diagnosed as the result of a physical illness) the visions temporarily cease. However, they begin again when he is out riding and Kitty calls off their engagement.

Pansay's disorientation is in part due to the fact that he is the only one who can see the ghosts and 'it seemed that the 'rickshaw and I were the only realities in a world of shadows' (p. 29). However, Pansay's attempt to assert an alternative reality only refers to the very limited world of the Anglo-Indian. He tries to restore his sanity by attempting 'to recollect some of the gossip I had heard at the Club: the pieces of So-and-So's horses – anything, in fact, that related to the workaday Anglo-Indian world I knew so well' (p. 30). However, he finds himself trapped between two worlds: 'By day I wandered with Mrs. Wessington almost content. By night I implored Heaven to return me to the world as I used to know it' (p. 33). Dr Heatherleigh, who had previously treated him, suggests sending Pansay back to England, however 'Heatherleigh's proposition moved me almost to hysterical laughter' (p. 33) because he knows that he cannot escape his punishment for abandoning Mrs Wessington.

The comedy in 'The Phantom 'Rickshaw' is a consequence of Pansay being trapped between two worlds: the Anglo-Indian and the Gothic. Both of them seem utterly risible to Pansay, who dies because of the presiding 'Powers of Darkness' (p. 34). Finally, the hysterical laughter which characterises the tale becomes one of despair but, as in the other tales discussed here, such laughter is non-cathartic as it is associated with the liminality of the Anglo-Indian.

Ultimately, images of laughter in Kipling represent a highly politicised language of male hysteria in which men's sense of social identity becomes compromised because it is either subject to mimicry or otherwise merely present as a nervous projection.

How to read the ghost story in its colonial contexts reveals how images of spectrality articulate the feelings of unease that accrue to the colonising subject. Dickens uses the figure of the ghost in order to peculiarly empower his account of America in which he asserts a seemingly 'superior' national difference. For Le Fanu political history and the ghost are closely associated because for him the political history of Ireland is spectral. His tales also work through images of humour and suppressed hysteria which are closely linked to the spectre as they make emotionally present the mood of anxiety which the invisibility of the ghost conjures. Kipling runs together comedy and the Gothic in order to dwell on the irrationality of the colonial subject whose only knowledge of 'Otherness' so often appears as a projected version of themself. In these instances spectrality becomes a language without transcendence.

Nationhood and history are also issues which have shaped criticism on M.R. James, and how his spectres function as literary and historical entities will be the subject of the following chapter.

Notes

1 Homi K. Bhabha, 'Of Mimicry and Man: The Ambivalence of Colonial Discourse' in *The Location of Culture* (London: Routledge, 1995) pp. 85–92, p. 85. All subsequent references are to this edition and are given in the text.

2 Avril Horner and Sue Zlosnik, *Gothic and the Comic Turn* (Basingstoke: Palgrave, 2005) p. 166.

3 Charles Dickens, *American Notes for General Circulation*, ed. and introd. John S. Whitley and Arnold Goldman (Harmondsworth: Penguin, [1842] 1985). All subsequent references are to this edition and are given in the text. Please also note that my reading of Dickens is based on my previously published 'Colonial Ghosts: Mimicking Dickens in America' in Avril Horner and Sue Zlosnik (eds), *Le Gothic: Influences and Appropriations in Europe and America* (Basingstoke: Palgrave, 2008) pp. 185–97.

4 Sigmund Freud, 'The "Uncanny"' in *Art and Literature: Jensen's* Gradiva, *Leonardo Da Vinci and other works*, Penguin Freud Library vol. 14, trans. James Strachey, ed. Albert Dickson (Harmondsworth: Penguin, 1985) pp. 339–76.

5 A point also made by John S. Whitley and Arnold Goldman in their introduction to *American Notes*, p. 31, n. 59.

6 Letter dated 22 March. Cited in *American Notes*, p. 316.

7 This use of the ghost is quite different to how Dickens uses ghosts in, for example, *A Christmas Carol* (1843), where they become devices to scare Scrooge into living a better life. Dickens does not really believe that there is a ghost in the State Penitentiary or intend to imply that there might be one there; instead the ghost is designed as an image to rhetorically capture the experience of isolation.

8 Steven Marcus, *Dickens from Pickwick to Dombey* (London: Chatto and Windus, 1965) p. 246.

9 W.J. McCormack, *Dissolute Characters: Irish Literary History through Balzac, Sheridan Le Fanu, Yeats and Bowen* (Manchester: Manchester University Press, 1993) see pp. 2–11.

10 Jarlath Killeen, 'Irish Gothic: A Theoretical Introduction', *Irish Journal of Gothic and Horror Studies*, 1 (October 2006), 1–7, 2. All subsequent references are to this edition and are given in the text.

11 Robert Tracy, 'Undead, Unburied: Anglo-Ireland and the Predatory Past', *LIT: Literature, Interpretation, Theory*, 10 (1999), 13–14, 14. All subsequent references are to this edition and are given in the text.

12 Sally Harris, 'The Haunting Past in J.S. Le Fanu's Short Stories', *Le Fanu Studies*, 2 (November 2006), 1–12, 1.

13 Victor Sage, 'Gothic Laughter: Farce and Horror in Five Texts' in Allan Lloyd Smith and Victor Sage (eds), *Gothic: Origins and Innovations* (Amsterdam: Rodopi, 1994) pp. 190–203. See also Jack Sullivan, *Elegant Nightmares: The English Ghost Story from Le Fanu to Blackwood* (Athens: Ohio University Press, 1978) pp. 43–5, p. 67, pp. 85–7.

14 Luke Gibbons, '"Some Hysterical Hatred": History, Hysteria and the Literary Revival', *Irish University Review*, 21.1 (1997), 7–23, 23.

15 Sheridan Le Fanu, 'The Child that went with the Fairies' in *Madam Crowl's Ghost: and Other Tales of Mystery*, ed. and introd. M.R. James (Ware, Hert: Wordsworth, [1923] 1994) p. 50. All subsequent references are to this edition and are given in the text.

16 See Tracy, 'Undead, Unburied', 23. Indeed *Carmilla* helps to re-establish the view that Le Fanu conjures the *sidhé* as representative figures of a territorialism that pre-dates the Anglo-Irish. In *Carmilla* Laura notes that 'My father is English, and I bear an English name, although I never saw England', however in Styria they have been able to purchase a castle because 'here, in this lonely primitive place, where everything is so marvellously cheap' they are at an economic advantage. In *Carmilla* it is Laura and her father who represent the alien elements within the place (even if they are distant relatives of the Karnsteins, which include Carmilla), whereas Carmilla is directly descended from an ancient family that has a clearer association with the area. Sheridan Le Fanu, *Carmilla*, in *The Penguin Book of Vampire Stories*, ed. Alan Ryan (Harmondsworth: Penguin, 1987) pp. 71–137, p. 72.

17 See W.J. McCormack, *Sheridan Le Fanu* (Guernsey: Sutton, [1980] 1997) pp. 203, 269.

18 Sheridan Le Fanu, 'Ghost Stories of Chapelizod', pp. 86–107, 'The Spectre Lovers', pp. 97–107, *Madam Crowl's Ghost: and Other Tales of Mystery*, ed. and introd. M.R. James, (Ware, Herts: Wordsworth, [1923] 1994) p. 106. All subsequent references are to this edition and are given in the text.

19 Sheridan Le Fanu, 'An Account of Some Strange Disturbances in Aungier Street', in *Madam Crowl's Ghost: and Other Tales of Mystery*, ed. and introd. M.R. James (Ware, Herts: Wordsworth, [1923] 1994) p. 68. All subsequent references are to this edition and are given in the text.

20 This is a view which echoes Scrooge's in *A Christmas Carol* (1843) when he tells Marley's ghost, ' "There's more of gravy than of grave about you" '. *A Christmas Carol* in *The Christmas Books*, vol. 1, ed. and introd. Michael Slater (Harmondsworth: Penguin, 1985) pp. 45–134, p. 59.

21 This section reworks some of my earlier 'Kipling's Gothic and Postcolonial Laughter', in *Gothic Studies*, 11.1, special issue on 'Theorising the Gothic', ed. Jerrold E. Hogle and Andrew Smith (May 2009), 58–69.

22 Bart Moore-Gilbert, *Kipling and 'Orientalism'* (New York: St Martin's Press, 1986) p. 188. All subsequent references are to this edition and are given in the text.

23 Lewis D. Wurgaft, *The Imperial Imagination: Magic and Myth in Kipling's India* (Middletown, CT: Wesleyan University Press, 1983) p. 127.

24 Cited in Wurgaft, *The Imperial Imagination*, p. 129. Italics in original.

25 Rudyard Kipling, 'The Strange Ride of Morrowbie Jukes' in *The Phantom 'Rickshaw and Other Ghost Stories* (Fairfield CT: 1st World Library, [1885], 2007) pp. 45–72, p. 48. All subsequent references are to this edition and are given in the text.

26 Baidik Bhattacharya, 'Jokes Apart: Orientalism, (Post)colonial Parody and the Moment of Laughter', *Interventions: International Journal of Postcolonial Studies*, 8.2 (2006), 276–94, 280. All subsequent references are to this edition and are given in the text.

27 Maurice Bloomfield, 'On Recurring Psychic Motifs in Hindu Fiction, and the Laugh and Cry Motif', *Journal of the American Oriental Society*, 36 (1916), 54–89, 55. All subsequent references are to this edition and are given in the text.

28 Harish Trivedi, 'Colonial Influence, Postcolonial Intertextuality: Western Literature and Indian Literature', *Forum for Modern Language Studies*, 43.2 (2007). Trivedi's reference to an 'Oriental Renaissance' refers to Raymond Schwab's 'There is an Oriental Renaissance' from his *The Oriental Renaissance: Europe's Discovery of India and the East 1680–1880* (New York, 1984) pp. 11–20 and passim. Cited in Trivedi at 123.

29 Trivedi, 'Colonial Influence, Postcolonial Intertextuality', 127.

30 Sudipta Kaviraj, 'Laughter and Subjectivity: The Self-Ironical Tradition in Bengali Literature', *Modern Asian Studies*, 34.2 (May 2000), 379–406, 388. All subsequent references are to this edition and are given in the text.

31 Rudyard Kipling, 'My Own True Ghost Story' in *The Phantom 'Rickshaw and Other Ghost Stories* (Fairfield, CT: 1st World Library, [1888] 2007) pp. 35–44, p. 35. All subsequent references are to this edition and are given in the text.

32 Rudyard Kipling, 'The Phantom 'Rickshaw' in *The Phantom 'Rickshaw and Other Ghost Stories* (Fairfield, CT: 1st World Library, [1888] 2007) pp. 7–34, p. 7. All subsequent references are to this edition and are given in the text.

8

M.R. James's Gothic revival

This book has explored how a variety of socio-political concerns became articulated through a discourse of spectrality between 1840 and 1920. This discourse of spectrality is in many respects an essential characteristic of those socio-political issues as in, for example, the instance of economics. We have also explored how such concerns shaped gender scripts and informed discussion of national identity. However, with M.R. James the picture appears to be much less complex because critical analysis of his tales has tended to emphasise their apparent lack of overt or covert political engagement. This chapter outlines the reasons for this prevailing view of James, and argues that his writings should be understood as a critical, perhaps conservative, response to modernism. This requires a close analysis of the structure of his tales and in particular how he employs embedded Gothic narratives. However, the reason why James has seemingly posed a problem for scholars of the Gothic has its origins in a response to the ghost story itself.

David Punter in *The Literature of Terror* (1996) argues that during the early part of the twentieth century the ghost story entered 'a highly mannered phase'[1] which culminated in 'the shockingly bland tones of M.R. James' (p. 68). For Punter, this matter of tone is a consequence of the stories' apparent 'self-conscious fictionality' (p. 68), which does not invite the Coleridgean suspension of disbelief upon which the Gothic so typically depends. Indeed, James's settings are often little more than 'Gothic stereotypes' (p. 89) and although his formulaic constructions might possess a certain Gothic style, they are fundamentally devoid of radical content: 'They *work* well, but they *mean* almost nothing' (p. 90, emphasis in original). In *The Gothic* Punter and Glennis Byron summarise this view by suggesting that James's tales do not invite the reader to 'dwell too long on horrors' because this 'would be entirely out of keeping with the scholarly, or gentlemanly, ambience of the tales'.[2] For William Hughes, 'James's tales construct an almost idyllic late-Victorian and Edwardian world' consisting of the quiet 'College Combination Room, the library, or the cathedral close'.[3] Even the Gothic's typical fascination with extreme mental states is missing because as Julia Briggs claims, in James's tales 'psychology is totally and defiantly excluded'.[4]

Clive Bloom has argued that this critical frustration with James is because his tales seemingly refuse to yield up the covert and often conflicted political messages that typically characterise the Gothic. He notes that for such critics 'there is an embarrassment of literary form over sociological content'.[5] For Bloom, James should be seen in the context of an Edwardian rural revivalist culture which looked back to a halcyon version of the eighteenth century, one which is referenced in the urbane and distinctively English voices of James's narrators. James's tales are therefore grounded in 'an aesthetic based on the pleasure of avoidance of deeper symbolic meaning' (p. 67), so that 'they refuse to be read as sexual, psychological or social allegories' (p. 70).

This version of James implies that the highly politicised narratives of the ghost story which we have so far addressed disappear within a mannerist aesthetic that has been purposefully designed to marginalise any troubling Gothic elements because James's nostalgia refers to 'a world both slower and more stable' than the 'modernistic' (Bloom, p. 69) period in which he was writing. This issue of the retrospective nature of James's writing and how it relates to modernism is one that will be returned to. However, the idea that James's tales represent stable worlds is a problematic claim given the prevalence of death, abduction, and demonic hauntings. The past is a dangerous place in his tales but, as we shall see, this is related to a response to modernism that relocates its apparent amorality within the seemingly urbane narratorial voices.

According to the prevalent critical view, then, with M.R. James the ghost story becomes hollowed out, or manifested as little more than a repetitive narrative mannerism, and yet some of these same critics have also acknowledged that there is more to James than just this. Punter, for example, claims that 'almost all of the stories are structurally identical' (p. 86), but that the tales do generate a sense of unease even if 'it is curiously difficult to find within his texts the exact grounds of his effectiveness' (p. 87). One reason might be 'the mixture of the comforting and the disturbing' (Punter, p. 87) which characterises the tales and which, as Hughes acknowledges, points towards the presence of the uncanny.[6] Dani Cavallaro has commented on how James's characters 'come across as relatively flat', but that 'the pursuit of allusive vagueness' (also noted by Bloom) 'results in descriptions which evoke a powerful impression of physicality and even revulsion'.[7]

These hints of a critical ambivalence about James imply that there is a hidden complexity to the writings which has not yet been quite grasped. The role of the uncanny helps to draw out these complexities. In particular, an exploration of how James implicitly claims that uncanniness is central to the history of the Gothic helps us to appreciate that far from bringing the Gothic to an end he is attempting to revive an earlier, eighteenth-century, Gothic tradition. My argument is that this Gothic revival in privileged, often Oxbridge, milieux challenges the seemingly comfortable world of polite academic discussion by suggesting the presence of a barbarism that can be recorded and understood, but which cannot be defeated. This is not an Edwardian revivalist narrative, but one which is grounded in a critique of modernism.

The tales which best exemplify this attempt to resurrect the Gothic are 'Canon Alberic's Scrap-Book' (1895), 'Lost Hearts' (1895), 'The Mezzotint' (1904), and

'The Haunted Dolls' House' (1925). The different levels at which uncanniness is manifested are also significant. The uncanny appears in the content of the tales, and is also apparent in the disjunction between their rhetorical tone (familiar and conversational) and their subject matter (abduction and murder). What is revealing across these tales is how James locates fear in relation to either the narrator, or to the earlier teller of the tales. James's complex narrative structure has often been regarded as a means of distancing horror. However, changes in this structure, particularly in the later tales, implicate the reader in a voyeurism that is meant to unsettle the idea that 'horror' can be contained by the urbane narratorial voice. It is that very urbanity which generates the horror, a position which is clear in 'The Haunted Dolls' House'. Such tales are also not necessarily specifically about ghosts in any conventional sense; they also concern, as do the writings of Wilkie Collins, other images of haunting (James's figures are not just haunted by ghosts, but often by other demonic entities).

Freud claims that the uncanny represents our inability to escape the past, but it is also characterised by how the apparently homely and familiar (*heimlich*) becomes progressively sinister and uncomfortable (*unheimlich*). Indeed, it suggests that within our notion of the familiar there exists another thinly concealed presence that disturbs us, haunts us, and yet defines us. This position could almost be read as a summary of the disjunction between the narrators and the plots of James's tales. Such tales might be narrated from a position of comfort but this does not negate the effects of horror within the tales themselves.

Narrating monsters

In 'Canon Alberic's Scrap-Book' the anonymous narrator recounts a tale told to him by a Cambridge collector of antiquities, Dennistoun, about the strange experiences he had in France when collecting the scrap-book of the title. Such a device might seem to distance the reader from the 'horror' of the tale, but it is not the case that the narrator escapes unscathed. The tale is about the effects of horror, and how only a proximity to the supernatural events can create any genuinely lasting feelings of having entered a Gothic world. Dennistoun ostensibly shares the narrator's sense of distance as he initially assigns the suggestions of terror to prosaic origins. When, for example, he is taken round St. Bertrand's church by the verger, he notes the verger's terror: 'He was perpetually half glancing behind him; the muscles of his back and shoulders seemed to be hunched in a continual nervous contraction, as if he were expecting every moment to find himself in the clutch of an enemy'.[8] Dennistoun is not sure of the source of such terror and believes that he may be 'an unbearably henpecked husband' (p. 2), even if 'the impression conveyed was that of a more formidable persecutor [. . .] than a termagant wife' (p. 2). These initial uncertainties are contributed to by the narrator, who stresses that Dennistoun is in France and implies that such confusions might be due to national differences. The narrator also indicates that Dennistoun is not the real name of the main protagonist, and that he wishes to refer to the verger as a sacristan because 'I prefer the appellation, inaccurate as it may be' (p. 2). Such interventions imply a tidying up of the narrative, although one which cannot quite dispel the tale's Gothic content.

Dennistoun becomes increasingly pulled into a Gothic environment which, at this stage, is represented by the effect that it has on the verger and the lack of effect which it has on Dennistoun. Behind the altar is 'a large dark picture [. . .] well-nigh indecipherable' (p. 4) which is meant to represent St. Bertrand conducting one of his miracles. The painting reduces the verger to 'a suppliant in agony', whereas Dennistoun asks himself, ' "Why should such a daub of this kind affect anyone so strongly?" ' (p. 4). Represented worlds become real worlds when the verger sells Canon Alberic's scap-book to Dennistoun. The scrap-book contains 150 pages of assorted rare items including extracts from an eighth-century Bible, an English Psalter, and a 'very early unknown patristic treatise' (p. 9). The final two pages are the most recent; one is a plan of the south aisle and cloisters of the church, the next represents four soldiers (with a fifth lying dead) who are attempting to restrain a seemingly supernatural figure that has been brought before King Solomon to face judgement. The figure is described in ways which paradoxically suggest both its supernatural provenance and its reality. It is also described in terms of how it is seen, of how it becomes visual:

> At first you saw only a mass of coarse, matted black hair; presently it was seen that this covered a body of fearful thinness, almost a skeleton, but with the muscles stand-ing out like wires. The hands were of a dusky pallor, covered, like the body, with long, coarse hairs, and hideously taloned. The eyes, touched in with a burning yellow, had intensely black pupils, and were fixed upon the throned King with a look of beast-like hate. (pp. 11–12)

What is striking is how this representation of the fantastical is granted a strange reality due to the wealth of detail that is conferred upon the figure. According to the narrator, everyone who is shown the illustration remarks that ' "It was drawn from the life" ' (p. 12), even though, in a twist which reworks James's use of narratorial distance, people are only shown a photograph of the illustration as Dennistoun has destroyed the original. The photograph captures the sense of the scene's central Gothic drama, but with the destruction of the original a super-natural curse relating to ownership of the illustration (in which the figure haunts the owner) is brought to an end. The photograph, like the use of the narrator, therefore functions as an attempt to contain the troubling aspects of the inner Gothic tale. However, this is only a partially successful strategy of containment. The narrator has seen a photograph of the picture and observes:

> I entirely despair of conveying by any words the impression which this figure makes upon anyone who looks at it. I recollect once showing the photograph of the

drawing to a lecturer on morphology – a person of, I was going to say, abnormally
sane and unimaginative habits of mind. He absolutely refused to be alone for the rest
of that evening, and he told me afterwards that for many nights he had not dared to
put out his light before going to sleep. (p. 11)

Here, the problem seems to be being 'abnormally sane and unimaginative' because
it ill-equips the viewer to conceptually understand what they are observing. The
same is true of Dennistoun, who once he has purchased the scrap-book reluctantly
takes a crucifix from the verger's daughter which she has intended to protect him.
According to the narrator, 'Well, really, Dennistoun hadn't much use for these things'.
Dennistoun expresses suspicion of an alternative motive by questioning, 'What did
mademoiselle want for it?' (p. 13).

Dennistoun and the narrator appear to inhabit a culturally shared world which
this 'Well, really' implies. However, it is Dennistoun who is subject to a Gothic
presence when he purchases the scrap-book and the creature in the illustration
(prior to the illustration being photographed and destroyed) is manifested in
Dennistoun's hotel room. The narrator comments that:

The feelings with which this horror stirred in Dennistoun were the intensest physical fear and the most profound mental loathing. What did he do? What could he
do? He has never been quite certain what words he said, but he knows that he spoke,
that he grasped blindly at the silver crucifix, that he was conscious of a movement
towards him on the part of the demon, and that he screamed with the voice of an
animal in hideous pain. (p. 16)

Dennistoun's two rescuers do not see the creature although they are conscious that
something rushed between them when they opened the door. The significant
factor here is Dennistoun's apparent descent down an evolutionary ladder from
Cambridge archivist to 'an animal'.[9] The creature represents the presence of a physicality which is otherwise absent from the tale. When staring into the demon's eyes,
Dennistoun notes that 'There was intelligence of a kind in them – intelligence beyond that of a beast, below that of a man' (p. 16). Dennistoun's very brief and
temporary descent is an enforced transcendence of his detached, scholarly world.
This brief, explicit version of extreme fear in turn threatens to compromise the
detached narrative voice because of the shared values which exist between the
narrator and Dennistoun.

In this instance the reader is left with the impression that the means of Gothic
containment has to consist of more than an urbane slant on the events of the story,
because it depends upon controlling the Gothic content by taking a photograph
of the illustration and destroying the original. In this instance the distancing of
the Gothic is effected in problematic ways because the narrator is at only one remove
from Dennistoun's drama. Distance is only manifested through representational
forms: the illustration, the photograph of the illustration, the narrator's account
of Dennistoun's version of events. However, even this type of distance does not

generate a convincing containment because at one level what is horrific is that the creature escapes. This means that throughout there is a tension between the 'reality' of the creature and the narrative forms (such as the illustration) which have unsuccessfully attempted to contain him. The tale can thus be read as a conceit for how Gothic horror eludes a series of representational strategies because even they generate horror, as witnessed by the reaction of the frightened morphologist.[10]

The issue of visibility is important here because it implies that the reader becomes a voyeur of the events, whereas the narrator's detachment is problematised by their proximity to the action. The issue of narratorial proximity plays a crucial function in James's tales and will be explored in depth in some of his later narratives. However, another tale published in 1895, 'Lost Hearts', addresses the idea of horror and its physical immediacy in ways which suggest a critique of the scholarly detachment that ostensibly pervades many of James's tales.

Revisioning the demon

'Lost Hearts' focuses on the activities of the reclusive Mr. Abney, Professor of Greek at Cambridge. He lives in some comfort at Aswarby Hall in Lincolnshire and has servants who look after his domestic needs. This wealthy and privileged world has been periodically disturbed by the presence of three children who over a twenty-year period have been invited by the professor to reside with him. The first two children are outsiders to this privileged world. One is 'a wandering Italian lad named Giovanni Paoli' who played the hurdy-gurdy for money and who had disappeared twenty years ago.[11] Ten years later the second child, 'one Phoebe Stanley, a girl of gispy extraction' (p. 34), was brought into the house only to disappear in similarly mysterious circumstances. The final child is Stephen Elliott, an orphaned cousin of Abney's, who is perceived by the locals as a potentially unsettling presence within the apparently scholarly world of Abney.

For the locals, Abney 'was looked upon, in fine, as a man wrapped up in his books, and it was a matter of great surprise among his neighbours that he should even have heard of his orphan cousin, Stephen Elliott, much more that he should have volunteered to make him an inmate of Aswarby Hall' (p. 22). Abney's very bookishness implies a detachment from the world that does not permit this kind of benevolent involvement. Whilst this functions as a critique of his attachment to scholarship it is also based on ignorance of what Abney's studies consist of. Abney's researches include analysis of various ancient occult philosophies of magic which indicate that transformations including the ability to fly, invisibility, and the capacity to 'assume any form he pleased' (p. 33) will be possible if the hearts of three children are consumed. Abney records that his choice of children has been determined by the fact that they 'could conveniently be removed without occasioning a sensible gap in society' (pp. 34–5). Abney's scholarship therefore drives the Gothic narrative rather than contains it. It is through Stephen that the

Gothic appears as a series of frightening dream visions in which he encounters what appear to be the physical remains of the children. However, an additional factor is the revenge that the children are seeking by looking to replace the hearts which have been stolen from them. Ultimately the revenge is appropriately directed at Abney, but even Stephen has been attacked in a manner which anticipates the final assault on Abney. Stephen requests that Mrs Bunch, the housekeeper, repairs his pyjamas because of what the narrator notes as the presence of 'a most destructive and apparently wanton series of slits or scorings in the garment, which would require a skilful needle to make good' (p. 27). Whereas in 'Canon Alberic's Scrap-Book' there is an ostensible disjunction between scholarship and the Gothic (ostensible because Dennistoun is, after all, terrified by his experiences), in 'Lost Hearts' the uncanny disjunction is between the practical demands of domesticity (Mrs Bunch's complaint about having to repair the nightdress: ' "what trouble you do give to poor servants" ' (p. 27)) and the supernatural force which has caused the tears.

That the supernatural might be a consequence of Abney's experimentation is in part underlined by the suggestion that the place is besieged by tragic ghostly presences. On the night when Stephen is Abney's intended victim he looks out into the park which surrounds the house and 'felt as if an endless procession of unseen people were sweeping past him on the wind, borne on resistlessly and aimlessly, vainly striving to stop themselves, to catch at something that might arrest their flight and bring them once again into contact with the living world of which they had formed a part' (p. 30). Such a vision is not intended to be directly threatening because the spectres represent the presence of alienation, being described as 'lost and despairing wanderers' (p. 31). These spectral visions are contrasted with the physical presence of the ghosts of the earlier children which Stephen also sees: 'the girl stood still, half smiling, with her hands clasped over her heart, the boy, a thin shape, with black hair and ragged clothing, raised arms in the air with an appearance of menace and of unappeasable hunger and longing' (pp. 31–2). The figure of the boy develops the image of the demon in 'Canon Alberic's Scrap-Book' and it suggests the insistent presence of a kind of physical horror that is often overlooked in accounts of James.[12] The children represent a physical rather than a strictly psychological danger. Ghosts therefore take on material forms in order to enact their revenge. The tale indicates that the revengeful spirit of Giovanni carries out the final attack on Abney, after which, 'Mr. Abney was found in his chair, his head thrown back, his face stamped with an expression of rage, fright, and mortal pain. In his left side was a terrible lacerated wound, exposing the heart' (pp. 34–5).

The reader is not meant to sympathise with Abney because this murderous assault is the only means by which Stephen (despite an earlier assault upon him) can be saved. The question of where 'evil' lies in this is clear. It is Abney's reading of occult philosophies which has been responsible for the killing of the children, in what has been a spirit of intellectual curiosity. He describes his killing of the children and consumption of their hearts as an 'experiment' meant to test the truth of these occult theories (p. 33). In that regard an abstract academic mode of inquiry constitutes an amorality that generates, rather than contains, the Gothic. In 'Canon Alberic's Scrap-Book' the scholarly world represented by Dennistoun can only effect a problematic containment of the horror represented by the demon; in 'Lost Hearts' it creates the grounds under which horror appears. This demonising of academic inquiry is repeated throughout James's tales.

The fundamental issue concerns emotional detachment. The seemingly urbane tones of the narrator appear to be in stark contrast to the Gothic drama within the tale. However, such a view overlooks how this very detachment plays a part in generating the horror within such tales. Superficially it might appear that such a disjunction between tone and content helps to give a sharper focus to the embedded Gothic narratives. However, such a seemingly detached tone creates the possibility of horror because of its refusal to commit to any meaningful moral or intellectual system. In this way the narrators of James's tales generate horror and it requires an examination of the uncanny in order to appreciate this.

Distant voices

Freud's account of the uncanny identifies a disjunction between the familiar and the unfamiliar. However, the latter is freighted by the possibility of a return of a past experience which transforms the unfamiliar by claiming that within it exists an older repressed memory. It is this tension between the past and the present which is reworked by James in 'The Mezzotint' and 'The Haunted Dolls' House'.

The narrator of 'The Mezzotint' relates the experiences of Williams, who is responsible for collecting engravings for the university museum at Cambridge. The tale centres on a drama which takes place in the mezzotint of the title (an engraving that Williams was considering purchasing for the museum). The beginning of the tale focuses on the museum in a way which evokes the uncanny. For Freud, 'the uncanny is that class of the frightening which leads back to what is known of old and long familiar'.[13] In 'The Mezzotint' this is initially implied by the ambience of the museum. Williams is pleased that he did not have to embark upon a search for artefacts for the museum on the continent. Instead:

> He was glad to be obliged at the moment to confine his attention to enlarging the already unsurpassed collection of English topographical drawings and engravings possessed by the museum. Yet, as it turned out, even a department so *homely* and *familiar* as this may have its dark corners, and to one of these Mr. Williams was unexpectedly drawn.[14]

The mezzotint is brought into this museum, or mausoleum. The engraving dates from the early nineteenth century (the end of the Gothic heyday) and appears to Williams to be unremarkable, and he is surprised by the high price requested for it. The mezzotint is described as dull, both aesthetically and in terms of its content (a representation of a large country house): 'It was a rather indifferent mezzotint, and an indifferent mezzotint is, perhaps, the worst form of engraving known' (p. 39). Williams complains to Professor Binks, ' "It's a wretched engraving, and there aren't even any figures to give it life" ' (p. 40). This moribund illustration represents, in the tale, certain Gothic possibilities which become reanimated. Professor Binks replies, ' "I don't think it's so badly done . . . and I should have thought that there *were* figures, or at least a figure just on the edge in front" ' (pp. 40–1, italics in original), and so the mezzotint is aesthetically transformed and begins telling a Gothic tale concerning murder and abduction. Williams, however, looks for another opinion of the merits of the engraving and the amateur art historian that he shows it to tells him, ' "It's really a very good piece of work, Williams, it has quite a feeling of the romantic period. The light is admirably managed, it seems to me, and the figure, though it's rather too grotesque, is somehow very impressive" ' (p. 42). Williams is forced to acknowledge that the mezzotint is no longer an indifferent, lifeless, piece of work as the Gothic narrative within it comes to life and transforms it.

The illustration periodically traces the progress of a skeletal figure that heads towards the house in the mezzotint: 'It was crawling on all-fours towards the house, and it was muffled in a strange black garment with a white cross on the back' (p. 43). The question with which Williams and his colleagues are concerned relates to the significance of this narrative, in particular whom it is meant for and whether they have become complicit in its unfolding. Nisbet, one of Williams's colleagues, comments that ' "it looks very much as if we were assisting at the working out of a tragedy somewhere" ' (p. 46). For Williams it is also the case that the narrative is developed for the viewer's benefit, because the progress of the figure towards the house, its entry and its subsequent departure with a baby, are carefully staged so that they miss no part of the sequence, although they never see the movements taking place. As Williams says, ' "I rather imagine that we're meant to see the whole thing" ' (p. 47).

Williams and his colleagues carry out some research which enables them to locate the whereabouts of the house represented in the engraving. As a consequence they discover that the mezzotint is playing out a drama from 1802 when Arthur Francis (the engraver of the mezzotint) had his son seemingly abducted by the ghost of a man named Gawdy. Gawdy had been sentenced to death for killing one of Francis's gamekeepers, and he was therefore taking his revenge against Francis.

Throughout, the tale focuses on the idea of potentially moribund lives. We discover that the Francis family, which had displaced the Gawdys as the principal landowners, had died out as the abducted baby represented the last of the line (and because Francis did not have any more children). However, the executed Gawdy was also 'the last of his line' (p. 53), and so the tale addresses the idea of death at many different levels. The tale within the mezzotint is a Gothic narrative concerning revenge in which two families become extinct, but it also introduces the idea of death into the world of Williams and his colleagues, who occupy the position of the readers of a Gothic narrative.

The uncanny works on different levels here. Freud stated that 'death and the re-animation of the dead have been represented as most uncanny themes' (p. 369). The mezzotint, by coming to life, represents a resurrection of an earlier Gothic narrative. In effect James reanimates this earlier tradition as an object of curiosity for Williams and his colleagues, and this interpolation of a Gothic tale into their world also constitutes a moment of uncanniness. Freud argued that in the uncanny the homely (*heimlich*) and the unhomely (*unheimlich*) are conflated, so that the familiar becomes sinister. In the tale there exists a disjunction between the scenes within the mezzotint and the language used in the common room. Indeed the gravity of the Gothic narrative starkly contrasts with the self-consciously playful references to golf, which dominates much of the conversation. At one point the narrator observes, 'tea was taken to the accompaniment of a discussion which golfing persons can imagine for themselves' (p. 40). Later, over Sunday morning breakfast, 'Hardly a topic was left unchallenged, from golf to lawn-tennis' (p. 44). The implied point is that it is Williams and his colleagues who represent an 'indifferent' world (not the mezzotint), one which is amoral and associated with triviality. In essence they are lifeless figures who are forced, even if only temporarily, out of their complacency. Talk of golf therefore becomes a marker not of leisure but of moral vacuity.[15] The ending of the tale suggests this ambivalence as it indicates that perhaps the drama of the mezzotint informs them about their own sense of sterility: 'though carefully watched, it has never been known to change again' (p. 53).

'The Mezzotint' is a tale *about* the Gothic, rather than an explicitly Gothic narrative. The process of narration in which a tale witnessed by Williams is retold to a friend and then told to the narrator creates a distance from the inner Gothic tale. This is not to say that James's revival of a Gothic narrative for a later audience is without significance. Far from trying to lay the Gothic to rest, as Punter suggests, James is attempting to bring it back to life, and its resurrection does touch the apparently bland lives of Williams and his colleagues. In some respect the process of distancing the central narrative is in keeping with the type of subtle gestures and implied dangers that characterised the Radcliffean Gothic. James claimed in 'Some Remarks on Ghost Stories' (1929) that he was deliberately trying to avoid the explicitness which seemed to him to characterise contemporary Gothic. Like Radcliffe, he appears to have been an advocate of the subtleties of Terror rather than a champion of the explicitness of Horror: 'Reticence may be an elderly doctrine to preach, yet from the artistic point of view I am sure it is a sound one. Reticence conduces to effect, blatancy ruins it, and there is much blatancy in a lot of recent stories'.[16] This reticence is not associated with the alleged narrative blandness of the tales; rather it suggests the presence of a coyness that conceals one of the central mechanisms of the uncanny: repetition. In 'The Mezzotint', history in the form of the story of Francis and Gawdy is repeated. In a wider sense James's Gothic tale, which raises issues about power and legitimacy amongst feuding landowners, captures some of the spirit of the late eighteenth century and early nineteenth century Gothic, here repeated as an eloquent dumb show which does much to draw attention to the moral limitations of Williams and his colleagues.

One of the interesting features of 'The Mezzotint' is that it retells a Gothic narrative, and in the process repetition comes to an end. The Gothic tradition is reasserted and then disappears. James returned to this theme with 'The Haunted Dolls' House', where he makes some concluding remarks which acknowledge that the tale is a variation on 'The Mezzotint', although he hopes that 'there is enough of variation in the setting to make the repetition of the *motif* tolerable'.[17] The resurrection of the Gothic in 'The Mezzotint' is therefore itself resurrected, although in the later tale there is a more self-conscious sense of reviving the Gothic.

In 'The Haunted Dolls' House' Mr Dillet, a collector of antiques and curiosities, buys a dolls' house which is described as 'a museum piece', echoing the presence of the museum in 'The Mezzotint'. Mr Dillet takes the dolls' house home and unpacks it. The narrator states, 'it would have been difficult to find a more perfect and attractive specimen of a Dolls' House in Strawberry Hill Gothic' (p. 475). The house consists of a chapel, a main building with Gothic arches, and a stable. Mr Dillet comments that it is 'Quintessence of Horace Walpole, that's what it is: he must have had something to do with the making of it' (p. 476). Within this self-conscious Gothic setting he also finds a household of characters who play out a particular narrative at one o'clock in the morning every day. On the first occasion of this happening, Dillet notes that the house looks as though it has come alive: 'He seemed to be conscious of the scent of a cool still September night. He thought he could hear an occasional stamp and clink from the stables, as of horses stirring' (p. 478). As in 'The Mezzotint', there is the sense that the narrative requires a viewer to complete it; Dillet intuits, 'You mean to show me something' (p. 479). The tale that he bears witness to reveals that an old and ill man is poisoned by his daughter and her husband. In revenge the old man comes back as a ghostly form the night after he has been murdered and kills their children.

As in 'The Mezzotint', the tale unfolds in a particular way. The first scene concerns the murder of the old man, whose death throes were 'a sad and terrible sight – flushed in the face, almost to blackness, the eyes glaring whitely, both hands clutching at his heart, foam at his lips' (p. 481). However, in keeping with the Gothic, this is only the start of the tale and this is self-consciously referenced through Dillet's response to the murder: 'he had rightly guessed that there would be a sequel' (p. 482).

As discussed earlier, for Punter M.R. James's formalism seems to negate the possibility of true horror. However, although Dillet's familiarity with the Gothic implies that he expects the narrative to develop in a certain way, it also indicates that like 'The Mezzotint' the tale is not so much Gothic as *about* the Gothic. This sense of playing with the Gothic form is also indicated by what happens next in the dolls' house. The triumphant parents are joyfully conversing with their children, who are lying in bed before they go to sleep. During this playful scene the father stealthily leaves the room and returns with a sheet over his head, pretending to be a ghost. The 'joke' scares the children, who 'were in agonies of terror, the boy with the bedclothes over his head, the girl throwing herself out of bed into her mother's arms' (pp. 483–4). The children are placated, but this mock Gothic moment is quickly followed by the murder of the children by their grandfather. It is a moment in which the observer's role registers the horror of the scene without explicitly developing it:

> The door was opening again. The seer does not like to dwell upon what he saw entering the room: he says it might be described as a frog – the size of a man – but it had scanty hair about its head. It was busy about the truckle-beds, but not for long. The sound of the cries – faint, as if coming from out of the vast distance – but even so, infinitely appalling, reached the ear. (p. 484)

The final scene focuses on the coffins of the children being taken out of the house for burial. As in 'The Mezzotint' some historical research reveals the significance of the tale. The dolls' house was made by James Merewether, the father of the two children. It transpires that the grandfather was murdered because he was considering leaving his descendants out of his will.

History comes to repeat itself in a mock version of Strawberry Hill. The Gothic in this instance appears, superficially, as a parody in which Walpole's grand Gothic folly is represented as a child's toy. However, this literal diminution is used to chilling effect. Children are murdered in the doll's house, in what is a mock building far removed from the representative images of domesticity which such 'toys' usually connote. Instead of parody, James revives the Gothic and places explicit emphasis on Dillet's experience as a Gothic reader. Dillet is deeply disturbed by his sight of this drama, which leaves him 'in a disquieting state of nerves' (p. 485). However, this is all represented in the tale in a distanced way. Dillet's anxieties are not ours and this creates an unusual tension which has its roots in the earlier tales.

In 'The Mezzotint' uncanniness infiltrates the regulated, socially familiar lives of Williams and his colleagues. In doing so the fundamental amorality of the viewers of the mezzotint is brought into focus. They are not disturbed by the unfolding of the narrative in the way that Dillet is. The damaged nature of their lives is registered in this amorality, and the tale represents an attempt to repair this by introducing them to an extreme human drama which might provoke a response that transcends their fascination with golf. In 'The Haunted Dolls' House', it is the narrator who dispassionately relates the events, but this in turn suggests that it is the reader's world which is not to be disturbed. Dillet's sense of horror is distanced through James's use of a reticent narrator. This locates the reader of 'The Haunted Dolls' House' in an unusual position in that they are constructed as a passive voyeur of Dillet's despair. The tale therefore forces the reader to occupy the position of Williams and his colleagues in 'The Mezzotint'. The reader is made peculiarly complicit with the process of narrative distancing (indeed, Nisbet had acknowledged their complicity with the Gothic tale in 'The Mezzotint'), although crucially their implied comfort is rendered uneasy by the fact of the tale's incompleteness.

In 'The Mezzotint' the narrative of the engraving is told once, whereas the tale of the dolls' house repeats itself at one o'clock in the morning every day. Dillet puts the dolls' house into storage as the contrite previous owner agrees to find a new buyer for it in America. However, the unease which the tale generates is directed outwards towards the reader, rather than inwards at the other characters as it is in 'The Mezzotint'. This raises the question of why James would imply that the reader's voyeurism constitutes an amorality that distances them from the repetitive drama of the narrative of the dolls' house. This is because James does, despite Briggs's claim about his robust exclusion of psychological factors, focus on the traumatised Dillet, who is forced to seek recuperation in a seaside town. In doing so the Gothic is, in this instance, used in order to suggest that it represents a model of trauma which has, at least for Dillet, a reality to it. This psychological drama is distanced from the reader because we are never given direct access to Dillet's inner life. The tale therefore subtly poses particular demands on the reader, whose passive voyeurism contrasts with the troubled gaze of Dillet. This new turn in these later tales can be explained by relating James to a literary and artistic movement which was historically contemporaneous with him, but with which he is not usually associated: modernism.

Modernism

In Chapter 4 May Sinclair's ghost stories were explored in terms of a modernist aesthetic. The close relationship between modernism and the Gothic is evidenced in a range of narrative forms encompassing poetry, novels, film, and music. T.S. Eliot, for example, in *The Waste Land* (1922), makes a specific reference to *Dracula* (1897):

> A woman drew her long hair out tight
> And fiddled whisper music on those strings
> And bats with baby faces in the violet light
> Whistled, and beat their wings
> And crawled head downward down a blackened wall
> And upside down in air were towers
> Tolling reminiscent bells, that kept the hours
> And voices singing out of empty cisterns and exhausted wells.[18]

The lines refer to Jonathan Harker's sight of the count crawling head downwards down one of the towers at Dracula's castle. They also make reference to the insistent presence in Stoker's novel of images of maternalism, although here this image is somewhat pathologised in its association with vampirism. Eliot's use of the Victorian Gothic within his account of modern decay suggests the continuing significance of the apparently 'low' Gothic form within the 'high' modernist text, in which the Gothic provides a model of instability (both social and psychological) that illustrates an aspect of the fragmented modernist self.[19] James Joyce in *Ulysses* (1922) makes a more jocular reference to *Dracula*, writing, 'He comes pale vampire, through storm his eyes, his bat sails bloodying the sea, mouth to her mouth's kiss. Here. Put a pin in that chap, will you?'[20] German Expressionist films such as Wiene's *The Cabinet of Dr Caligari* (1919), Wegener's *The Golem* (1920), and Murnau's *Nosferatu* (1921) exploited a Gothic aesthetic in their attempts to relate a fractured modernistic sense of the self to Gothic excess. In addition, in music Schoenberg produces a piece entitled 'A Theme Tune for an Imaginary Horror Film'.

The demands which such modernist texts as Eliot's and Joyce's place upon the reader require them to undertake a complex semiotic journey through revitalised mythologies that dwell on the emptiness (consider Eliot's 'The Hollow Men' (1925)) and moral confusion of modern life. The Gothic is resurrected in modernist texts in a way which has some similarity to James's use of the Gothic in 'The Haunted Dolls' House'. There James uses a Gothic drama in order to address contemporary concerns about amorality and modern waste lands *and* places a special demand on the reader in suggesting their complicit voyeurism. As in modernism, the Gothic provides a focus for a debate about the loss of value (moral and social) – a debate that has its roots in the discussions about golf in 'The Mezzotint' and which culminates in the voyeurism of 'The Haunted Dolls' House'. It is for this reason that James's alleged 'blandness' is misleading. He is not bringing the Gothic to an end by containing its subversive or transgressive energies through his self-conscious narrative formalism, but rather using the Gothic as the counterpoint against which a modern (bland) amorality appears to be developing.

This is not to suggest that James should be properly read as a neglected modernist; his robust formalism precludes such literary experimentation. Nevertheless at one level he is engaging with some of the issues which were of concern to the modernists, and although he does not experiment with form, he does play with it. His self-consciously constructed literary worlds, perhaps most clearly illustrated in his turning of Walpole's Strawberry Hill into a dolls' house, suggest the figural (and in this instance oddly literal) diminishing of the Gothic. However, this is for a particular purpose; the playfulness disguises the horror.

Recent critics have explored how modernism became haunted by earlier, nineteenth-century, Gothic tropes. Such hauntings suggests that the past has not quite been laid to rest. For Bloom, as we saw at the beginning of this chapter, James's interest in the past was based on an avoidance of the future. However, James's

Gothic revival suggests that his version of the past is more Gothic than halcyon and through it he manifests the kinds of anxieties which more usually typified modernist narratives. Such anxieties suggest that the past has become a burden which the modernist attempts to alleviate. As discussed in Chapter 4, David Glover in an argument concerning the representation of spectrality in early modernism has claimed that 'the Gothicisation of the past stands as a sign of the radical unavailability of a definite break with what has gone before'.[21] In James this is manifested as a paradox because his tales suggest the inescapability of the past *and* that the past dramatises the Gothic potentialities of his abstracted, amoral, narrators (which implies projection). For Glover such tales 'adumbrate the fear of a generalised breakdown in the narrative of progress' because even imagined versions of the future 'would recapitulate, yet also dramatically reconfigure, the worst features of the past' (p. 42). Although Glover is specifically referring to Conrad and Ford Maddox Ford, this sense of a corrupted future which is a projection of a corrupted present captures Bloom's notion that James's writings are fundamentally retrospective. It is because James cannot imagine a future that is not touched by the past that he addresses this lack of progress in the way he does. In this sense the Gothic functions as a sceptical vision of the modernist fascination with novelty and innovation. The Gothic represents a fragmented present which cannot be developed into a coherent vision of the future. James's references to scraps of old documents, and time-worn illustrations, also suggests this.

As we have seen, in James images of fragmentation are expressed in the relationship of the past to the present. The problem is that these older narratives, as in 'Canon Alberic's Scrap-Book', 'Lost Hearts', 'The Mezzotint', and 'The Haunted Dolls' House', have a vitality and uncontrollability that is the product of the present rather than the past. James projects a modernist anxiety about fragmentation back into the past which suggests, in the later two tales, the inability to transcend this fragmentation. The way in which the reader is progressively repositioned in the tales is key to this, because the reader's alignment with an amoral voyeuristic position on horror makes them complicit with its production. The presence of the uncanny is crucial here as the distance between reader, narrator, and protagonist paradoxically asserts that it is an amoral distance which creates horror in the first place. At one level this is to claim the critical commonplace that the Gothic cultivates ambiguity. However, such ambiguity is also a feature of modernism, and significantly it is the figure of the ghost which effects this ambiguity because its very presence suggests that reality itself has become unreal. Punter in an account of ghosts in modernist literature develops this point when he quotes Lukács's view on Kafka and ghosts. For Luckács, 'The word "ghostly" is interesting. It points to a major tendency in modernist literature: the attenuation of actuality [. . .] the realistic detail is the expression of a ghostly unreality, of a nightmare world, whose function is to evoke *Angst*'.[22] Although Punter stresses that he wants to avoid simplifying modernism into 'the ordered and the ghostly' (p. 21) nevertheless there is a relationship between the two because the notion of 'order' is in reality 'a perversion of progress that gestures to the building of a new world on the shattered remains – shattered by war and by the withdrawal of religious conviction – of an older one' (p. 21). The roots of this anxiety predate the First World War and are to be found in the images of fear which haunt James's protagonists. As in Kafka, the attenuation of reality creates anxiety, and this is a direct and immediate source of fear for Dennistoun in 'Canon Alberic's Scrap-Book' and Dillet in 'The Haunted Dolls' House'. it is also suggested in 'Lost Hearts' in Stephen's sight of the spirits who 'aimlessly' walk past and yet attempt 'to catch at something that might arrest their flight and bring them once again into contact with the living world' (p. 30). Estrangement from reality might be a specifically Gothic characteristic but with M.R. James this is also associated with his implicit critique of a modernist subjectivity which in its claims for coherence (its urbanity) generates an amoral view of the world that creates a Gothic fragmentation. In this sense modernism is a Gothic mode *par excellence*.

It is clear that in M.R. James his formalism becomes another source of the uncanny. It implies a familiarity in form and tone, although one which is at odds with the *unheimlich* place of the Gothic narratives *within* these tales. This idea, of hidden Gothic narratives which come to define the amorality of the ostensible norm, also colours much later, twentieth-century, Gothic texts. It has been noted, for example, that *Night of the Demon* (1957), the film version of James's 'Casting the Runes' (1911), possesses a Hitchcockean ambience.[23] What is often overlooked, however, is that the film also uses, without attribution, a scene concerning mediums from Robert Bloch's short story 'The Indian Spirit Guide' (1948).[24] The narratives of James and Bloch dovetail seamlessly, which suggests that James's tale of evoking the demonic and Bloch's post-war American Gothic have some kind of relationship. Indeed James's implicit critique of 'normalised' amorality and Bloch's representation of doubled but curiously empty figures such as Norman Bates have more in common than their specific settings suggest.

James's early tales such as 'Canon Alberic's Scrap-Book' and 'Lost Hearts' differ from the later tales such as 'The Mezzotint' and 'The Haunted Dolls' House' because the self-referential qualities of the latter can be explained as a critique of modernism. Ultimately, however, James's great contribution to the Gothic is to be found in his self-conscious revival of it. As he noted in his introduction to Le Fanu's *Madam Crowl's Ghost and Other Tales of Mystery* (1923), 'the ghost story is in itself a slightly old-fashioned form; it needs some deliberateness in its telling'.[25] It is this deliberateness which resurrects the Gothic and so brings the 'old-fashioned' up to date in order to address the concerns of the present.

Notes

1 David Punter, *The Literature of Terror: The Modern Gothic* (London and New York: Longman, 1996) vol. 2, p. 67. All subsequent references are to this edition and are given in the text.

2 David Punter and Glennis Byron, *The Gothic* (Oxford: Blackwell, 2004) p. 133.
3 William Hughes, in Marie Mulvey-Roberts (ed.), *The Handbook to Gothic Literature* (Basingstoke: Macmillan, 1998) p. 143.
4 Julia Briggs, *The Rise and Fall of the English Ghost Story* (London: Faber & Faber 1977) p. 135.
5 Clive Bloom, 'M.R. James and his Fiction' in Clive Bloom (ed.), *Creepers: British Horror & Fantasy in the Twentieth Century* (London: Pluto, 1993) p. 69. All subsequent references are to this edition and are given in the text.
6 Hughes, p. 143. Hughes also notes that beneath their surface charm the tales raise difficult questions of Anglicanism, p. 144.
7 Dani Cavallaro, *The Gothic Vision: Three Centuries of Horror, Terror and Fear* (London: Continuum, 2002) pp. 66 and 67.
8 M.R. James, 'Canon Alberic's Scrap-Book' in *The Collected Ghost Stories of M.R. James* (London: Edward Arnold, [1931] 1970) pp. 1–19, p. 2. All subsequent references are to this edition and are given in the text.
9 The scene does not make clear who is actually screaming at this point. However, the ambiguity is one which aligns Dennistoun with the figure (and vice versa).
10 See also Jack Sullivan's reading of M.R. James in *Elegant Nightmares: The English Ghost Story from Le Fanu to Blackwood* (Athens: Ohio University Press, 1978) pp. 69–90. See esp. pp. 81–2, which discuss how the reader becomes complicit with the horrors generated by James's seemingly urbane narrators.
11 M.R. James, 'Lost Hearts' in *The Collected Ghost Stories of M.R. James* (London: Edward Arnold, [1931] 1970) pp. 20–35, p. 34. All subsequent references are to this edition and are given in the text.
12 Although this is a factor noted by Cavallaro in her reading of 'The Treasure of Abbot Thomas' (1904); Cavallaro, *The Gothic Vision*, p. 67.
13 Sigmund Freud, 'The Uncanny' (1919) in *Jensen's* Gradiva, *Leonardo Da Vinci and Other Works*, trans. J. Strachey, ed. Albert Dickson (Harmondsworth: Penguin, 1985) pp. 339–76, p. 340. All subsequent references are to this edition and are given in the text.
14 M.R. James, 'The Mezzotint' in *The Collected Ghost Stories of M.R. James* (London: Edward Arnold, [1931] 1970) pp. 36–53, p. 37. Emphasis mine. All subsequent references are to this edition and are given in the text. Please note that I have also discussed the links between 'The Mezzotint' and 'The Haunted Dolls' House' in 'M.R. James's Gothic Revival', *Diegesis*, 7 (Summer 2004), special issue on 'Horror' ed. Gina Wisker, 16–22. I also discuss these tales in *Gothic Literature* (Edinburgh: Edinburgh University Press, 2007) pp. 124–5.
15 There is also a class issue here. The only character who does respond with horror at the sight of the mezzotint is Filcher, the college servant; see pp. 48–9.
16 M.R. James, 'Some Remarks on Ghost Stories', cited in Cavallaro, *The Gothic Vision*, p. 68.
17 M.R. James, 'The Haunted Dolls' House' in *The Collected Ghost Stories of M.R. James* (London: Edward Arnold, [1931] 1970) pp. 472–89, p. 489. All subsequent references are to this edition and are given in the text.
18 T.S. Eliot, *The Waste Land*, in *Selected Poems* (Harmondsworth: Penguin, [1952] 1948) v. ll.377–85.

19 For an extended examination of this influence see Andrew Smith and Jeff Wallace (eds), *Gothic Modernisms* (Basingstoke: Palgrave, 2001). I have also discussed these links to M.R. James in *Gothic Literature*, pp. 123–30.

20 James Joyce, *Ulysses* (Oxford: Oxford University Press, 1993) p. 47.

21 David Glover, 'The "Spectrality Effect" in Early Modernism', in Smith and Wallace (eds), *Gothic Modernisms*, pp. 29–43, p. 32. All subsequent references are to this edition and are given in the text.

22 David Punter, 'Hungry Ghosts and Foreign Bodies', in Smith and Wallace (eds), *Gothic Modernisms*, pp. 11–28, p. 21. All subsequent references are to this edition and are given in the text. The original quotation is from Georg Lukács, *The Meaning of Contemporary Realism*, trans. John and Necke Mander (London: Merlin, 1963) pp. 25–6.

23 See Leslie Halliwell, *Halliwell's Film Guide*, 8th edn (London: HarperCollins, 1992) p. 802.

24 Robert Bloch, 'The Indian Spirit Guide', repr. in *The Living Demons* (London: Sphere, 1970) pp. 17–33. Significantly the part of the tale which has been used in the film refers to exposing a medium as a fraud. In its own way it is a moment which, like much of James's writings, is therefore *about* the Gothic, rather than Gothic.

25 M.R. James, intro. to Sheridan Le Fanu, *Madam Crowl's Ghost and Other Tales of Mystery*, ed. M.R. James (Ware, Herts: Wordsworth, 1994) p. i.

Conclusion

This book has proposed a number of ways of reading the political significance of the spectre during a period when a range of political issues were projected and reconstituted into other (ghostly) forms. The issue of projection and doubling is central to this process. Freud's model of the uncanny, discussed in Chapter 1, seems particularly relevant to our analysis as he argues that the uncanny is experienced 'in the highest degree in relation to death and dead bodies, to the return of the dead, and to spirits and ghosts'.[1] However, the uncanny is so much more than this because it is also 'that class of the frightening which leads back to what is known of old and long familiar' (p. 340). The ghost is thus a double and whilst Freud's model is an attempt to account for a perceived psychological phenomenon, it also functions as a conceit for the political projection of spectrality. This aspect of the spectral was clear during periods of economic crisis when money in general, and more often paper money in particular, seemed to become ghostly because its reality or solidity was in question.

Dickens, Collins, and Riddell, at different levels of explicitness, explore how consciousness in a money-based society was constructed as if it were like money because it reflected feelings of disembodiment and alienation which rework the abstract qualities of money. Tricia Lootens in her account of 'Commodity Gothicism' sees the nineteenth century as a period driven by abstractions when she claims that 'With its Crystal Palace, department stores, and novels awash in consumer items, the Victorian period notoriously marks the development of commodity culture – a development dependent on the process of abstraction'.[2] Money by itself is useless and only takes on significance when it is translated into another form (when it is exchanged for goods). The issue of exchange, as Lootens notes, articulates a model of the abject in which 'objects' are transformed 'into commodities by occluding their physical materiality and precise social origins' (p. 149). For Kristeva abjection is a process in which a culture banishes what it needs to exclude (death, waste, bodily fluids), in a process that both confirms a 'norm' and reveals how it is defined by what it expels. Identity thus appears as a lack (by what it has abjected), just as commodity production conceals the origins of the object and so relies on the type of concealments which abjection problematically polices.

Whilst this is not the place to introduce a new theory of the spectral it is note-worthy that Kristeva's account of abjection fundamentally reworks the principles of doubling that defined the uncanny. Kristeva, for example, notes that in nausea 'I expel *myself*, I spit *myself* out, I abject *myself* within the same motion through which "I" claim to establish *myself*'.[3] The other, as in the uncanny, merely becomes another aspect of the self, one in which for Kristeva there is 'a kind of *narcissistic crisis*' (p. 14, italics in original). However, although Freud's essay struggles to elaborate convincing non-literary examples of uncanniness, Kristeva optimistically asserts that 'Abjection is a resurrection that has gone through death (of the ego). It is an alchemy that transforms death drive into a start of life, of new significance' (p. 15). The ghost as a liminal, abjected figure represents this 'new significance' as it suggests an alternative view of identity, colonialism, and gender. The ghost is thus a disembodied body through which the wider body politic is radically reassembled in a projected form.

As we have seen, an examination of the spectral helps open up narratives about colonial and national identities. How Dickens, Le Fanu, and Kipling use the ghost to ambivalently either master (Dickens) or transform (Le Fanu and Kipling) the landscape functions as a critique of a threatened alienation. How the colonial out-sider reads the politics of place via the spectral enables this critical recomposition of the very origins of the colonial. The liminality of the Anglo-Irish or the Anglo-Indian thus becomes the vantage point from which the spectral can be developed. However, as in the example of Henry James, it is also the case that a hyphenated national identity leads to an estrangement from the past (Europe) and the present (America). Nevertheless the ghost retains its status as a vehicle through which a superior, because critical, insight into the past and the present can be established. The place on the social margins becomes transformed into a position of power as the ghost articulates the type of intellectual distance that would otherwise be impossible to assert. The ghost thus becomes an ambivalent figure, both powerful and powerless.

For Kristeva abjection is caused by 'What does not respect borders, positions, rules. The in-between, the ambiguous, the composite' (p. 4). The ghost questions such borders (whether they are metaphysical, or national) and this was an issue made clear in the work of Vernon Lee. In Lee's 'Amour Dure' (1887) we witnessed how Spiridion Trepka, her German-trained Polish historian, wrestled with writing a conventional history of an Italian city. Instead he engages with a different version of the past, one which seems to bring back to life an otherwise female-focused lost history of the city. This ghost of the Renaissance femme fatale, Medea, is in part a product of his delirious fantasies about her (rooted originally in a more prosaic ambition to develop a new historical method). However, the tale also concerns lost or spectral histories which can be uncannily brought back to life. In 'Prince Alberic and the Snake Lady' (1896) the past is reworked through a discourse of art in which history, as a ghostly presence, is associated with a particular type of aesthetic practice that challenges and redirects male notions of creativity (as in Keats and Pater). Charlotte Riddell had explored links between art and the marketplace through analogies to the female author suggested in *The Haunted River* (1877), and May Sinclair in 'The Token' (1923) also examined the exclusion of women from certain public, male, writing processes. The spectre is thus aligned with the cultural liminality of women, and that position is both radically questioned and subtly empowered as the spectre generates new histories and art forms, and challenges the generation of public knowledges.

Such fictional spectres become conduits for obliquely but highly critical political encounters. They also indicate, certainly in the case of Riddell, Lee, Sinclair, and Henry James, debates about the role of the author and the production of the literary text. These issues were also focused in a certain strand of spiritualism which accorded the 'other world' an imaginative power that George Eliot addressed in 'The Lifted Veil' (1859). That spirit messages require skills in literary interpretation is evidenced from the discussion in Lodge's *Raymond* (1916) which centred on the seemingly cryptic warning contained in some brief lines from Horace's *Odes*. How to interpret such messages was also explicitly the topic in Ames and Hayter's *The Book of the Golden Key* (1909), which self-consciously reflected on *how* it was to tell its tale, rather than developed a narrative in a coherent way. The fragmentary narrative was held together by an idea that the spirit transmitting the messages was also in control of how they needed to be reassembled. Literary production thus becomes a matter of spirit direction, which could imply that creativity is granted a mystique were it not the case that the material focus on the pragmatics of constructing the narrative emphasised the labour involved.

How to read spectrality thus also involved a focus on the relationship between the literary and the ghostly and the idea that the spectre needed to be decoded was given an innovative twist in the ghost stories of M.R. James. In James, history requires but seemingly eludes analysis. His scholars find themselves confronted by animated figures from their areas of historical expertise and the disjunction between their world of quiet scholarship and the embedded Gothic narratives is striking. However, in a tale such as 'The Mezzotint' (1904) James subtly displaces the ostensible Gothic narrative of the engraving with the seemingly amoral *milieu* of academic enquiry. His dons become truly Gothic due to their lack of basic human empathy. This assault on the apparent vacuity of those who make a superior claim on culture can in turn be read as James's conservative critique of modernism in which the complex narrative play of his tales functions as a lampoon of the type of demands that the modernist text places upon the reader.

This book has explored spectres in a variety of guises from the 1840s to the 1920s. This period can be read as a long nineteenth century in which even the late, and very different, voices of May Sinclair and M.R. James evidence an extended Victorianism which conditions their approach to modernism. The writers discussed here thus represent the end of a certain era. However, it is also an era which, given our culture's present interest in the neo-Victorian, may well be subject to a ghostly return.[4] In one way or another critically reading the Victorians and reworking their fictional preoccupations means that their spectres still speak to us.[5]

Notes

1 Sigmund Freud, 'The Uncanny' in *Art and Literature: Jensen's* Gradiva, *Leonardo Da Vinci and Other Works*, Penguin Freud Library vol. 14, trans. James Strachey, ed. Albert Dickson (Harmondsworth: Penguin, 1985) pp. 339–76, p. 364.

2 Tricia Lootens, 'Fear of Furniture: Commodity Gothicism and the Teaching of Victorian Literature', in Diane Long Hoeveler and Tamar Heller (eds), *Gothic Fiction: The British and American Traditions* (New York: MLA, 2003) pp. 148–58, p. 149.

3 Julia Kristeva, *Powers of Horror: An Essay on Abjection*, trans. Leon S. Roudiez (New York: Columbia University Press, 1982) p. 3.

4 See the journal *Neo-Victorian Studies* http://www.neovictorianstudies.com. Also see the tellingly titled *Haunting and Spectrality in Neo-Victorian Fiction: Possessing the Past*, eds Patricia Pulham and Rosario Arias (Basingstoke: Palgrave, 2009).

5 See the work of Sarah Walters in that respect, especially her neo-Victorian *Tipping the Velvet* (New York: Riverhead, 1998), *Affinity* (New York: Riverhead, 1999), and *Fingersmith* (New York: Riverhead, 2002).

Bibliography

Agnew, Lois, 'Vernon Lee and the Victorian Aesthetic Movement: "Feminine Souls" and Shifting Sites of Contest', *Nineteenth-Century Prose*, 26.2 (1999), 127–42.

Ames, Hugo and Flora Hayter, *The Book of the Golden Key: An Idyll and a Revelation Being a Message from the So-called Dead* (London: Kegan Paul, 1909).

Anon., 'The Ghost in the Bank of England' in *Victorian Ghost Stories* (London: Senate, [1936] 1996) pp. 242–87.

Anon., 'Stockbroking and the Stock Exchange', *Fraser's Magazine* n.s. 14 (July 1876), 84–103; repr. in Mary Poovey (ed.), *The Financial System in Nineteenth-Century Britain* (Oxford: Oxford University Press, 2003) pp. 149–73.

Arata, Stephen D., 'The Occidental Tourist: *Dracula* and the Anxiety of Reverse Colonialism', *Victorian Studies*, 33.4 (1990), 621–45.

Aytoun, W.E., 'The National Debt and the Stock Exchange', *Blackwood's Edinburgh Magazine*, 66 (December 1849), 655–78; repr. in Mary Poovey (ed.), *The Financial System in Nineteenth-Century Britain* (Oxford: Oxford University Press, 2003) pp. 127–48.

Baldick, Chris, *In Frankenstein's Shadow: Myth, Monstrosity and Nineteenth-Century Writing* (Oxford: Clarendon, 1987).

Banta, Martha, *Henry James and the Occult: The Great Extension* (Bloomington: Indiana University Press, 1972).

Baudrillard, Jean, *The Mirror of Production*, trans. Mark Poster (New York: Telos Press, [1973] 1975).

Beidler, Peter G., *Ghosts, Demons and Henry James 'Turn of the Screw' at the Turn of the Century* (Columbia: University of Missouri Press, 1989).

Benson, A.C., *Escape and Other Essays* (London: Murray, 1915).

Bentham, Jeremy, *An Introduction to the Principles of Morals and Legislation* in *Bentham's Selected Writings on Utilitarianism*, introd. Ross Harrison (Ware, Herts: Wordsworth, 2001) pp. 73–309.

Bhabha, Homi K., 'Of Mimicry and Man: The Ambivalence of Colonial Discourse' in *The Location of Culture* (London: Routledge, 1995) pp. 85–92.

Bhattacharya, Baidik, 'Jokes Apart: Orientalism, (Post)colonial Parody and the Moment of Laughter', *Interventions: International Journal of Postcolonial Studies*, 8.2 (2006), 276–94.

Bleiler, Richard, 'May Sinclair's Supernatural Fiction' in Andrew J. Kunka and Michele K. Troy (eds), *May Sinclair: Moving Towards the Modern* (Aldershot: Ashgate, 2006) pp. 123–38.

Bloch, Robert, 'The Indian Spirit Guide', repr. in *The Living Demons* (London: Sphere, 1970) pp. 17–33.

Bloom, Clive, 'M.R. James and his Fiction' in Clive Bloom (ed.), *Creepers: British Horror & Fantasy in the Twentieth Century* (London: Pluto, 1993) pp. 64–71.

Bloomfield, Maurice, 'On Recurring Psychic Motifs in Hindu Fiction, and the Laugh and Cry Motif', *Journal of the American Oriental Society*, 36 (1916), 54–89.

Botting, Fred, *Gothic* (London: Routledge, 1996).

Briggs, Julia, *Night Visitors: The Rise and Fall of the English Ghost Story* (London: Faber, 1977).

Briggs, Julia, 'The Ghost Story' in David Punter (ed.), *A Companion to the Gothic* (Oxford: Blackwell, 2000) pp. 122–31.

Brocklebank, Lisa, 'Psychic Reading', *Victorian Studies*, 48.2 (Winter 2006), 233–9.

Brown, Nicola, Carolyn Burdett and Pamela Thurschwell (eds), *The Victorian Supernatural* (Cambridge: Cambridge University Press, 2004).

Browning, Robert, 'Mr Sludge, "Medium"' in *The Poems of Robert Browning* (Ware, Herts: Wordsworth, 1994) pp. 499–518.

Buitenhuis, Peter, *The Grasping Imagination* (Toronto: University of Toronto Press, 1970).

Burke, Edmund, *A Philosophical Enquiry into the Origin of our Ideas of the Sublime and the Beautiful*, ed. and introd. Adam Phillips (Oxford: Oxford University Press, [1757] 1998).

Buse, Peter and Andrew Stott (eds), *Ghosts: Deconstruction, Psychoanalysis, History* (Basingstoke: Macmillan, 1999).

Cavallaro, Dani, *The Gothic Vision: Three Centuries of Horror, Terror and Fear* (London and New York: Continuum, 2002).

Collins, Wilkie, *Armadale*, ed. and introd. Catherine Peters (Oxford: Oxford University Press, [1866] 1989).

—— *Basil*, ed. and introd. Dorothy Goodman (Oxford: Oxford University Press, [1852] 2000).

—— *The Haunted Hotel: A Mystery of Modern Venice* (New York: Dover, [1878] 1982).

—— *The Letters of Wilkie Collins*, vol. 1: 1838–1865, ed. William Baker and William M. Clarke (Basingstoke: Macmillan, 1999).

—— *No Name*, ed. and introd. Mark Ford (Harmondsworth: Penguin, [1862] 1994).

—— *The Woman in White*, ed. and introd. Julian Symons (Harmondsworth: Penguin, [1860] 1985).

Davies, Owen, *The Haunted: A Social History of Ghosts* (Basingstoke: Palgrave, 2007).

Denisoff, Denis, 'The Forest Beyond the Frame: Picturing Women's Desires in Vernon Lee and Virginia Woolf' in Talia Schaffer and Kathy Alexis Psomiades (eds), *Women and British Aestheticism* (Charlottesville: University of Virginia Press, 1999) pp. 251–69.

Derrida, Jacques, *Specters of Marx: The State of the Debt, the Work of Mourning, & the New International* (New York and London: Routledge, 1994).

Dickens, Charles, *A Christmas Carol* in *The Christmas Books*, vol. 1, ed. and introd. Michael Slater (Harmondsworth: Penguin, 1985) pp. 45–134.

—— 'A Christmas Tree', published as 'Christmas Ghosts' in *The Signalman & Other Ghost Stories* (Stroud: Sutton, 1990) pp. 110–16.

—— 'A December Vision' in *Dickens' Journalism: The Amusements of The People and Other Papers: Reports, Essays and Reviews 1834–51*, vol. II, ed. and introd. Michael Slater (London: Dent, 1996) pp. 306–9.

—— *American Notes for General Circulation*, ed. and introd. John S. Whitley and Arnold Goldman (Harmondsworth: Penguin, [1842] 1985).

—— *Bleak House* (Harmondsworth: Penguin, [1853] 1985).

—— 'Lying Awake' in *Dickens' Journalism: 'Gone Astray' and Other Papers from Household Words 1851–1859*, vol. III, ed. and introd. Michael Slater (London: J.M. Dent, 1998) pp. 88–95.

—— *The Pickwick Papers*, ed. and introd. Mark Wormald (Harmondsworth: Penguin, [1837] 2003).

—— 'Review: *The Night Side of Nature; or, Ghosts and Ghost Seers* by Catherine Crowe in *The Examiner*, 26 February 1848' in *Dickens' Journalism: The Amusements of the People and Other Papers: Reports, Essays and Reviews 1834–1851*, vol. II, ed. and introd. Michael Slater (London: J.M. Dent, 1996) pp. 80–91.

—— 'The Signalman' in *The Signalman & Other Ghost Stories* (Stroud: Sutton, 1990) pp. 1–13.

Dickerson, Vanessa D., *Victorian Ghosts in the Noontide: Women Writers and the Supernatural* (Columbia and London: University of Missouri Press, 1996).

Doyle, Arthur Conan, *The History of Spiritualism*, vol. II (Teddington: The Echo Library, [1926] 2006).

Eagleton, Terry, *The Ideology of the Aesthetic* (Oxford: Blackwell, [1990] 2000).

Edel, Leon, intro. to *The Ghostly Tales of Henry James*, ed. and introd. Leon Edel (New Brunswick, NJ: Rutgers University Press, 1948).

Edmundson, Melissa, 'The "Uncomfortable Houses" of Charlotte Riddell and Margaret Oliphant', forthcoming in *Gothic Studies*, 10 (2010).

Eliot, George, *The Lifted Veil and Brother Jacob*, ed. and introd. Helen Small (Oxford: Oxford University Press, [1859] 1999).

Eliot, T.S., *The Waste Land*, in *Selected Poems* (Harmondsworth: Penguin, 1948 [1952]), part V, ll. 377–84.

Felman, Shoshana, 'Turning the Screw of Interpretation', *Yale French Studies*, 55/56 (1977), 94–207.

Fisher, Benjamin F., 'Mrs. J.H. Riddell and Late Victorian Literary Gothicism' in Felice A. Coles (ed.), *In Memory of Richard B. Klein: Essays in Contemporary Hilology* (Oxford: University of Mississippi, 2005) pp. 175–93.

Forster, Laurel, ' "Imagism . . . Is a State of Soul": May Sinclair's Imagist Writing and *Life and Death of Harriett Frean*' in Andrew J. Kunka and Michele K. Troy (eds), *May Sinclair: Moving Towards the Modern* (Aldershot: Ashgate, 2006) pp. 99–122.

Freud, Sigmund, *Beyond the Pleasure Principle* in *On Metapsychology*, ed. James Strachey and Angela Richards, Penguin Freud Library vol. 11 (Harmondsworth: Penguin, 1984) pp. 275–338.

—— 'The "Uncanny" ' in *Art and Literature: Jensen's Gradiva, Leonardo Da Vinci and other works*, Penguin Freud Library vol. 14, trans. James Strachey, ed. Albert Dickson (Harmondsworth: Penguin, 1985) pp. 339–76.

Gagnier, Regenia, *The Insatiability of Human Wants: Economics and Aesthetics in Market Society* (Chicago: University of Chicago Press, 2000).

Galvan, Jill, 'The Narrator as Medium in George Eliot's "The Lifted Veil"', *Victorian Studies*, 48.2 (Winter 2006), 240–8.

Gardner, Burdett, *The Lesbian Imagination (Victorian Style): A Psychological and Critical Study of 'Vernon Lee'* (New York: Garland, 1987).

Gibbons, Luke, '"Some Hysterical Hatred": History, Hysteria and the Literary Revival', *Irish University Review*, 21.1 (1997), 7–23.

Glover, David, 'The "Spectrality Effect" in Early Modernism' in Andrew Smith and Jeff Wallace (eds), *Gothic Modernisms* (Basingstoke: Palgrave, 2001) pp. 29–43.

Halliwell, Leslie, *Halliwell's Film Guide*, 8th edn (London: HarperCollins, 1992).

Handley, Sasha, *Visions of an Unseen World: Ghost Beliefs and Ghost Stories in Eighteenth-Century England* (London: Pickering & Chatto, 2007).

Harris, Sally, 'The Haunting Past in J.S. Le Fanu's Short Stories', *Le Fanu Studies*, 2 (November 2006), 1–12.

Hawthorne, Nathaniel, *The Scarlet Letter* (New York: Signet, [1850] 1959).

Heller, Tamar, *Dead Secrets: Wilkie Collins and the Female Gothic* (New Haven: Yale University Press, 1992).

Herbert, Christopher, 'Filthy Lucre: Victorian Ideas of Money', *Victorian Studies*, 44.2 (Winter 2002), 185–213.

Hogle, Jerrold E. (ed.), *The Cambridge Companion to Gothic Fiction* (Cambridge: Cambridge University Press, 2002).

Horner, Avril and Sue Zlosnik, *Gothic and the Comic Turn* (Basingstoke: Palgrave, 2005).

Houston, Gail Turley, *From Dickens to Dracula: Gothic, Economics, and Victorian Fiction* (Cambridge: Cambridge University Press, 2005).

Hughes, William, 'M.R. James' in Marie Mulvey-Roberts (ed.), *The Handbook to Gothic Literature* (Basingstoke: Macmillan, 1998) pp. 143–4.

Hughes, Winifred, *The Maniac in the Cellar: Sensation Novels of the 1860s* (Princeton: Princeton University Press, 1980).

James, Henry, *The American Scene* (Harmondsworth: Penguin, [1907] 1994), ed. and introd. John F. Sears.

—— 'The Art of Fiction' (1884) in *Henry James: Selected Literary Criticism* (Harmondsworth: Penguin, 1968) ed. Morris Shapira, pp. 78–97.

—— 'The Author's Preface to *The Turn of the Screw*', *Ghost Stories of Henry James*, introd. Martin Scofield (Ware, Herts: Wordsworth, 2001).

—— *English Hours*, ed. and introd. Alma Louise Lowe (London: Heinemann, [1905] 1960).

—— 'The Ghostly Rental' in *Ghost Stories of Henry James*, introd. Martin Scofield (Ware, Herts: Wordsworth, 2001) pp. 38–66.

—— *Hawthorne* (London: Macmillan, [1879] 1883).

—— *Italian Hours*, ed. and introd. John Auchard (Harmondsworth: Penguin, [1909] 1995).

—— 'The Jolly Corner', in *Ghost Stories of Henry James*, introd. Martin Scofield (Ware, Herts: Wordsworth, 2001) pp. 306–34.

—— *The Portrait of a Lady*, intro. and notes by Nicola Bradbury (Oxford: Oxford University Press, 1998).

—— 'The Private Life' in *The Altar of the Dead, The Beast in the Jungle, The Birthplace, and Other Tales*, vol. 17 of the *New York Edition of Henry James* (New York: Charles Scribner's Sons, [1909] 1937) pp. 215–66.

—— *Selected Letters*, ed. and introd. Leon Edel (London: Rupert Hart-Davis, 1956).

—— *The Sense of the Past* (Farifield, CT: Augustus M. Kelley, 1976).

—— *The Turn of the Screw* in *The Turn of the Screw and Other Stories*, ed. and introd. T.J. Lustig (Oxford: Oxford University Press, [1898] 1992) pp. 113–236.

James, M.R., 'Canon Alberic's Scrap-Book' in *The Collected Ghost Stories of M.R. James* (London: Edward Arnold, [1931] 1970) pp. 1–19.

—— 'The Haunted Dolls' House' in *The Collected Ghost Stories of M.R. James* (London: Edward Arnold, [1931] 1970) pp. 472–89.

—— Introduction, *Madam Crowl's Ghost and Other Tales of Mystery* by Sheridan Le Fanu, ed. M.R. James (Ware, Herts: Wordsworth, 1994) pp. i–ii.

—— 'Lost Hearts' in *The Collected Ghost Stories of M.R. James* (London: Edward Arnold, [1931] 1970) pp. 20–35.

—— 'The Mezzotint' in *The Collected Ghost Stories of M.R. James* (London: Edward Arnold, [1931] 1970) pp. 36–53.

Jevons, William, *The Theory of Political Economy*, ed. R.D. Collison Black (Harmondsworth: Penguin, [1871] 1970).

Joyce, James, *Ulysses* (Oxford: Oxford University Press, [1922] 1993).

Kane, Mary Patricia, *Spurious Ghosts: The Fantastic Tales of Vernon Lee* (Rome: Carocci, 2004).

Kaston, Carren Osna, 'Houses of Fiction in *What Maisie Knew*', *Criticism: A Quarterly for Literature and the Arts*, 18 (1976), 27–42.

Kaviraj, Sudipta, 'Laughter and Subjectivity: The Self-Ironical Tradition in Bengali Literature', *Modern Asian Studies*, 34.2 (May 2000), 379–406.

Keats, John, *Lamia*, in *Keats: Complete Poetical Works*, ed. H.W. Gorrod (Oxford: Oxford University Press, 1970) pp. 161–78.

Killeen, Jarlath, 'Irish Gothic: A Theoretical Introduction', *Irish Journal of Gothic and Horror Studies*, 1 (October 2006), 1–7.

Kipling, Rudyard, 'My Own True Ghost Story' in *The Phantom 'Rickshaw and Other Ghost Stories* (Fairfield, CT: 1st World Library, [1888] 2007) pp. 35–44.

—— 'The Phantom 'Rickshaw' in *The Phantom 'Rickshaw and Other Ghost Stories* (Fairfield, CT: 1st World Library, [1888] 2007) pp. 7–34.

—— 'The Strange Ride of Morrowbie Jukes' in *The Phantom 'Rickshaw and Other Ghost Stories* (Fairfield, CT: 1st World Library, [1885] 2007) pp. 45–72.

Lang, Andrew, *Cock Lane and Common-Sense* (London, [1894] 1896), 2nd edn.

Lee, Vernon, 'Amour Dure' in *Hauntings and Other Tales*, ed. Catherine Maxwell and Patricia Pulham (Peterborough, Ontario: Broadview, 2006) pp. 41–76.

—— *The Beautiful: An Introduction to Psychological Aesthetics* (Cambridge: Cambridge University Press, 1913).

—— *Miss Brown*, 3 vols (Edinburgh: W.M. Blackwood and Sons, 1884).

—— 'Prince Alberic and the Snake Lady' in *Hauntings and Other Tales*, ed. Catherine Maxwell and Patricia Pulham (Peterborough, Ontario: Broadview, 2006) pp. 182–228.

Le Fanu, Sheridan, 'An Account of Some Strange Disturbances in Aungier Street', in *Madam Crowl's Ghost: and Other Tales of Mystery*, ed. M.R. James (Ware, Herts: Wordsworth, [1923] 1994) pp. 68–85.

—— *Carmilla*, in *The Penguin Book of Vampire Stories*, ed. Alan Ryan (Harmondsworth: Penguin, 1987) pp. 71–137.

—— 'The Child that went with the Fairies', in *Madam Crowl's Ghost: and Other Tales of Mystery*, ed. M.R. James (Wares, Herts: Wordsworth, [1923] 1994) pp. 50-7.

—— 'Ghost Stories of Chapelizod', in *Madam Crowl's Ghost: and Other Tales of Mystery*, ed. M.R. James (Ware, Herts: Wordsworth, [1923] 1994) pp. 86-107.

—— 'The Spectre Lovers', in *Madam Crowl's Ghost: and Other Tales of Mystery*, ed. M.R. James (Ware, Herts: Wordsworth, [1923] 1994) pp. 97-107.

Leighton, Angela, 'Resurrections of the Body: Women Writers and the Idea of the Renaissance' in Alison Chapman and Jane Stabler (eds), *Unfolding the South: Nineteenth-century British Women Writers and Artists in Italy* (Manchester: Manchester University Press, 2003) pp. 222-38.

Lewis, Pericles, ' "The Reality of the Unseen": Shared Fictions and Religious Experience in the Ghost Stories of Henry James', *Arizona Quarterly*, 61.2 (2005), 33-66.

Lodge, Sir Oliver, *Raymond* (London: Methuen, [1916] 1917).

Lootens, Tricia, 'Fear of Furniture: Commodity Gothicism and the Teaching of Victorian Literature', in Diane Long Hoeveler and Tamar Heller (eds), *Gothic Fiction: The British and American Traditions* (New York: MLA, 2003) pp. 148-58.

Luckhurst, Roger, *The Invention of Telepathy* (Oxford: Oxford University Press, 2002).

Lukács, Georg, *The Meaning of Contemporary Realism*, trans. John and Necke Mander (London: Merlin, 1963).

Lustig, T.J., *Henry James and the Ghostly* (Cambridge: Cambridge University Press, 1994).

March-Russell, Paul, 'Introduction' to *Uncanny Stories* (Ware, Herts: Wordsworth, 2006) pp. 7-21.

Marcus, Steven, *Dickens from Pickwick to Dombey* (London: Chatto and Windus, 1965).

Marx, Karl, *Capital* in David McLellan (ed.), *Karl Marx: Selected Writings* (Oxford: Oxford University Press, 1977).

—— *Economic and Philosophic Manuscripts of 1844* (Moscow: Progress Publishers, [1844] 1967).

Maxwell, Catherine, 'Vernon Lee and the Ghosts of Italy' in Alison Chapman and Jane Stabler (eds), *Unfolding the South: Nineteenth-century British Women Writers and Artists in Italy* (Manchester: Manchester University Press, 2003) pp. 201-21.

McCormack, Peggy, *The Rule of Money: Gender, Class, and Exchange Economics in the Fiction of Henry James* (Ann Arbor: UMI Research Press, 1990).

McCormack, W.J., *Dissolute Characters: Irish Literary History through Balzac, Sheridan Le Fanu, Yeats and Bowen* (Manchester: Manchester University Press, 1993).

—— *Sheridan Le Fanu* (Guernsey: Sutton, [1980] 1997).

Mengel, Ewald, 'The Structure and Meaning of Dickens's "The Signalman" ', *Studies in Short Fiction*, 20 (1983), 271-80.

Myers, F.W.H., *Human Personality and Its Survival of Bodily Death* (London: Longmans, [1903] 1907).

Milbank, Alison, *Daughters of the House: Modes of Gothic in Victorian Fiction* (Basingstoke: Macmillan, 1992).

Moore-Gilbert, Bart, *Kipling and 'Orientalsim'* (London: Croom-Helm, 1986).

Moretti, Franco, 'Dialectic of Fear' in *Signs Taken for Wonders: Essays in the Sociology of Literary Form* (London: Verso, 1983) pp. 83-108.

Oppenheim, Janet, *The Other World: Spiritualism and Psychical Research in England 1850–1914* (Cambridge: Cambridge University Press, 1985).

Owen, Alex, *The Darkened Room: Women, Power, and Spiritualism in Late Victorian England* (London: Virago, 1989).

Pater, Walter, *The Renaissance* (Oxford: Oxford University Press, [1873] 1986), ed. and introd. Adam Phillips.

Peterson, Linda H., 'Charlotte Riddell's *A Struggle for Fame*: Myths of Authorship, Facts of the Market', *Women's Writing*, 11.1 (2004), 99–115.

Poovey, Mary, *The Financial System in Nineteenth-Century Britain* (Oxford: Oxford University Press, 2003).

Psomiades, Kathy Alexis, ' "Still Burning from This Strangling Embrace": Vernon Lee on Desire and Aesthetics' in Richard Dellamora (ed.), *Victorian Sexual Dissidence* (Chicago: University of Chicago Press, 1999) pp. 21–41.

Pulham, Patricia, *Art and the Transitional Object in Vernon Lee's Supernatural Tales* (Aldershot: Ashgate, 2008).

Punter, David, 'Hungry Ghosts and Foreign Bodies' in Andrew Smith and Jeff Wallace (eds), *Gothic Modernisms* (Baskingstoke: Palgrave, 2001) pp. 11–28.

—— *The Literature of Terror: The Modern Gothic*, vol. 2 (London and New York: Longman, [1980] 1996).

Punter, David and Glennis Byron, *The Gothic* (Oxford: Blackwell, 2004).

Raitt, Suzanne, *May Sinclair: A Modern Victorian* (Oxford: Clarendon Press, 2000).

Ricardo, David, *On the Principles of Political Economy and Taxation* (London and Toronto: Dent, [1817] 1926).

Riddell, J.H., *The Haunted River* in *The Haunted River and Three Other Ghostly Novellas by Mrs. J.H. Riddell*, ed. and introd. Richard Dalby (Mountain Ash: Sarob Press, 2001) pp. 1–84.

—— 'The Old House in Vauxhall Walk' in *The Collected Ghost Stories of Mrs. J.H. Riddell*, ed. E.F. Bleiler (New York: Dover, 1977) pp. 85–101.

—— *The Uninhabited House*, in *Five Victorian Ghost Novels*, ed. E.F. Bleiler (New York: Dover, 1971) pp. 1–118.

Robbins, Ruth, 'Vernon Lee: Decadent Woman?' in John Stokes (ed.), *Fin de Siècle Fin du Globe: Fears and Fantasies of the Late Nineteenth Century* (Basingstoke: Macmillan, 1992) pp. 139–61.

Roberts, Adam, 'Browning, the Dramatic Monologue and the Resuscitation of the Dead' in Nicola Brown, Carolyn Burdett and Pamela Thurschwell (eds), *The Victorian Supernatural* (Cambridge: Cambridge University Press, 2004) pp. 109–27.

Russell, Norman, *The Novelist and Mammon: Literary Responses to the World of Commerce in the Nineteenth Century* (Oxford: Clarendon, 1986).

Sage, Victor, 'Gothic Laughter: Farce and Horror in Five Texts' in Allan Lloyd Smith and Victor Sage (eds), *Gothic: Origins and Innovations* (Amsterdam: Rodopi, 1994) pp. 190–203.

Seed, David, 'Mystery in Everyday Things: Charles Dickens' "Signalman" ', *Criticism*, 23.1 (1981), 42–57.

—— ' "Psychical" Cases: Transformations of the Supernatural in Virginia Woolf and May Sinclair' in Andrew Smith and Jeff Wallace (eds), *Gothic Modernisms* (Basingstoke: Palgrave, 2001) pp. 44–61.

Shand, Alexander Innes, 'Speculative Investments', *Blackwood's Edinburgh Magazine* 120 (September 1876), 293–316; repr. in Mary Poovey (ed.), *The Financial System in Nineteenth-Century Britain* (Oxford: Oxford University Press, 2003) pp. 173–200.

Sinclair, May, 'The Finding of the Absolute' in *Uncanny Stories* (New York: Macmillan, 1923) pp. 329–62.

—— 'The Token' in *Uncanny Stories* (New York: Macmillan, 1923) pp. 51–78.

Smajic, Srdjan, 'The Trouble with Ghost-Seeing: Vision, Ideology, and Genre in the Victorian Ghost Story', *English Literary History*, 70.4 (2003), 1107–35.

Smith, Andrew, 'Colonial Ghosts: Mimicking Dickens in America' in Avril Horner and Sue Zlosnik (eds), *Le Gothic* (Basingstoke: Palgrave, 2008) pp. 185–200.

—— 'Dickens' Ghosts: Invisible Economies and Christmas', *Victorian Review*, 31.2 (2005), special issue on 'Literature and Money', ed. Andrew Smith, 36–55.

—— *Gothic Literature* (Edinburgh: Edinburgh University Press, 2007).

—— *Gothic Radicalism: Literature, Philosophy and Psychoanalysis in the Nineteenth Century* (Basingstoke: Macmillan, 2000).

—— 'Kipling's Gothic and Postcolonial Laughter', *Gothic Studies*, 11.1 (May 2009), special issue on 'Theorising the Gothic', ed. Jerrold E. Hogle and Andrew Smith, 58–69.

—— 'M.R. James's Gothic Revival' *Diegesis*, 7 (Summer 2004), special issue on 'Horror', ed. Gina Wisker, 16–22.

—— *Victorian Demons: Medicine, Masculinity and the Gothic at the Fin de Siècle* (Manchester: Manchester University Press, 2004).

Smith, Andrew and Jeff Wallace, *Gothic Modernisms* (Basingstoke: Palgrave, 2001).

Stahl, John D., 'The Source and Significance of the Revenant in Dickens's "The Signal-Man"', *Dickens Studies Newsletter* (1980), 98–101.

Stallman, R.W., *The Houses that James Built, and Other Literary Essays* (East Lansing: Michigan State University, 1961).

Stead, W.T., *Real Ghost Stories* (New York: George H. Doran, [1897] 1921).

Stewart, Victoria, ' "War Memoirs of the Dead": Writing and Remembrance in the First World War', *Literature and History*, 14.2 (Autumn 2005), 37–52.

Sullivan, Jack, *Elegant Nightmares: The English Ghost Story from Le Fanu to Blackwood* (Athens, OH: Ohio University Press, 1978).

Sword, Helen, *Ghostwriting Modernism* (Ithaca and London: Cornell University Press, 2002).

Talairach-Vielmas, Laurence, 'Victorian Sensational Shoppers: Representing Transgressive Femininity in Wilkie Collins's *No Name*', *Victorian Review*, 31.2 (2005), special issue on 'Literature and Money' ed. Andrew Smith, 56–78.

Tracy, Robert, 'Undead, Unburied: Anglo-Ireland and the Predatory Past', *LIT: Literature, Interpretation, Theory*, 10 (1999), 13–14.

Trivedi, Harish, 'Colonial Influence, Postcolonial Intertextuality: Western Literature and Indian Literature', *Forum for Modern Language Studies*, 43.2 (2007), 121–33.

Vicinus, Martha, 'The Adolescent Boy: Fin-de-Siècle Femme Fatale' in Richard Dellamora (ed.), *Victorian Sexual Dissidence* (Chicago: University of Chicago Press, 1999) pp. 83–106.

Voskuil, Lynn M., 'Feeling Public: Sensation Theater, Commodity Culture, and the Victorian Public Sphere', *Victorian Studies*, 44.2 (Winter 2002), 245–74.

Wallace, Diana, 'Haunted by History: Vernon Lee's "Fantastic Tales" ' in Wallace, *Female Gothic Histories*, m.s. in progress (Cardiff: University of Wales Press, forthcoming 2012) p. 8.

—— 'Uncanny Stories: The Ghost Story as Female Gothic', in *Gothic Studies*, 6.1 (May 2004), special issue on the 'Female Gothic', ed. Andrew Smith and Diana Wallace, 57–68.

Willburn, Sarah A., *Possessed Victorians: Extra Spheres in Nineteenth-Century Mystical Writings* (Aldershot: Ashgate, 2006).

Williams, Frederick S., *Our Iron Roads: Their History, Construction and Administration* (London: Frank Cass & Co., 1968).

Willis, Martin, 'Clairvoyance, Economics and Authorship in George Eliot's "The Lifted Veil"', *Journal of Victorian Culture*, 10.2 (2005), 184–209.

Winter, Jay, *Sites of Memory, Sites of Mourning: The Great War in European Cultural History* (Cambridge: University of Cambridge Press, 1995).

Wolfreys, Julian, *Victorian Hauntings: Spectrality, Gothic, the Uncanny and Literature* (Basingstoke: Macmillan, 2001).

Wurgaft, Lewis D., *The Imperial Imagination: Magic and Myth in Kipling's India* (Middletown, CT: Wesleyan University Press, 1983).

Zorn, Christa, *Vernon Lee: Aesthetics, History and the Victorian Female Intellectual* (Athens, OH: Ohio University Press).

Index

abjection 186–7
Agnew, Lois 79–80
Ames, Hugo 7, 119n.20
   The Book of the Golden Key 7, 97, 105–10,
      112, 113, 116, 118
Anon, 'The Ghost in the Bank of England'
      49, 63–6
   see also Collins, Wilkie
anti-Semitism 19–20
Aytoun, W.E. 19–20

Baldick, Chris 13, 14
Banta, Martha 128
Barthes, Roland 98
Bayfield, M.A. 111
Beidler, Peter G. 128
Benson, A.C. 7, 97, 104, 114, 116
   Escape and other Essays 114–16
   see also Browning, Robert
Bentham, Jeremy 10, 23, 26, 27, 28, 29
   *An Introduction to the Principles of Morals
      and Legislation* 23–5
Berman, Marshall 90
Besant, Walter 162
Bhabha, Homi, K. 8
   The Location of Culture 143–4, 145, 146,
      148, 153, 159, 160
Bhattacharya, Baidik 160
Bleiler, Richard 86, 92
Bloch, Robert
   'The Indian Spirit Guide' 183
Bloom, Clive 168–9, 181, 182
Bloomfield, Maurice 160–1

Bosschère, Jean de 86
Botting, Fred 12
Braddon, Mary Elizabeth 51, 69, 122
Briggs, Julia 4, 14, 15, 168, 180
Browing, Robert 6, 97, 103–5, 115–16
   'Mr Sludge, "the Medium"' 103–4, 115, 116
Buitenhuis, Peter 124
Byron, Glennis 168
Byron, George Gordon 105

Carlyle, Thomas 51
carnivalesque 144, 160
Cavallaro, Dani 169
Charcot, Jean-Martin 152
Conrad, Joseph 182
   Heart of Darkness 90
Crowe, Catherine 1, 2
Collins, Wilkie 5, 6, 7, 11, 18, 27, 28, 47,
      49–68, 70, 76, 87, 121, 186
   Armadale 49, 53, 56–8, 60, 65
   Basil 50, 51
   The Haunted Hotel 49, 58–63, 64, 65
   No Name 49, 53, 54–6, 58, 60, 65, 72,
      93n.9
   The Woman in White 49, 51–4, 56, 63,
      70, 72
   see also Anon 'The Ghost in the Bank of
      England'
   see also Sensation fiction

Davies, Owen 3
Defoe, Daniel 3
De la Mare, Walter 14

Denisoff, Denis 85
Derrida, Jacques 4, 39, 90
    Specters of Marx 4, 5, 16–17, 18
Dickens, Charles 1–2, 3, 5, 7, 11, 14, 17, 18,
        21, 22, 27, 28, 29, 32–48, 51, 76, 87,
        121, 122, 144, 151, 165, 186, 187
    A Christmas Carol 2, 3, 4, 5, 18, 34,
        35–41, 42, 43, 44, 45, 46, 72, 73, 74,
        75, 127
    'A Christmas Tree' 33, 45
    'A December Vision' 5, 14, 34, 41–4, 45,
        46
    American Notes for General Circulation
        7–8, 143, 144–50, 157
    Bleak House 32–3, 42
    Hard Times 34, 42
    The Pickwick Papers 33, 34
    'The Signalman' 5, 6, 34–5, 44–7
Dickerson, Vanessa, D. 69, 92, 93n.5
Donne, John 133
Doyle, Sir Arthur Conan 98–9
Du Maurier, George
    Trilby 107

Eagleton, Terry 12
Edel, Leon 120–1, 128, 129–130, 131
Edwards, Amelia B. 50
Eliot, George 5, 6, 97, 104, 105
    'The Lifted Veil' 7, 99–103, 108, 109, 110,
        113, 115, 116, 118n.12, 188
Eliot, T.S. 93, 181
    The Waste Land 90, 180–1
    see also modernism
Ellis, S.M. 70
Engels, Friedrich 41

Felman, Shoshana 127–8
Fisher, Benjamin F. 70
Ford, Ford Maddox 182
    The Inheritors 90
Forster, E.M. 14
Forster, Laurel 86
Frazer, James 38, 39, 40
Freud, Sigmund 5, 16, 25, 38, 39, 40, 120,
        160

Beyond the Pleasure Principle 10, 27–8
    'The Uncanny' 14–16, 17, 22–3, 24, 26, 27,
        28, 145, 170, 175, 177, 186, 187

Gagnier, Regenia 14, 29n.7, 31n.22
Galvan, Jill 99
Gardner, Burdett 77
Gaskell, Elizabeth 76
Gibbons, Luke 152, 153
Glover, David 90, 182
Gore, Catherine 51

Haggard, Sir Henry Rider
    She 106, 107
Handley, Sasha 2–4
Hardy, Thomas 5
Harris, Sally 151
Hawthorne, Nathaniel 121, 122, 124, 134,
        140, 142n.30
    The Scarlet Letter 122
Hayter, Flora 6, 7, 199–20
    The Book of the Golden Key 7, 97, 105–10,
        112, 113, 116, 188
Heller, Tamar 50–1, 51–2, 63
Herbert, Christopher 38, 39, 40, 42
Hoffmann, E.T.A. 14–15
Hogle Jerrold E. 127
Home, Daniel Dunglas 103
Horner, Avril 8
    Gothic and the Comic Turn 144, 153, 160,
        161
Housten, Gail Turley 14
Hughes, William 168, 169, 184n.6
Hughes, Winifred 49–50
hysteria 144, 152, 155, 156, 157, 158, 165

James, Henry 3, 4, 7, 11, 14, 23, 27, 28, 76,
        86, 94n.14, 97, 115, 116, 120–42, 143,
        150, 187, 188
    The American Scene 132–4, 136
    English Hours 125, 129, 130, 131–2, 136,
        142n.30
    Hawthorne 122, 134
    'The Ghostly Rental' 121–4, 127, 131
    'The Jolly Corner' 134–7, 139

The Portrait of a Lady 124–7, 131, 133, 139
'The Private Life' 104–5
The Sense of the Past 137–40
The Turn of the Screw 122, 124, 125,
    127–32, 133, 134, 136, 139
James, M.R. 4, 8, 14, 23, 114, 168–85,
    185n.24, 188
    'Canon Alberic's Scrap-Book' 170–3, 174,
        175, 183
    'Casting the Runes' 183
    'The Haunted Dolls' House' 175, 178–80,
        181, 182, 183
    'Lost Hearts' 173–5, 182, 183
    'The Mezzotint' 175–80, 181, 182, 188
Jevons, William 10, 23, 28, 29
    The Theory of Political Economy 25–7
Joyce, James
    Ulysses 181

Kafka, Franz 182, 183
Kane, Mary Patricia 78, 79, 85
Kant, Immanuel 16, 89, 92
Kaston, Carren Osna 120
Kaviraj, Sudipta 161
Keats, John
    Lamia 81, 82–3, 84, 85, 95n.29, 188
Killeen, Jarlath 151, 155
Kipling, Sir Rudyard 7, 8, 143, 144, 151,
    157–65, 187
    'My Own True Ghost Story' 162–3, 164
    'The Phantom 'Ricksaw' 163–5
    'The Strange Ride of Morrowbie Jukes'
        158–60, 161
Kristeva, Julia 186–7

Lamia 81–4
Lang, Andrew 3
Lawrence, D.H. 14
Lee, Vernon 2, 4, 6, 14, 66, 67, 76–85, 89,
    91, 92, 93, 94n.14
    'Amour Dure' 6, 77–81, 84, 187
    Miss Brown 85
    'Prince Alberic and the Snake Lady' 81–5,
        187–8
    see also modernism

Le Fanu, Sheridan 7, 8, 143, 144, 150–7,
    165, 183, 187
    'An Account of Some Strange Disturbances
        in Aungier Street' 155–7
    Carmilla 153, 166n.16
    'The Child that went with the Fairies'
        152–4, 155, 156
    'The Spectre Lovers' 154–5, 157
Leighton, Angela 78, 79
Lewes, G.H. 50
Lewis, Pericles 123
Lodge, Oliver 7, 99, 110
    Raymond 7, 98, 99, 100, 104, 105, 110–14,
        115, 116, 188
Lootens, Tricia 13, 186
Luckás, Georg 182
Luckhurst, Roger 98, 99, 112, 117n.4
Lustig, T.J. 121, 122–3, 124, 126, 129, 136

MacDonald, George
    Lilith 81
Macready, W.C. 149
March-Russell, Paul 92
Marcus, Steven 149–50
Marx, Karl 5, 10, 11–14, 15, 17, 23, 25, 28,
    35, 37, 39, 41, 54
    Capital 11–12, 13, 16, 18, 22, 36, 43
    *Economic and Philosophic Manuscripts of
        1844* 57–8, 59, 64, 65
Maxwell, Catherine 80
Mayhew, Henry 38
McCormack, Peggy 126, 127
McCormack, W.J. 150–1, 153, 155
Mengel, Ewald, 4, 5
Milbank, Alison 32, 33, 50
modernism 85–92, 93, 117n.4, 168, 169,
    180–3, 188
Moore-Gilbert, Bart 157–8, 160, 164
Moretti, Franco 20
Mulock, Dinah Maria, 51
Murnau, F.W.
    Nosferatu 181
Myers, F.W.H. 98, 99, 110, 111
    *The Human Personality and Its Survival of
        Bodily Death* 116

Oliphant, Margaret 93n.1
Owen, Alex 102

Pater, Walter 81, 84, 85, 188
  The Renaissance 78–9
Peterson, Linda H. 76
Poovey, Mary 17–18, 40
Psomiades, Kathy Alexis 77, 81, 84–5
Pulham, Patricia 80, 81
Punter, David 10–11, 12, 168, 169, 177, 178,
    182–3

Radcliffe, Ann 177
Raitt, Suzanne 92, 95n.37
Reade, Charles 51
Ricardo, David 11, 25
Riddell, Charlotte 5, 6, 7, 11, 18, 21, 28, 51,
    66, 67, 70–6, 87, 92, 93, 121, 186
  The Haunted River 71–2, 75–6, 188
  'The Old House in Vauxhall Walk' 73–5
  The Uninhabited House 6, 70–3
Robbins, Ruth 81, 82
Roberts, Adam 103
Rossetti, D.G.
  'Eden Bower' 81
Ruskin, John 38
Russell, Norman 51

Sage, Victor 152
Schoenberg, Arnold
  'A Theme Tune for an Imaginary Horror
    Film' 181
Seed, David 46, 86
Sensation fiction 49–51
  see also Collins, Wilkie
Shakespeare, William
  Hamlet 16
Shand, Alexander Innes, 21–2
Sinclair, May 6, 66, 67, 77, 85–92, 93, 180,
    188
  'The Finding of the Absolute' 86, 89–92
  'The Token' 86, 87–8, 91, 93, 188
  see also modernism
Slater, Michael 2
Smajic, Srdjan 46–7

Smith, Adam 11
Society for Psychical Research 3, 77, 86, 100,
    114, 163
Spiritualism 97–119
Stahl, John D. 45
Stallman, R.W. 120
Stead, W.T. 97
Stoker, Bram
  Dracula 20, 152, 180, 181
Stott, Andrew 4
Sullivan, Jack 9–8, 184n.10
Sword, Helen 103, 117n.4

Talairach-Vielmas, Laurence 55
Tennyson, Alfred, Lord 5
Tourneur, Jacques
  Night of the Demon 183
Tracy, Robert 151, 152, 153
Trivedi, Harish 161

uncanny 123, 143, 145, 148, 157–8, 160, 169,
    170, 174, 175, 178, 179, 182, 183, 187

Vicinus, Lynn M. 77, 81, 84
Voskuil, Lynn M. 36, 37

Wallace, Diana 69, 80, 81
Walpole, Horace 178, 181
  The Castle of Otranto 127, 138
Wegener, Paul
  The Golem 181
Wells, H.G. 128
  The Time Machine 90
Wiene, Robert
  The Cabinet of Dr Caligari 181
Willis, Martin 118n.12
Wolfreys, Julian 5, 99–100
Woolf, Virginia 85, 93
Wood, Ellen (Mrs Henry) 51, 69
Wurgaft, Lewis D. 158

Zlosnik, Sue 8
  Gothic and the Comic Turn 144, 153, 160,
    161
Zorn, Christa 78

CPSIA information can be obtained at www.ICGtesting.com
Printed in the USA
BVOW010248190213

313634BV00002B/8/P

9 780719 087868